Dog Stags
&
NAAFI Growlers

By James Marc Ivimey

Dog Stags & NAAFI Growlers

By James Marc Ivimey

Dog stag (n): Guard duty, usually armed, on the unpopular graveyard shift (0200-0400hrs)

NAAFI (n): Navy, Army and Air Force Institutes. Set up in 1921 to run recreational establishments needed by the British Armed Forces and to sell goods to servicemen and their families

NAAFI growler (aka NAAFI pie) (n): A staple snack for drunken squaddies. The 'growler' is a soggy, greasy pasty from a NAAFI vending machine or fast-food counter containing suspicious lumps of assorted colours and textures, ranging from nearly frozen chunks through to boiling soft bits, all wrapped in oily pastry. Usually served in a paper bag to ensure the greasiness is obvious to the consumer, who would otherwise think he had been sold a substandard growler (according to the Army Rumours Service).

See Glossary for terms and abbreviations

iii

Matador
9 Priory Business Park
Kibworth Beauchamp
Leicestershire LE8 0RX, UK
Tel: (+44) 116 279 2299
Fax: (+44) 116 279 2277
Email: books@troubador.co.uk
Web: www.troubador.co.uk/matador

ISBN 978 1783065 905

British Library Cataloguing in Publication Data.
A catalogue record for this book is available from the British Library.

Printed and bound in the UK by TJ International, Padstow, Cornwall

Matador is an imprint of Troubador Publishing Ltd

In memory of my mum and dad, Vinny
and David Ivimey, who were willing me
on for every moment of my military
career. Without their support I wouldn't
have made it past week one.

"It's so much darker when a light goes
out than it would have been if it
had never shone."

John Steinbeck
The Winter Of Our Discontent

Foreword
Colonel Bob Stewart DSO MP

Jim Ivimey joined my regiment, the 1st Battalion the Cheshire Regiment, when I was posted away from it in early 1985. In his training he had been awarded the Gale Cup, for being the best infantry recruit. His first posting was in Hong Kong and he threw himself into all aspects of Battalion life – especially the social side in downtown Hong Kong, resulting in a spell in the local prison for alleged assault. Of course, I know he was totally innocent of the charge!

Actually, I first met Jim when I returned as Second in Command a year later, when the battalion had returned from the Far East and was positioned at Caterham in Surrey on public duties in London. I soon came to know the guy; he was difficult to miss. As today, he is a larger than life man with great style and a joy of life, which shows in everything he did and continues to do.

Jim was a natural non-commissioned officer and it didn't take him long to advance up the ranks to the Warrant Officers' and Sergeants' Mess, traditionally the backbone of any regiment.

We served together in Caterham, Chester, Northern Ireland and Belize. There were few people I would have trusted more in an operational situation than Jim Ivimey. Despite his very best efforts, as he was posted away, he was not allowed to come back to the battalion when I, then Commanding Officer, deployed to Bosnia in 1992. This was a desperate disappointment to him (and me, actually). In my view he should have stayed in the Army and made a full career of it.

Clearly, Jim thoroughly enjoyed his time in uniform and that shows in the way he remembers and writes about his experience as a grass roots member of the poor bloody infantry for over 10 years, from 1983 to '94.

I really enjoyed reading this book. It gives an excellent insight into the views of infantry life from ground level, which gives it both realism and charm – despite the sometimes fruity imagery and language!

Charities

I have published this book myself, with the
help of many great friends but out of my
own pocket. If I'm fortunate enough
to recoup my costs and more, I will donate
a proportion of any profits made from
sales to the following charities:

Help for Heroes
helpforheroes.org.uk

The Mercian Regiment Benevolent Fund
justgiving.com/mercianbenevolentcharity

Acknowledgements

I'd like to thank a number of people for their help and support over the many years it has taken me to complete this book. My beautiful wife Jenny has probably heard these stories more than most. She has shown immense patience in me continually returning to this project and helped me to turn my raw diaries into the book you see today. Thankfully it's now been put to bed while I can still remember the details and before I've started to elaborate on the facts.

I first spoke to Colonel Bob Stewart about this book more than 10 years ago. Through his unwavering support of the regiment (Cheshires) he has been a constant reminder of why I needed to get this finished.

Andy Bunyan took all of my photos newspaper clippings and documents and stitched them together. He showed superb design skills and patience throughout.

Polly Courtney for convincing me I could get over the finish line and her editor Joy Tibbs, who sharpened it all up and made it readable for the non-military people out there.

Finally, the men of the 22nd (Cheshire) Regiment; it was a true family and a fantastically memorable experience for 10 years of my life.

Part One – Hong Kong

Contents

Part one – Hong Kong

Chapter 1: Banged up in a Chinese prison

When the barred door rolled shut behind me, I was still in shock. I couldn't believe what had happened to us. Jacko was close; next door in fact. I could hear him but I couldn't see him. My immediate surroundings were grim and the harsh reality of where we were still hadn't sunk in.

The cell was eight feet by six feet and the side next to the corridor was made up entirely of bars, leaving me totally exposed.

To the rear and left was a sink with running cold water. Next to this was a hole in the stone floor, which was to be my toilet. Running along the right-hand wall was a plastic bed. There was no mattress, but it had a blanket on top. At the back was a plastic table and chair, and on top was an upturned green plastic plate: my dinner. To my horror on lifting the plate, I found fish heads and cabbage; the smell of the revolting concoction almost made me vomit. This was the start of my short spell in a Chinese correctional facility in Hong Kong along with Simon Jackson, also of the Cheshire Regiment.

Jacko and I had both been sentenced to three months for actual bodily harm (ABH) and three months for common assault, and the sentences were to run concurrently. We had arrived fairly late in the evening and BBC Radio 2 was already being piped through the internal speaker system.

We were sent to the jail from the local magistrates' court and in the cells below the courthouse our laces, belts and ties had been removed. Jacko and I were still together, and right then that was a major comfort.

Two policemen had led us down from a stunned and silent

courtroom. My left and Jacko's right hands had been cuffed together, but the handcuffs had since been removed. In the court cell I was in deep shock and Jacko was probably the same, but it affected us in quite different ways. I couldn't speak, while Jacko began to cry uncontrollably.

I think he did the crying for both of us. I could hear him in the next cell and even see his hands, but I couldn't see his face. The smell of bodies was ever-present; powerful and lingering. This was it now and we weren't going anywhere. Sleeping and eating were hard to contemplate, but what choice did we have?

Breakfast was served in the cells the next morning. I can't remember what it was, but I didn't eat it. The smell was similar to that of the previous night's delights and I knew I wouldn't be able to hold it down. Fear kept me functioning; this was way worse than basic training. We didn't know what to expect from anybody: the inmates or the prison officers. Probably because of the way the Chinese write their names with the surname first, the guards addressed me and Jacko by our first names, Simon and James. It wasn't exactly a remission in sentence, but it was comforting in a strange sort of way.

One thing we noticed straightaway was the lack of white faces. We had been sent to a youth correctional centre on Kowloon, and as far as we knew, the last non-Chinese (gweilo) inmate was a Scots Guard who had tried to steal an aircraft in 1982. He had apparently worked in the cookhouse. One other gweilo was incarcerated at the same time as us: a Maori lad from a New Zealand ship who was on remand for murder. We had seen him briefly on the way in, but he had been led away to the maximum-security wing.

I remember the night his alleged victim was killed, downtown in the Wan Chi. She worked in the Popeye Bar and was found strangled in one of the rooms upstairs. The Maori lad had been

the last person seen with her, hence why he was in prison, and
he had been inside since October. He was eventually cleared and
released in April, when it turned out the Triads had killed her.
But that's another story…

Most of the lads were Chinese, aged sixteen to twenty-five, and
the most common offences were either drugs (eight to ten years) or
armed robbery (more than ten years). This made the three months
that Jacko and I had to serve seem rather pathetic. Most of them, we
quickly found out, were prepared to have sex with one another, so
once out of the cells Jacko and I stuck as close together as possible.

On that first full morning inside we were taken to see the prison
governor. It was outside my cell that I got my first chance to look
at Jacko again. He was as ugly as ever, only with no hair. But then
I probably didn't look much better.

This prison was a sort of Borstal, and one of the aspects of
discipline involved all the inmates marching everywhere when they
were out of their cells. Well, that was something we could do well.
Jacko was at the front, being shorter, and I was always at the back.
This gave us both a chance to see where we were going.

The governor, an intelligent-looking Indian, was rather apologetic
about our situation. He said that no preparations had been made for
our arrival because he didn't know we were coming. That sounds
about right. He explained that mattresses would be provided and
that the food would be changed to suit a European palate. It was
a sort of pep talk: "We hope we can make it as comfortable for
you as we can, blah, blah. Any problems, please call."

Actually, he was very nice and, in for a penny in for a pound,
Jacko and I thought we might as well ask if we could be moved
into the same cell. Well, if you don't ask, you don't get. He
explained that this was a non-starter on account of the homosexual
tendencies of European men. We both wanted to laugh, but decided

against it as this had landed us in trouble before. We were thanked for our time and marched back to the cells.

The first few days are a bit of a blur, really. This was the induction period, when the guards show the new prisoners how to conduct themselves. Most of the time was spent sitting in small groups of six or eight with one guard giving the lecture. This was a slow and drawn-out process, as once it had been mapped out in Chinese, the English version had to be given to us. There was sport, too: football once a week on a pitch that resembled a building site. Jacko played but I couldn't – they didn't have training shoes big enough to fit my size eleven feet – but I watched him and he managed to hold his own.

On a normal working day, half the time was dedicated to classroom work and the other half was spent at a workshop. We asked to be put into the bookbinding workshop and we got our wish. It wasn't going to be a lot of use in the Army, but our careers were effectively over anyway. Any solider who receives a prison sentence, even if it's suspended, is booted out of the British Army. That's it, bye bye. This led me to contemplate joining the French Legion, as I could see that this was the only way to carry on in the military.

I didn't know what was going on in Jacko's head. We had both become withdrawn while on Stonecutters Island (more on that later) waiting for our day in court. We were still mates and always would be, but part of this was personal and private; it could only be processed inside our own heads. The future looked bleak. We no longer had careers ahead of us and, more pressingly, how were we going to get ourselves out of this mess and clear our names?

****

I had passed out of training from the Prince of Wales' Division depot at Litchfield on December 20, 1984, and after extended duties at the Selection Centre in Sutton Coldfield over New Year (the IRA had promised to blow something up in the UK), I flew out to join 1 Cheshire on February 10, 1985.

In the past there have been many different Cheshire battalions, and 1 Cheshire was the regiment's regular battalion. In 1900, the Second Battalion fought in South Africa and during the First World War, thirty-eight battalions of the Cheshire Regiment were raised. At the close of the Battle of Mons on August 24, 1914, the 1st Battalion was left exposed to the attack of two German Army corps in the Belgian village Audregnies. The battalion's heroic stand saved the British Expeditionary Force from disaster, but they sustained seven hundred and fifty casualties. This day is celebrated as a second Regimental Day. The Cheshires were involved in every major action in France throughout the war and won thirty-five battle honours.

Post-war, Cheshire's battalions were reduced to two: the Fourth/ Fifth and the Seventh, while the Sixth became Royal Artillery. Just prior to the Second World War, all battalions were converted to a support machine gun role (with the Vickers medium machine gun) and the regiment became a support regiment for the duration of the war. On the eve of the Second World War, the Territorial Army was doubled, so our four battalions – Fourth, Fifth, Sixth and Seventh – all reappeared.

I was seventeen years old and had finally achieved something. I don't mean passing out of basic training as the Gale Cup Winner (Best Recruit), although I had indeed done this. No, it was a first for me to finish anything at all.

I had initially been at college with my best friend of nine years, Paul. However, the Royal Signals wasn't really where I wanted to be. I had always wanted to be a Royal Engineer (a pipefitter;

basically a plumber), but as vacancies were tight, I eventually accepted a place at Harrogate as a telegraphist. To be fair, I had only gone that way because Paul was doing the same. His dad, Des, had been part of the Parachute Signal Squadron (Para Sigs), dropping at Suez in 1956. Paul was following him to the Sigs, and with nothing on at Chepstow I opted to go with my best mate.

Paul really did follow in his dad's footsteps. He passed Pegasus Company (P Coy) at the second attempt and went Para himself, touring in Iraq and Afghanistan. As far as I know, he left as a Sergeant after twenty-two years of service. If it hadn't been for Paul, I wouldn't have made it out of college and on to the Cheshires because the Army Apprentices College in Harrogate was a fucking nightmare, and for anyone who came from a 'normal' family, like me, it was a huge shock to the system.

But here I was studying telecommunications. Where was all the digging of holes and getting dirty? It had nothing to do with soldiering, either. So after eight unbearable months and a number of letters and interviews, I transferred to my county regiment: the 22nd Cheshire Regiment of Foot (known as the 22nd of Foot). Despite not really being the right kind of person for the Signals, it was difficult to leave the college, mainly because Paul – who had got me through those tearful early days – wasn't coming with me. However, passing out of basic training was like removing a weight from my chest. I had made it to the end.

Chapter 2: Basic training

I turned up at the Army Apprentices College on January 6, 1984. It seemed like a good idea at the time. In the first instance, I had been drawn to the Royal Marines as my dad had been in the Marines and I had gone to their recruiting office in Liverpool a year earlier. I remember the first thing they asked me to do was some pull-ups on a bar in the office. I took the test, which went well, then was given the news that there was a two-year wait to join up. This was because the Royal Marines' success in the Falklands had seen their popularity soar. Being the impatient sixteen-year-old that I was, I thought, 'Sod that!' So one summer's day I was sitting in the middle of my hometown, Chester, with Paul and we decided to go and take the Army test.

It had been drilled into us at school that we needed to have a trade to get by in life and I had pushed hard to get a place as an apprentice so that I could learn one. However, ending up at Harrogate could be considered to be this advice coming back to haunt me. The college was a bleak factory for turning out tradesmen; some of whom would be good soldiers and some of whom would be rubbish.

Mum cried at the front door when I was picked up by Paul's dad. We were full of anticipation on the way to the station, and when we got on the train we stuck our heads out of the window and he said to us: "I'm sure it'll be fine, just like going to college."

We were picked up in a minibus by a member of the Provo staff (the Provos are members of a regiment or corps and are not members of the Royal Military Police) and driven up to a grey set of blocks on a hill that appeared to be in the middle of nowhere, although it was only a few miles outside Harrogate. It was on Penny Pot Lane and the camp shared this name. It was used as a test run site for the RAF, so aircraft buzzed by on a regular basis. Half a

7

mile down the road was Queen Ethelburga's College for young ladies, a private independent school. There were tales of apprentices going missing in the school never to be seen again, having been devoured by young nymphs. Sadly, nothing that exciting ever happened to me.

It rained all the time and the regime seemed relentless. We were constantly harassed during the day and the evenings were even worse. Under this system, apprentices who had junior rank and had been there a year or so would be put in charge of whole squadrons. This was fantastic for them, and they took great delight in messing us around for hours at night – introducing quick-change parades (during which we would have to change from combat gear to PE kit to working dress) and the making of bed blocks – because they could. Occasionally, they would go to the NAAFI, have a few beers and then come back and knock us around. Making us stand to attention at the end of our beds and then punching us as hard as they could in the solar plexus was a favourite. Watching and listening to the air go out of a poor combat recruit of war (CROW) when he hit his pit (bed) was a sad sight. This was usually the finale after a few rounds of quick-change parades, and it was usually followed by a room inspection.

At full capacity, there were six hundred apprentices at the college. We would queue up for breakfast, dinner or tea and the ranked junior would go to the front of the queue. Then, by the time we got to sit down with our food, they would shout 'five minutes' and we had to be ready to move. I had always been a fussy eater at home, but I learnt quickly that if I was going to survive I would have to eat what I had in front of me and get it down me quickly.

The behaviour of the junior ranks was petty and, for the best part, unnecessary. A Boy Lance Corporal or a Boy Corporal was in charge of each room, which included three or four recruits. There would also be a Boy Sergeant or Colour Sergeant in a bunk at the end of the corridor. We had to stand up each time they came into the room, go to and from the NAAFI for them, and clean and iron their kit. But the real ball-breakers were the quick-change parades; they could go on for thirty minutes or more. You could be wearing anything in the corridor, from PE kit to full combats.

Then there were the locker inspections. First our lockers would be destroyed, then they would call a snap locker inspection. I wouldn't have found this so distressing if it hadn't been for the fact that it was being carried out by a bunch of knobs who had never done anything or been anywhere. They had merely been at the college a bit longer than we had. I had taken some of Dad's old kit with me, including a clasped knife, fork and spoon that were stamped with the year 1944. The Lance Corporal (Lance Jack) who ran our room took a shine to these and asked if he could use them when he was next on exercise. I had no choice but to give them up, and they were never seen again. As I said, this was all unnecessary.

I had a hard time, and I don't mind admitting it. I realised early on that I had made a mistake in joining the Sigs, but I was trapped and had to get on with it. I would phone my mum from the NAAFI at night crying and say that I wanted to come home and go to college "in the real world". She always told me the same thing: life was going to be tough and that I had made a decision so I had to stick by it.

It must have been difficult for her to listen to me blubbing down the phone, but she was right. It was my mum's support and having my best mate with me that made me stick it out. Paul was a lot tougher than me and I tried my best to stick close to him. I was on a downward spiral at this point and was sinking fast. I remember getting a bad cold and convincing myself I had the flu. Of course, being a young lad, I just wanted my mum.

****

However, there was one good thing to come out of this whole sorry experience. There was a Boy Sergeant Major, let's call him 'W' (he knows who he is), who particularly enjoyed smacking us around. Years later (in 1989), I was on exercise in the Falklands. We were out there for a few weeks live firing and I was stagging on (performing guard duty) in Signals Comcen. An Argentine boat had sailed into the exclusion zone and all hell had broken loose. I was a Full Corporal (Full Screw) at the time and I was walking along a corridor when a Full Screw from the Sigs walked past in the opposite direction. The difference was that the Sigs boys had their names on their jumpers and 'W' had an unusual name. I called this bloke back and asked if he was ex-Harrogate, and he said that he was. I then asked if he remembered knocking the shite out of the 84A intake in Bradley Squadron. There was no reply, but I deduced from his silence that he remembered well enough.

The psychology of violence is interesting for me. In many cases you don't have to raise a finger, but you let people work out for themselves what might be about to happen to them. By now I was about two stone heavier than this dickhead and about six inches taller. I got close so that he and only he could hear, and I told him very firmly to do one. There was no swearing and nothing more was said. He quickly left to go to the toilet and I left feeling much better. I'd got my own back all those years later.

****

So being pissed around went on at night, while in the day we were marched down to the training blocks where we had lessons in telegraphy, radio masts and morse code. These were all useful skills, but I was set on being a soldier, and for me that involved weapons and carrying heavy kit. Then, after dinner on Friday nights, Paul and I would get a taxi into Harrogate for a few beers. There were plenty of pubs that were out of bounds – where locals would fight with squaddies – but we wanted to steer clear of all that anyway. We favoured a quiet bar called Gladstone's, which had a three-quarter-size snooker table. We would sink a couple of beers, play a few frames and head back; it just gave us a few hours away from the grim reality of the camp. Saturday morning was drill and Sunday was the church parade, which I loved. It was the only time I got to sit on my own and wasn't shouted at. Bliss!

We passed out of basic recruit training on March 31, 1984. My mum, dad, oldest sister Tilly, brother Rob and his wife Lynne all came to the parade. As usual, the wind was shocking and they handed out extra blankets to keep the guests warm on the square. Looking back at the photos, everyone looks cold, and Paul and I looked like we had just got out of a prison camp. That night we were allowed to go out with our families and we went to an Italian, Casa Romana Ristorante, in Cheltenham Crescent. The bill was £18.95; when you think about prices today it was pretty good. For me, after weeks of not really getting enough to eat, it was a feast, especially considering the dubious quality of food in an Army cook house. Plus it was great to get out. It had been a big day and after a few hours I was so tired they had to take me back to camp.

As I said before, my mind was made up and I wanted to go and do some real soldiering. At the time, this was probably the most difficult decision of my life. My best mate had helped me get through, but I knew I had to leave. His heart was always in it, he wanted to be there, but I didn't. After many interviews, I finally got one at Empress State Building on August 6, 1984. This would allow me to transfer to the infantry and to the Cheshire Regiment.

I saw Captain Pigeon, the infantry's special personnel staff officer (SPSO), in room 1115. Dad had done me some notes so I could revise: Colonel-in-Chief, battle honours and so on, as it's taken as a given that every solider should know the names of the top brass and the history of their regiment. It seemed to work, as I got my wish; the transfer was accepted and I left Harrogate a few weeks later.

We got late passes and I had one last night out with my mates. First we went to a bar in Harrogate for a few warmers, then we took a taxi to Leeds and went to a German bar. We went to a club to finish and I remember trying to dance to Gloria Estefan's "Dr. Beat" but really making a dog's ear of it because I was so pissed. We had a great time getting bladdered, singing and dancing. We were really going for it in the German bar; the steins were flowing and I got one in the face at some stage as they were being flung around, sort of in tune to the music. Despite that it was a great send-off.

On my last day I was driven down to the station and sent on my way to Litchfield. The Squadron was formed up to march down to the trade blocks and Paul and I said our goodbyes. I was on my own now, and whatever the infantry wanted to throw at me I had to do it without my best mate.

Chapter 3: Now for the real soldiering

Whittington Barracks in Litchfield was where the real training began: eighteen weeks of infantry training at the home of the Prince of Wales Division, which included the Cheshire Regiment, where I was hoping to go. This was regular Army training, which involved men from a minimum age of seventeen to a maximum of twenty-five; the difference being that after training these men would join combat infantry regiments, some of which would go straight to Northern Ireland. There was no time for the sort of fucking around they did at Harrogate.

The instructors were fully qualified weapons instructors and the buildings were Victorian stone brick, so they were very cold in winter. When I went through basic with Gheluvelt Platoon in the autumn of 1984, they began to build state-of-the-art modern accommodation. There was no such luck for us. Apart from when we got back from Battle Camp in December, we had to run across the square with our washing and shaving kits to get a decent shower before we went out on the piss.

I joined the platoon as its members were just coming up to the badging parade (Passing off the Square). At this point recruits stop wearing a CROW cap – the peaked cap worn by all new recruits – and are allowed to wear a beret. You're judged in groups of four on the drill square; kit first and then marching, turning and saluting. It's the first test in uniform and, if you pass, not only are you allowed home for the weekend, you also get your headdress. I turned up with a beret with a Sigs cap badge, but this was duly handed in and I too was given a CROW cap. There were no problems there.

It was tough training and a packed programme. Weapons training took place in the keep: a dark, sober, stone multi-storey construction at the top of the square. The training room was bleak and dark and fitted the sombre mood; there was no room for messing around. The Army 'factory' is designed to turn out soldiers with a basic understanding of it all: weapons; map training; field craft; nuclear, biological and chemical (NBC) defence; and, of course, military fitness. If you don't make the grade, you're out. Gheluvelt Platoon started off with fifty-two recruits, but only thirty-four made the platoon photo and about the same number passed out. The same applied for lads from other platoons. They didn't make the cut at some point and were 'back-squadded'.

There was a long straight road with a huge dip that ran from the guard house, NAAFI and bar up to where the blocks began. There were two phones behind the guard room (this was long before everyone had a mobile phone) and we all queued up to put a call in to our parents. Later on, we got clued up to the fact that there was a family NAAFI at the back of the camp, and that going through the back provided access to a better shop and a phone that was hardly ever used.

Most stuff we needed was inside the camp; I hardly ever went outside unless I was heading back to Chester. I had made a big decision not to drink during basic as I knew it was going to be tough and I didn't need a bad head as well. I went out with the lads but didn't touch a drop until we got back from battle camp. Then I got slaughtered!

On the Friday we got back, threw our kit down and hit Litchfield for beer and a curry. The next day we were practising drill for the passing-out parade, but that night we hired a car to run us to Birmingham. First we went clubbing, then we ended up in a curry house that was owned by the cousin of the lads we had eaten with the night before. Or so they claimed! It was fantastic to see the joy and relief in the lads' faces that basic training was finally finished. Brecon had been a slog and it was great to be back in the real world with some pretty girls to look at, a few ales to sink and a good curry warming us through. One of the lads opted for the hottest, a Vindaloo. He shovelled it in pretty quickly, but there was a delayed reaction before the power of the curry kicked in. Have you ever seen anyone try to sink their entire tongue into a glass of beer? It was a good effort!

The camp had a familiar feel in terms of the support team, partly because it was just the Army way that everyone was called John regardless of their actual names. So when you went to get a hair-cut, there was John the barber, while the mobile chip wagon was manned by John the chippy. No one ever asked if these were their real names, and they always responded to John so it didn't matter. (Only in the Army!) Being in a hostile and strange environment it made me – and I'm sure the same applied for many other lads – feel a bit better about it all.

On Wednesday nights the camp hosted a disco in the NAAFI, which was known as the Dogs' Ball. All of the local 'talent' came along to drink and get shagged by the troops. I'm pleased to say I never went to one; I think I stuck my head around the door one night and shit myself! Never again.

I seemed to spend all my time cleaning stuff. We trained all day and then after tea put on our coveralls and cleaned for most of the night. Every now and again someone would troop off to the NAAFI to collect chocolate and Pot Noodles and we cracked on. Saying that, we had a laugh. We had a black-and-white portable TV I had brought from home and a boogie box for tunes. I remember Chaka Khan's "I Feel for You" being a huge hit at the time, so there was plenty of spinning around on the floor on our backs, which was good for polishing it up, along with the bumpering (a huge, mop-like thing we loaded up with polish and used to make the floor shine).

There was a lad in our platoon, Tim (who was badged Staffordshire Regiment), who to me at the time seemed quite old. He was twenty-five! He had a motorbike and in the later stages of training he would ride down to Litchfield to buy us kebabs. He would keep them warm inside his leather jacket on the run back. He really knew how to ride, and he took me to collect the snap one night. It was not for the fainthearted. On another occasion I was relieved of my money (probably about £2.50) by some trained soldiers on a trip to the NAAFI one night. I'm sure this was pretty common; CROWs are easy pickings for lads from regiments that are back for a training course. It must have been the shock of being fleeced as I can't remember what the lads looked like. I had hoped to catch up with them again when I got to the regiment, but I suppose this was the order of things.

As mentioned, there was a lot of fitness. I struggled after sitting on my arse learning Morse at Harrogate, and infantry fitness requires a certain level of commitment. After we had done the customary few weeks in the gym running up and down, climbing ropes and pretending to stab rabbits between our legs, it was on to the real stuff. Our webbing (kit) had to weigh 26lbs, and add to this the 9lbs a self-loading rifle (SLR) weighs, it was the standard 35lbs for our runs. We got to know the roads and small holding pretty well around the barracks. You formed up at the gym with the physical training instructors (PTIs), who all looked very smart with their white vests or blue jackets (depending on the temperature). The markers (training Non-Commissioned Officers, or NCOs) would have high-visibility vests and the medic would be in the Land Rover. You would weigh your kit on fishing scales and then you would be off: out of the gates at a march and when you hit the lane that ran alongside the barracks you would break into the double march, a brisk run. We had to complete three, five, seven

16

and nine-mile runs at speed, as well as longer-distance tabs of ten and fifteen miles. The big one, twenty-five miles, was at Battle Camp (more on that later).

We would usually lose two or three on a run as they would flake out and be put inside the Land Rover. The platoon ended up being spread out and a few stragglers would be encouraged to catch up by the NCOs, who would double backwards and forwards from the main group as if it were a Sunday afternoon stroll. During one seven-mile tab I weighed my kit incorrectly and ended up carrying 35lbs as well as the rifle, so 44lbs in total. I was really biffing and moaning, but just about got round.

When I got back to camp it was lunchtime and after the PTIs fell us out (dismissed us from that session) we marched back to the blocks and we fell out for lunch. I was in bits and went down to the phone near the guard room and phoned Mum in tears. I said I couldn't do it; that I wasn't strong enough. Unbeknown to me, she then phoned my Platoon Commander, Lieutenant Kingsberry (Glosters) and said she was worried about me. I only found out at my passing-out parade that he had told her I would finish in the top three. He was right.

****

We had a few Cheshires in the platoon including Mickey Roberts and Ray Hubbard, who was from Ellesmere Port. Ray had an old Mini and I couldn't drive, so when we were fallen out for the weekend we jumped into his car. He put his foot down and we knew we would be back in Chester in a few hours' time. He agreed to pick me up at the back of the Gateway Theatre on Sunday afternoon for the return trip.

It was during one of these weekends back in Chester that I met

Helen for the first time. We had gone to the same school, but as she was a year younger we had not had much to do with each other. It was teed up for me to turn up at her place of work, a shoe shop, to ask her out. She accepted and that was that.

She was a good laugh; lively on account of her red hair, and pretty. It was a no-brainer for me. I was getting fucked around all week, so when I did get home I wanted to spend time with my folks, but a pretty girl was a bonus of course. She wanted to do the same stuff as I did at the weekend: have a drink, a laugh and a roll around. That was Helen. We stuck together throughout my basic training and I was smitten.

Perhaps it wasn't meant to last. She eventually copped off with Paul, my best mate, when I was stagging on at Sutton Coldfield on New Year's Eve. Being uncharacteristically diplomatic and grown up about it at the time, I didn't say anything, despite knowing about it, because I didn't want to lose either of them. She came to my passing-out parade and waved me off to Hong Kong. I had a picture of her on my wall and she had also sent me a pair of her stockings, which I had on the wall next to her photo to remind me of her beautiful legs. Anyway, at some point during the tour I got the 'Dear John' letter. It was over.

****

The last weekend before we flew to Hong Kong, Mickey came back to Chester and he, Ray and I went on the piss. We had a great night at The Strawberry pub near Ellesmere Port. Mickey decided to get a tattoo to celebrate finishing basic and visited the parlour on the Fountains Roundabout in Chester during the afternoon. He got a bulldog on his arm with 'Mick' and 'Cheshires' inked underneath. We got to the battalion in Hong Kong and Ray and I went to B

Company (B Coy), Mickey to A Coy.

Some years later, after the Belize tour, Ray died while on leave in Cyprus after falling off a balcony. I carried the coffin at his funeral in Ellesmere Port, which was tough. It wasn't a full military funeral as his death didn't happen while he was on active service, but all the coffin bearers were in No.2 service dress and he had the best bugle player in the regiment playing the "Last Post". We (Whistler, the bugle player from the Pipes and Drums, and I) had gone out on the piss the night before in Chester, but it was one of those nights where the ale stuck in your throat.

Whistler was really good musically, but he struggled to get the "Last Post" out. A Union Jack, belt and Dress Hat were placed on top of the box. As expected, Ray's mother was in bits. We weren't the very best of mates, but he was a good lad. We served together in B Coy and I suppose you keep reasonably close links with the people you train with. We stumped up to Hong Kong together and he didn't deserve to go out like that.

****

In training we seemed to spend a disproportionate amount of time on the ranges. It was always raining and bloody freezing. You would drive out on coaches, if you were lucky, but more often than not on a four-tonne truck. This wasn't the interesting close quarter battle (CQB) stuff with different terrains and firing positions; this was 100 metres, 200 metres and so on, with a magazine load of twenty rounds, prone position down. We would spend all day out there, usually taking shelter in a range hut. We were either firing or fixing the targets (targets up!) and using a huge arrow to point out where the rounds were striking. We drank cups and cups of stewed tea out of an urn and ate range stew, which was beef (I think).

I once had a negligent discharge (ND) on the range, and this was a big no-no. I was standing on the firing point and my SLR went off. When this happens, the rifle is taken away so it can be tested by an armourer, as it should take 7lbs of pressure on the trigger to fire a round. I cried on the four-tonner all the way back to camp. A few days later I was marched in front of the Commanding Officer (CO), Lucy Lockhart, and charged. You live and learn.

Pre-battle camp came in week twelve and was carried out at the Sennybridge Training Area in Powys, Wales. As you cross the cattle grid at the start of area, anyone who has served will know you could quite easily be about to go through four seasons within thirty minutes. It's all the good stuff up there – field craft, weapons, map reading and living in the field – and it was at this point that we all had the feeling that it was starting to come together. There is, of course, the loss of dead wood as lads leave or are back-squadded.

Our platoon had one incident around this time. There was a lad there, Christy, who saw himself as a bit of an Arthur Daley. He quite often mentioned that he had opened his own enterprise called Christy's Stores, where he would sell on kit he had 'acquired'. He pushed his luck a little too far one day and one of the NCOs gave him a slap on a Range Day. He complained and there was an investigation: the NCO was returned to unit (RTU'd) and Christy didn't make it much further through the process, either.

The real one – Battle Camp – came in December. It was bloody freezing in camp and it was much colder when we got up onto the training areas in the hills of Wales. The drive up was bleak, with frost and ice on the roads, and the coach made its way with thirty or so excited but extremely apprehensive young soldiers-in-training on board. Once we got to the camp we were given the familiarisation tour of the guard room, cookhouse and so on, and then we were left to our own devices. We walked into the NAAFI bar, which had the standard pool table, dartboard, juke box and a lone girl serving drinks. It was as though time had stood still; this could have been any scene from any post-war film about soldiers in the UK doing their national service (think *Carry On Sergeant* and you're on the right page!). It had a tired look about it, with a musty, slightly damp smell to it. The furniture looked as if it was on its last legs – very 'lived in' – and the patterned fabrics were like something your great-aunt would have in her dining room.

After grabbing some food, most of us hit the NAAFI again and strangely, with soldiers inside it, it looked and felt better. I wasn't drinking, but most of the lads were and some were settling in for a session in front of the barmaid, who was joined by a partner in crime. An hour or so later I made my way back to the old Nissen hut we were sleeping in, got into my pit and tried to get some rest before the twenty-five-mile bash in the morning. I'm not sure how much time had passed, but I was asleep and some of the lads were still in the NAAFI when the door was kicked open by one of the Full Screw instructors. He had all his kit on – including combats and webbing – and said: "Get your kit on, get down to the NAAFI and get them back here now." And that's what happened. We got on the back of the four-tonners with some of the lads looking slightly the worse for wear, then drove on to the training area, debussed and started the twenty-five miler in the middle of the night. It was a beautiful cold but crisp night. The clear sky was dark and we tabbed and tabbed. 'TAB' stands for 'tactical advance to battle' and typically involves a long march carrying a large load. Occasionally we'd break into the double, but the main aim was just to keep going.

At one stage, the chance of a drink at The Drovers Arms was offered up by one of the instructors. It must have been the same stunt he pulled with every training platoon, but we started to think we were actually going to get a drink in the warmth of a pub. The excitement grew until we finally got to 'The Drovers Arms', a fighting in built-up areas (FIBUA) house. It was a breeze block shell of a building with old pyrotechnics on the floor and the remains of burnt tyres lying around. What an anti-climax! That said, it was a little warmer than being outside, so we did actually get a chance to rest up for a few minutes.

As long as we kept moving we stayed warm, but as soon as we stopped our sweat grew cold and so did our bodies – very quickly. We lost a few during the course of the night who couldn't make it and ended up in the back of the safety Land Rover. At one stage, my mate Aussie (Geoff) was taking his turn carrying the 84mm rocket launcher (Carl Gustav, 34lbs) on top of his webbing, helmet and the rest. Unfortunately, at this stage we had also had a call of "Gas, gas, gas!" so we all had our respirators on. We broke into the double and he fell over. I managed to haul him up and we kept going until we broke back into a tab again, but he clearly wasn't having a good time.

What was left of the platoon stopped just outside camp in the early hours of the morning so we could all get a shave in the stream. I was never the best at shaving (I'm still not that good now!) but being white as a ghost, dehydrated and trying to shave in a freezing stream at 0600hrs was more than enough. We formed up and tabbed back in; the first bit was done. After breakfast the rest of Saturday was ours before we started live firing on the Sunday. I remember we had a jerry can of rifle oil in the block and an extremely free-flowing amount of oil was used to clean our rifles. I got into my gonk bag and slept.

The live firing was to take place in field conditions. We would get up, eat breakfast and then tab or be carried on a four-tonner to the training area. We were engaging in CQB with SLRs, sub-machine guns (SMGs), general-purpose machine guns (GPMGs) and two-inch mortars (with two live grenades each). It was cold and we spent a lot of time in a range hut preparing our kit before we went up, but it was really exciting. Putting those hours of static range work behind us and applying the skills in the field was what it was all about. We would tab back, clean the weapons, drop them at the armoury, eat and then sleep again.

The second week we tabbed on to the training areas as a platoon and set up a patrol base on the forward slope of a hill. We dug in to stage two, which meant corrugated sheets and steel pickets recovered with tons of earth and then returned; we slept inside. Then we patrolled for five days from this position. I was given the job of Patrol Commander, so I was positioned in the middle of a reverse triangle formation with the GPMG set up behind me at the highest point. I had a two-inch mortar, which we were able to use with smoke to try to locate teams that were carrying out close target recces on our location. We, in turn, would patrol day and night. I took a close target reconnaissance (CTR) out on the 'enemy' during the day and we got close enough to see them in balaclavas before we were fired out and forced to bug out.

Each night we would stand to as the darkness set in; this is traditional for British troops wherever they are in the world. We suffered from our own blue-on-blue one night. As the returning patrol took off their helmets and went back to their trenches, the GPMG opened up. We were learning, and at least it was only loaded with blanks!

The NCOs were nearby in a tented area. They would stump up in the morning after we had all endured another extremely uncomfortable night inside a trench. By this stage, all of our kit was wet and there was no chance of anything drying out. I had two pairs of long johns on as well as two pairs of tights, none of which came off until I got back to Whittington. The NGOs would stroll over at dawn (usually still eating their hot, buttery toast), stand to and ask how we were. There was a regulation response to this, which had to be, "As warm as toast, Corporal", and it had to be given with a smile on your face. You couldn't lose face and let them know how bad you were feeling.

The recce work was undertaken in preparation for the culmination of the exercise: a platoon attack on the enemy troops, who were dug in inside a FIBUA house. I went in with our Platoon Commander and I remember him giving me a thunder flash, a hand-thrown device that is used to provide realistic battle simulation. It's a big noisy firework, but my hands were so cold I couldn't get it to strike. Finally he called "End Ex" (end of exercise) and it was over, we had finished. Weapons were cleared and we went back to Sennybridge Camp, got on the coach and drove back to Whittington.

On the drive back we were all knackered and slept for chunks of the journey. It was strangely quiet as people either tried to gather their thoughts or catch a few zeds. I could see Christmas trees in the windows of the houses we passed; we hadn't even had a chance to think about it, but it would be Christmas in a few weeks' time. When we got back, we handed our weapons in and threw our kit behind our beds. We ran over to the square to where the CROWs were in the new blocks to get a hot shower and then we went out on the piss. Even I sank a few beers.

The next day (Saturday) we lined up in open order outside the block, ready to get to the square and start practising for the passing-out parade. As he walked in and out of the ranks, Platoon Sergeant Kennedy (Royal Welch Fusiliers, or RWF) called out the various awards that would be presented at the passing-out parade, for example Best Shot. At the exact time he was calling out the name of each winner, Corporal Thomas (Royal Regiment of Wales, or

RRW) stood behind that person, who would then receive a huge punch to the kidneys and end up on the floor. He went through the list until he got to the Gale Cup Winner (the most prestigious award for the best recruit) and the next minute I was on the floor. It was me; I was getting it!

There were four days to go until the passing-out parade, but I didn't tell Mum and Dad I had won. (When it was all over, Mum said I sounded different when I called her during that last week; perhaps because there was no longer any pressure.) During those four days it was all kit and drill. I was asked to visit the Padre, who presented me with a Bible and asked if I would read the lesson in church after the parade. It was Colossians chapters one to six, which I practised in the lines (accommodation) and at night. It drove the lads mad. I would say: "Hold on, I've just got to run something by you," and then start. I would usually get stuff thrown at me!

By the morning of the parade we were finally ready. After breakfast I marched the lads over to the training wing for a final brief from the Lieutenant Kingsberry. On the way back we doubled and passed the road that leads down the slope to the main gate. People were starting to arrive and the excitement was building. We got our kit on: No.2 belts, buckles and our best boots. All the NCOs looked especially smart with their medals on. The Platoon Sergeant took the platoon round to the back of the blocks and behind the new accommodation so no one would catch sight of us. When we got behind the main stand on the square it was really quiet and I thought not many people had come along. We formed up and marched out. It was absolutely packed and I was shitting myself.

Brigadier Mike Dauncey, Distinguished Service Order (DSO), from the Cheshire Regiment, was the Inspecting Officer. When he came past me, he said: "I hear you've done pretty well," which was a lovely thing to say. When the time came, I grounded my rifle and marched out to collect the Gale Cup from him. I saluted him and my dad, who was watching in the stand, was crying. Next it was hats off and church, and after I'd struggled through the lesson we had lunch in the cookhouse. Lieutenant Kingsberry came and introduced himself to Mum, and then the conversation they had had weeks earlier – when she was worried I wasn't coping – was revealed to me.

Next there were a few beers in the NAAFI, some photos and then I got the train home with Mum, Dad, Tilly and Helen. There was a feeling of loss at the end as I knew I would never see most of the lads I had spent so much time with in those last few months again. I was very quiet on the train. Aussie had been my best mate at Whittington; he had come back to Chester at weekends when we were off and we had been close. Unfortunately, he didn't pass out. He had struggled with the fitness, particularly towards the end of training, and was medically discharged before the parade. He became an estate agent in Swindon before emigrating to Australia, when we lost touch. Before then he had a lovely habit of calling my mum's house every Christmas morning when I was on leave. He would ask for Corporal Ivimey and start speaking to me with his best officer impersonation until we both started laughing and had a proper catch-up. He was a cracking bloke.

Saying I wouldn't see the platoon again was premature as we were reformed and called back from leave on New Year's Eve. The IRA had threatened to blow up a barracks in the UK, so the threat level had risen. We were called back to stag on at the Army Selection Centre in Sutton Coldfield. We did day-on, day-off for a month. It was freezing, and one night the temperature dropped to -12°C in the Midlands and one person died in the area. But nothing much happened besides that. The coppers were using the Selection Centre to get their breakfast before they went to knock the shite out of some miners on the picket lines. There was also a huge fire at an industrial block next door, which made us all a little nervous. It wasn't the IRA, though.

Chapter 4: Politics and music in 1984

Hitting the headlines

January 15: Left-wing rebel Tony Benn wins the Labour Party's nomination for the Chesterfield by-election, eight months after losing his seat as MP for Bristol in the general election.

February 12: Austin Rover announces that the Triumph marque will be discontinued after 63 years, and that the Triumph Acclaim's successor will be sold as a Rover.

March 12: The miners' strike begins and pits the National Union of Mineworkers against Margaret Thatcher's Tory government, which was intent on closing most of Britain's coal pits.

April 17: WPC Yvonne Fletcher is shot and killed during the Libyan embassy siege. Eleven others are shot but survive.

May 8: The Thames Barrier, designed to protect London from flooding, is opened by the Queen.

October 12: The Provisional Irish Republican Army attempts to assassinate the British Cabinet in the Brighton hotel bombing. Prime Minister Margaret Thatcher escapes injury, but Norman Tebbit is trapped among the rubble and his wife Margaret is left paralysed. Five people, including MP Anthony Berry, are killed.

November 12: The English one pound note is withdrawn after 150 years in circulation.

November 29: The Band Aid single goes on sale.

What I was listening to at the Army Apprentices College at Harrogate and the Prince of Wales' Division depot in Litchfield:

When Doves Cry by Prince

What's Love Got To Do With It by Tina Turner

Against All Odds (Take A Look At Me Now) by Phil Collins

Footloose by Kenny Loggins

Ghostbusters by Ray Parker, Jr.

I Just Called To Say I Love You by Stevie Wonder

Out Of Touch by Daryl Hall and John Oates

Say Say Say by Paul McCartney & Michael Jackson

I Feel For You by Chaka Khan

Caribbean Queen (No More Love On The Run) by Billy Ocean

The Wild Boys by Duran Duran

Hold Me Now by the Thompson Twins

Oh Sherrie by Steve Perry, Randy Goodrum, Craig Krampf and Bill Cuomo

99 Luftballons by Nena

Drive by The Cars

Here Comes The Rain Again by Eurythmics

Breakdance by Irene Cara

I'm So Excited by The Pointer Sisters

Thriller by Michael Jackson

Doctor! Doctor! by the Thompson Twins

Love Will Find a Way by Lionel Ritchie (we were feeling sorry for ourselves in the Battle Camp huts!)

Chapter 5: Hong Kong – new in and clueless

I arrived in Hong Kong on a wet Tuesday evening ten days before
my eighteenth birthday. Thinking myself a bit of a smart arse, Gale
Cup winner and all, I came back to reality with a sharp bump when I
realised that I knew nothing at all. Being a 'NIG' (New in Germany),
as the new lads were called, I didn't speak until I was spoken to.

The garrison in Hong Kong was represented by all three services:
the RAF at Seckong; Royal Navy/Royal Marines at the land-based
HMS Tamar; and the Army, with several Gurkha camps on the New
Territories/in Kowloon, although the one and only resident bat-
talion was based at Stanley Fort. This is the most southern tip of
Hong Kong Island, and is on top of a huge hill overlooking Stanley
Village and the South China Sea.

The main responsibility of the resident battalion is to support the
Royal Hong Kong Police in carrying out their duties. The second is
to patrol the Chinese border and prevent the entry of illegal immi-
grants into the old colony.

The New Year's Eve gig at Litchfield, courtesy of the IRA,
meant all postings had been delayed, and once we had been stood
down it meant a few extra days before we were shipped off to our
respective battalions. The three Cheshires – me, Ray and Mickey
– were joined by a serving member of the battalion, Tate, who had
been back to the depot and was now returning to Hong Kong.

We set off from Litchfield on the train to London. This in itself
was an adventure, with a few beers and a couple of games of cards.
In the back of my mind I didn't really know what to expect. I had
spent weeks and weeks keeping my head down, getting on with it,
and the end result was a trip into the unknown. Britannia Airways
had won the contract to fly service personnel on long-haul, so what
they saw in us was probably a common occurrence. On arrival at

the RAF check-in desk at Heathrow, Ray was wearing a Union Jack flat cap. One look from the check-in clerk and he was reminded that he would be going nowhere with that on his head – charming! We were set free in the big city for a few hours, and then that was it.

It's worth pointing out that this was my first trip on a plane. The furthest I had been before this was to France on my Uncle Geoff's boat! Sixteen hours in the air is a fair schlep, and it's even longer when you're sitting with the lads you've just spent sixteen weeks with in basic. I'm not sure how it works now, as Britannia has relinquished its contract for HM Forces long-haul, but back in 1985 it meant you could drink as much as you wanted. This was music to a soldier's ears! However, on the way to join the 1st Battalion in Hong Kong I didn't really know what to expect. It had sometimes been said in training that you don't start learning until you reach your battalion, so with this in mind I decided not to get bladdered on the plane. This wasn't going to stop the others, though. The call button on the arm of Tate's chair was going into overdrive. At one stage the hostess arrived with her arms full of lager cans, which she threw into Tate's lap. She promptly told him not to call again for a while. Good effort!

The stop en route was Dubai Airport. We arrived mid-afternoon, and walking down the steps of the plane I was met by a tremendous heat. I thought it was coming from the engines, but it was just the sun. Questions about what would be better between a warm or a cold-climate posting rushed into my mind.

The rest of the flight was much of the same, until the approach to Kai Tak Airport. The pilot informed us that this was his first land-ing here, and it was onto a runway that sticks out into the South China Sea. It was probably all routine, but the skyscrapers looked pretty close to the wing tips on the run in. After all the formalities, I was left standing outside the terminal building at about 2200hrs in the heat, which was damp and rather stifling. Welcome to Hong Kong! A Land Rover picked us up with all our kit and we set off through the tunnel to Stanley Fort.

****

Being a NIG in the Cheshire Regiment meant we had a whole new language to learn: 'choggies' (café) and 'bondhook' (rifle) to name just two. But the first port of call was to keep our mouths shut so we didn't get 'filled in' for being gobby CROWs. After spending a night in a spare room behind HQ lines, we were quickly marched in front of the CO.

When talking to any serving member of the regiment who had been back to the UK on courses, they had always explained the company system in the same way:

A Coy: training company (bullshitters)
B Coy: full of bad bastards (mainly nutters)
C Coy: sports/athletics company

In my head I knew where I desperately wanted to go – it had to be C Coy – but it was never wise to say much to the Commanding Officer. He would talk at us and we would say: "Yes sir, no sir, three bags full sir," and then we were off. In front of the great man, Lieutenant Colonel Henderson, I was asked what sports I had played. I responded with rugby for Chester's under-16s and the Royal Signals Corps championship for tennis. Like a shot he was on the phone, first to the battalion's Chief Clerk (a big tennis player) and next to Major David Colebourn, Officer Commanding B Company and a rugby man. By the time he got off the phone my fate was sealed, probably because of the tennis; I was to join the

Busy Bs. It's strange as I did play for the battalion in Caterham, but it was never really a focus. Major Colebourn was a larger-than-life character – the classic English gentleman – and to a seventeen-year-old CROW he was one cool bloke; he reminded me of James Bond. He was a big man, six foot plus with broad shoulders. There were always rumours of his antics in the Officers' Mess – racing his 500cc motorbike around the camp against the clock with young officers on the back hanging onto the fans as they span around – that sort of thing. If you got up to this kind of thing in the NAAFI it would be called unacceptable behaviour, but in the Mess it was 'high spirits'.

Colebourn had a number of trademark expressions. One was, "Close in, I don't want to shout," another, "If there's one thing that grips my shit," when he was annoyed about something. Probably the best one (used when B Coy fucked up) was, "If any of you fucks want to have a go, I'll take you around the back and knock the shit out of you. And if I can't do it, I'll get Fox (the battalion heavyweight) to do it." There was one brilliant episode in Fiji when he went out riding with Major Brown, a Cheshire officer but also a local Fijian, who was a living god in those parts. But more on this later…

****

Ray was coming with me to B Coy and Mickey Roberts was off to A. There was no time to hang about; I had to move my kit immediately into B Coy lines. I was off to Six Platoon on the top floor. I was doing my best to keep my head down, but I was attracting attention without even trying. This had something to do with the huge Royal Signals badge on the side of my suitcase. I opened the door and was met by Lance Corporal Walker, 'Wacker' to his mates, who was holding a baseball bat. What a lovely welcome.

When you first arrive in a unit, everyone else knows what to do and where to go and you spend most of your time playing catch-up. This is where I was, running around like a headless chicken. Dave Sherlock was B Coy Company Sergeant Major (CSM). He'd been a flyer in his day and eventually made Regimental Sergeant Major (RSM), then went on to get a commission. I met him for the first time down on the square after he'd just finished his basic fitness test (BFT). I was in sports kit, which is never a good start. Straight away he asked why Ray and I weren't in the correct kit for the BFT. See what I mean about not knowing the score and running around?

The disorientation soon passed and I was quickly thrown in to battalion life; doing a bit of work, but mainly going out and hitting the town, and getting to grips with the fact that it wasn't going to be that easy to get home and see my mum.

Chapter 6: Guardians of the fence

The border fence was about twenty-two miles long and a battalion would usually have two stints on the wire during a twelve-month period. Each period of duty would last between six and eight weeks, during which time all day and night-time locations were occupied along the border. Manning was minimal during the day, which was when the troops would get most of their sleep. When somebody hit the fence it was usually at night. Only on a few occasions did people swim the river or try to climb or cut the fence during daylight hours.

So it was at night that most people would make their attempts on the fence, and that's when the troops came alive and everybody went out capturing 'gooks'. While we were in Hong Kong, it was said that the Cheshires held the record for the highest number of captures during a tour on the fence: some six hundred plus. This was relevant because it was estimated that any force on the fence would only stop fifty percent of those trying to get through.

On seeing a chance of freedom and a new beginning, Chinese nationals would do whatever was necessary to get away. I myself saw a man run, leaving behind his wife and children; that's how desperate these people were. The fence itself was between ten and twelve feet high, with razor wire at the top and bottom. When it was breached it was occasionally cut, but more often than not a man would get up and over – without any shoes or gloves – in about ten seconds. My first experience of the border was at Man Kam To, facing the Special Economic Zone (SEZ) of Shenzhen. The last time I was up there was at Lok Ma Chau.

Being on the border was a real pain in the arse: we were living out of a kit bag for weeks on end and sleeping in dirty sleeping bags with no sheets and filthy mattresses. These were the centralised platoon (or sometimes two platoon) locations, which were just like big dormitories. Occasionally this sort of accommodation would be situated near a police station and there would invariably be a stagging on tower for two men to work long shifts, sometimes for up to ten hours. Inside, the official equipment would be powerful binoculars; sometimes 20/120 Nikons, log sheets and brewing equipment, plus comms by means of a very high frequency (VHF) radio. Unofficial equipment comprised a boogie box of some kind and a couple of dirty magazines.

As well as this type of location, there were also Mackenzie Forts: concrete constructions that were usually found in the middle of a field looking out over the fence and river. They were manned by a four-man team (two on, two off), but were independent with a small kitchen/living area and a similar type of stagging arrangement. As the name implies, these were well fortified and would only have one entrance.

At irregular intervals along the fence there were also towers that were made from wood and resembled scaffolding. Between twenty and thirty feet high, these would be manned by two or maybe three men who would spend up to forty-eight hours at the location. However, these weren't independent and food was brought out to them with the Land Rover run.

The final type of position was an ambush position – arguably the best and most exciting. During the day we did as little as possible, but there was always the danger of being caught and told to help in the kitchens or operations (ops) room. It was after our evening meal that it began to get exciting, as the camouflage cream competitions to see who could paint their face in the most warlike manner started. The kit was handed out and the teams were allocated to ambush sites.

The video player was always on the go. If it wasn't showing porn, it showed some form of gratuitous violence to get the lads fired up for the night's work. A two or three-man team would go out with a 349 handheld radio, shark eye torch, a baton/gook stick each (I know, I know, but we weren't operating in a politically correct environment) and plenty of plastic cuffs. The battalion started its third (my first) border tour with BMX bikes, but these were later taken away from us because troops began to spend too much time perfecting their tricks rather than doing their work. Backing up the troops on the fence were helicopters with thermal night-viewing kit as well as sweep and tracker dogs. (A sweep dog is a knackered tracker dog; it can be used to clear a general area, but not to follow a specific trail.)

The rhythm of being out at night involved troops smoking, getting bitten to death by mosquitoes, eating and listening to some sounds on the radio, and now and again grabbing a few minutes' sleep. From time to time, one or two call signs were instructed to check the fence at a particular zone (although they didn't always follow orders if a match was on TV in one of the MacKenzie Forts. Generally a huge hole would be found in the wire the next day. I took a bollocking on this account, as most of us did, but so what? Somebody had made it to Hong Kong Island looking for a better life). Once in a while it was a mad dash, but more often than not it involved lots of skulking around fishponds trying not to fall in. On one particular occasion, Five Platoon call signs came across a kung fu expert who gave a few lads a kicking, plus a dog accompanied by a handler!

Up to the point of actually catching a man with his wife and kids, and usually having to knock them down, this was exciting. But seeing a huddle of people crouching by a tiny hole – their fear quite evident as 'white perils' with painted faces came running at them – was sobering. And when you actually looked into these people's eyes and saw their terror and desperation, the excitement quickly evaporated and was swiftly replaced by a feeling of shame and disgust. I will readily admit, as I am sure others would, that I let people go. I had a quick look over my shoulder to check I wasn't being observed, then I let them disappear into the night. All these people wanted was their freedom; a break.

Those who were detained and processed were interrogated by the police and then handed back to a police station just over the International Bridge via Man-Kam To. There they were given into the 'care' of the People's Armed Police (PAP) and invariably had the shit kicked out of them. On average, the regiment would pull two bodies out of the river on each tour. These people either drowned crossing the river or were beaten and thrown in by the PAP.

Chapter 7: How we ended up in a Chinese glasshouse

A tour is physically and mentally demanding, so once a stint
was finished, the usual reward was five days' leave for the whole
battalion. This is where the trouble began: there were too many
troops with time on their hands, money in their pockets and
a need to let off steam.

The original plan for our break had been to go to the Philippines.
I had already missed my sister Sarah's wedding and opted to spend
two weeks' summer leave in Thailand.

We'd chosen Thailand because it was close; in fact, Hong Kong
to Thailand was like travelling from England to Spain. It took about
two hours. A few of us were going out: Ronnie Wilding, Spud
Huddleston, Dava and me. We had gone through customs at Kai
Tak Airport and we were sitting looking at this bloody huge Cathay
Pacific jumbo. We heard the tannoy announce a few times that it
was the last call for some passengers and we suddenly realised it
was us. Leg it! Typical troops on tour. We got a few disgruntled
looks from the other passengers we had kept waiting, but finally
got to our seats for takeoff.

We landed at Bangkok and transferred to Pattaya to a hotel on
Beach Road. We were on the main strip and when we stepped out
of the reception, the beach and the sea was just over the road.

It was standard stuff on tour: first, check out the bars; second, the
women; and then hire a motorbike and see the sights. Bear in mind
that Dava couldn't ride before we got out there, so the fact that he
managed to drive to Bangkok with Ronnie on the back before the
two weeks was up was a good effort. More on that later.

We drank in our rooms on the first few nights because it was
cheaper. Thai whisky and crisps were the order of the day, with a
club sandwich from room service. Then we would go out. During

the day we would chill by the pool, and because Spud was huge we would build a three-man tower; him at the bottom, me, then Dava. We would stagger to the edge of the pool and then tip forward and in. He dropped me once off his shoulders and I scraped my ribs on the side of the pool. No matter; the sun was out, we weren't wearing uniform and we were having a good time.

There was a notable incident when we caught up with Ray Beth, a Full Screw from B Company. He was out there at the same time as us, but he was with his rather glamorous wife. She had decided to go paragliding behind a speed boat. We were in the right place at the right time to see her get the harness on – wearing her usual full face of makeup and looking pretty hot. The lad who strapped her in gave the thumbs up and the boat set off. It didn't all go to plan, however, as the boat pulled her along but she didn't go up. In fact, it dragged her under the water for about five metres before she rose up in the air. Her makeup didn't look quite as good after that and we were pissing ourselves laughing. We hastily made our excuses.

I was arrested twice in Thailand. The first time I was being chased (pissed, don't ask) and I was running across a roof when the corrugated sheeting gave way and I fell, hitting my chest on a beam. This really knocked the wind out of me for a few minutes and I wasn't going anywhere. I was arrested and held at a beach holding point. After what seemed like ages nothing much was happening, so I got out my ID card and showed it to the police. They asked me to pay for the roof, which I did, and I was allowed to leave.

The second time, Ronnie and Spud had run out of money and had requested new funds to be wired to the bank in Bangkok some ninety-one miles away. We got there OK despite heavy traffic for the last ten miles. On the way out we made the mistake of going through a red light and got a pull. Luckily, the CO of the police station was Army trained, so he let us off – after inflicting about two hours of stories on us. We got going, but the final end to a shitty day came when I ran out of fuel about five miles out of town and it was raining. Dava's taillight disappeared in the night and I was on my own. I walked for a bit, pushing the bike, and thankfully a bloke with a low-backed truck stopped and gave me a lift back to Pattaya. I told him I had no money and he still took me, which restored my faith in human nature. When I got back after a ten-hour day, I looked in the mirror at the hotel and I was absolutely covered in shit. A quick clean-up and Dava and I were back on the piss.

At the end of our break we had all run out of money; we were skint. All we had was our airport tax, so this meant we spent thirty-six hours in a hotel in Bangkok before we got on the plane. The only thing we had to eat was the buffet breakfast.

On the flight back there was a massive storm around Hong Kong, which was locked down when we landed. The jumbo was being thrown around like a paper plane, but we got back in one piece to Kai Tak, which isn't the easiest airport for pilots to land at, as the one runway there sticks out into the sea. It was strange seeing so many shops closed down because of the storm as we headed back to camp and back to the grind. Anyway, that really is another story.

Before I left the Far East, it seemed only right that I should visit the Philippines. Many troops had fallen in love with the place and would go out at every opportunity, even for long weekends. But something went wrong – probably somebody's cash flow was suspect – so we didn't end up going. Instead, the self-styled 'Wrecking Crew' (me, Bomber, Scully, Bruce and Jacko) decided to spend the week drinking as much beer as we could in Hong Kong.

There were some real characters in Six Platoon, but then it doesn't matter where you serve; every platoon is filled with good blokes. Yes, there are lots of nutters and oddballs, but there are lots of good blokes too.

I had other mates outside of the 'Crew', but they had other things on their minds. Olly Almond had an English girlfriend, so he was sorted, while Tom Brown and Jimmy Baker were no doubt up to no good in the Wan Chi. Besides, this was an adventure for the Wrecking Crew. John Bailey, aka Bomber, was a funny lad from Knutsford. He was a sound Man United fan (yes, they do exist!). He was very friendly and his heart was in the right place; John wouldn't hurt a fly. He was a great long-distance runner, but his lack of coordination meant he was sometimes nicknamed Nerve Agent.

Andrew McCall, aka Scully, was a hard, wiry bastard. To Scully, everything was black and white. He had an answer for everything and everybody. We already knew of each other before Hong Kong, both of us coming from Chester. He was a good soldier and sportsman, but he was never really interested in the job; he just did enough to get by.

Bruce Turner was a bit of a strange one. I have some eye-popping mood swings, but I had nothing on Bruce. He was paranoid a lot of the time; always convinced that we were talking about him. But he was a solid soldier and was really fit.

Simon Jackson, aka Jacko, was a tough lad, built like a little bulldog. He was much wider than he was tall. Always up for a laugh, he took the rough with the smooth. Jacko was another fit bloke who had boxed in the junior Army finals. He was a good one to have on your side.

****

On Monday, the first day of our leave, we put our best kit on and went out on the town. This was to be an all-day affair and we started off in fine form: cheap beers in the China Fleet Club, ten-pin bowling, shopping, more beers and then the Star Ferry over to

Kowloon, where we carried on until we ended up in the Someplace Else bar under the Sheraton Hotel. As it was still the afternoon, pitchers of lager were half price, and the large bowls of salted popcorn that were thrown our way fuelled our thirst.

The mood was good and we began chatting across the tables to a group of Australian tourists. I knew that if it was going to go off at all, it would be between me and Bruce Turner – and it duly did. As usual, I had made a flippant remark at the precise moment Bruce was standing right over me. He landed a firm right hook to the side of my head. This was the only excuse I needed. I stood up and we traded several blows. I pushed Bruce backwards onto the bar, and when Bomber tried to intervene he got a smack as well.

The idea of troops fighting is bad enough, but it never looks good when they do it among themselves. Scully and Jacko finally got hold of us and put an end to the handbags, and still acting as a five-man unit we regrouped outside. The jugs and glasses had all been plastic, so there were no breakages. A few tables had been knocked over, but besides this there was no damage at all, so Bomber went back in to pay the bill and we thought that would be that. But a large group of people, mainly Chinese, began to gather around us. There was plenty of shouting and waving of arms from a group of men in suits, who were pointing in our direction. We thought they were regular citizens, but these men actually turned out to be internal security staff for the Sheraton.

It kicked off again when Scully decided he had had enough and punched a small, grey-haired man. Unfortunately, this was the head of security. What followed was the sort of fight you usually see on TV; all hands to the pump, every man for himself. Everybody went for it, punching and kicking in all directions, but from the outside looking in it probably resembled a scene from a *Carry On* film. As soon as there was a lull in the proceedings, Bomber led us off, running up a downwards escalator! What we didn't initially notice was that Bruce had been left behind.

We threw ourselves headlong up the downwards escalator. The adrenaline was pumping hard through my body. I had connected with something, but I wasn't sure who or what. It had really gone off. Lads talk about this sort of trouble but are rarely involved in it. We had lashed out and then legged it, but nobody knew the layout or where were we going. We could hear whistles being sounded behind us, and more and more security officers were arriving on the scene.

Scrambling up the escalator, Jacko had kicked backwards, knocking a security officer down to try to buy us more time. But even with a few extra seconds we had had it. We just seemed to run out of steam when we got to the next level. We stopped at some shop fronts and were almost immediately joined by the security officers. None of them attempted to get hold of us; they just stood by and blocked all the potential escape routes.

In no time at all the police arrived and started speaking to the security staff in Cantonese. It became clear that we weren't going to get a chance to explain this in English. The escalator we had had so much trouble running up had been stopped and two security officers led Bruce up it with his hands behind his back. Once he got up close, a third security officer punched him in the face. This happened in front of the police, who did nothing about it, so then it all kicked off again! This time we were in a rather confined space, heavily outnumbered and pretty much done for.

The five of us were bundled into a police wagon and driven away. Actually, Bomber started to get into the front passenger seat, which didn't go down too well!

We spent the night on the floor of a police station. There was no specific cell, just the floor with a number of desks and chairs scattered around. Our statements were originally written up in Cantonese, but we refused to sign them. They were then translated into English and we duly signed. What I can remember most is being very, very tired, but each time I tried to sleep I was woken up by one thing or another.

Bruce had come in for some pretty rough treatment. The security guards used small metal batons, which were about seven inches long and were kept on the wrist with small bands. When he had been left behind, these had come out and the damage was visible on his ribs and face. He had needed hospital treatment for this and, to our surprise, so had seven security officers.

In the early hours of Tuesday, I remember seeing a shiny pair of hobnail boots from my position on the floor. They belonged to Lance Corporal Latham of the Cheshire Regimental Police. 'Lathe' was the battalion heavyweight and nobody messed him around. We must have looked a right sight: my best shirt had been torn open and I had bruise marks around my neck where the gold chain my mum had bought me for my eighteenth birthday had been ripped off. We all looked bedraggled, unshaven, dirty and very tired. Despite this, they put us in jail again when we finally got back to Stanley. The regimental police fucked us around for a bit, asking us where we got our tattoos and that sort of thing. Before we knew it, we had been summoned by the adjutant, who is responsible for discipline in each battalion. We told our stories and, to our surprise, he said that we had been believed and would receive the support of the regiment.

It was also divulged that the Military Police had been called to an incident at the Someplace Else bar earlier in the day, and that incident had been nothing to do with us.

We were still on leave, sort of, so that night and the next we went for a few beers. Keeping as far as possible from the Sheraton Hotel, we headed for Mad Dog Come (Mad Dogs) in Mid-Levels, a very English bar that was frequented by middle-class Brits. We sat quietly with a pint and each told the story the way we had seen it: who was where, who did what and who hit what. The conclusion we came to was that we all got stuck in. Each one of us had hit somebody when we had thought we were going to get a kicking.

A legal representative was appointed: Squadron Leader Charles (RAF) from HMS Tamar. Tall, blond and fortyish, he was a good man. He sat back and allowed us to explain what had happened.

After our week's leave, we went back to work with everybody else. Nothing had really changed except that we had been charged. On the appointed evening we all turned up at the police station where we had spent the night and we were met there by Squadron Leader Charles. We thought this was a formality; we had all been involved, so we all expected to get something. But this was not quite the case.

Only two people were charged: me and Jacko. Jacko was on four charges of ABH and one of common assault, while I was charged with one of each. I was absolutely gobsmacked, but what could I do? Photos and fingerprints were taken and we were out of there, just waiting for a date to appear at a formal hearing. Work went on as normal, besides the occasional meeting with Squadron Leader Charles at Battalion HQ. Once it was established that Scully, whether provoked or not, had landed the first punch, he had to be withdrawn from any sort of defence plan we were mounting, and then there were four.

The final border tour took place in November, and before we knew it we were into December. Our regiment was to be the first line regiment to take over two years of ceremonial duties in London the following February. In December, Colonel Sergeant Fibbs (Coldstream Guards) arrived for the start of the Cheshires' ceremonial initiation. It was crazy. We did drill morning, noon and night.

It was only a taste of what was to come, but they were trying to put us in the picture. "Right, imagine this is the thrust of St James's Palace," they would say. Yeah, right – no problem at all! It's 27°C in the shade, we're all sweating our nuts off and this is supposed to be a royal palace. All we had to help us were a few traffic cones!

Besides the drill, we were set a number of dates to appear in court between December and February. We turned up every time in best bib and tucker, only for it to be adjourned to a later date. Cheshires were starting to leave Hong Kong for Caterham in Surrey, and likewise Guardsmen from the UK were starting to appear. We were running out of time if we wanted to head home with the rest of the Cheshires. In the meantime, the intercompany competition had taken place: B Company was champion company, and Six Platoon was champion platoon.

The Commander of the British Forces (CBF) had turned up one day at Stanley to present the intercompany shield and let the regiment know what a good tour we had had. This was also when our incident was reported at the highest level. The CBF had asked the CO/adjutant whether there was any news. He had been told about the delays and apparently was not happy. In turn, the CBF had spoken to the Governor of Hong Kong, who said that he wanted the matter closed off before the regiment officially left. A new court date was set for February 20. We were on...

Chapter 8: Getting the girl

While this whole shit storm was happening in Hong Kong, my thoughts often drifted to back home and the people I had left behind. I had had an on-off flirtation for years with a girl I was at school with, 'G'. It was a love-hate thing with us, and for ages she wouldn't even admit she was interested. That said, there was never a dull moment. Once we were out drinking in Chester and a lad pulled a pistol on me in the Snooty Fox pub. He said he was with the police and that I had to go with him. It didn't ring true for a minute, and as he frogmarched me down to the station near the racecourse I tried to put him through one of the giant, plate-glass windows of Iceland. He just bounced off so I ran. As I set off, he called for me to stop and he must have fired, because I heard the gun go off. I could only have been seven or eight metres away, so either he was a terrible shot, or more likely it was only firing blanks. Either way, I didn't stop to find out. When I did eventually stop to get my breath back, I was nearly sick. After a few minutes of rest I finally caught my breath and retraced my steps. I found G near the bus station in a right state and sent her home. I was walking home past the police station, when who should walk up the steps of the nearby car park but my assailant. I chased him right into the cop shop and they locked him up. As I was pissed, they sent me home. I never heard any more about what happened to the lad with the gun or why he was targeting me. I got away safely, that was the main thing.

Anyway, I digress. I finally managed to sweet-talk G into bed just before I flew out to Hong Kong. Once there, I was in a tower on the border stagging on when my mail arrived. It was a letter from G informing me that she was pregnant. I fell off my stool, then spent the next four hours writing her a letter: pages and pages of rambling incoherent assurances that I would support her in whatever she wanted to do. A baby wasn't my desired outcome from a roll around, but I wanted her to know that despite all the back chat and sniping that had become a feature of our relationship, I was there for her. Babies would be a bit of a game changer at eighteen, but I knew I wanted fatherhood to figure in my life at some point. If she chose to go through with the pregnancy, I could carry on with my career, but life would never be quite the same for G again. What did she want?

She didn't really enlighten me, but it was my best guess that she didn't want a baby and she didn't want me, either. Convincing her to sleep with me was one thing, but spending an extended period of time, possibly years, with me? It was a non-starter. That said, if she had surprised me and said, "OK Jim, let's give it a go," I would have stepped up to the plate.

I asked to be allowed home to sort things out, but B Coy CSM Dave Sherlock said it was a bad idea and that I should stay put. He was right and I did. G's response to my letter was a very short one, saying she had had an abortion. It seemed pretty clear she wasn't inviting any further correspondence, so I didn't write back and neither did she. It was more than a year later that I finally got back to the UK and went to see her. We went out for a drink and talked over what had happened, but only that once. After that we remained friends, but we weren't close. The pregnancy had effectively put an end to any romantic possibilities as far as she was concerned, so we never slept together again, which was probably a smart move.

Chapter 9: Wan Chai Warriors

With it being so relentlessly hot, lessons and training sessions were normally restricted to the morning unless we were on exercise or training for a particular event. During the afternoons we played as much sport as we could get out hands on. We were fit back then: we did military fitness, running in boots and battle PT in the morning and then football in the afternoons.

Official 'work' would knock off at about 1600hrs, when the 'pads' (married men) would go home and the barrack room would be left to us singles. Before tea we'd get close to a TV to watch cartoons, take a turn on the iron or stick some washing on. To go to the cookhouse (if you could be bothered – the food wasn't that good) you had to be dressed in either uniform or trousers/jeans and a top. No tracksuits were allowed. This was a bit of a pain and sometimes I couldn't be bothered, so I would get a sandwich at the NAAFI or choggies – a small shop on the lower-ground floor of A Company block. The shop sold sandwiches, cigarettes, drinks and chocolate. All of this could be run up on a tab, which was dangerous.

Things always got more exciting after tea. For me and many others, this was the first major trip away from home, because during training we went home most weekends. Here we were left to our own devices. One thing was a given, though; nobody ever had any money, and most of the lads were up to their eyeballs in hock with the camp trader, Jimmy Lamb, for TVs, videos and stereos. I didn't have any of that stuff and I still never had any money, but I loved going out.

Olly Almond usually got us all out of trouble. He was very frugal with his money and always had cash, mainly because he didn't go out much; well, not until he pulled an English girl about two months before we came home. We would all march up to him at the same time – Scully, Bruce, Jacko, Bomber and me – and ask him for a 'borrow' and he would hand out $100 bills so we could hit the town. He was a top bloke.

Getting ready to go out was almost as good as being out on the town; it was the anticipation of it all. We would shower, shave and work out what civvies were clean. Did these trousers look good with this shirt? What a bunch of girls! But it was all important for the elusive pull. I actually had some hair on the top of my head at the time, a flat top. I found the best way to make it flat on top was to wear my No.2 dress hat for twenty minutes. I applied plenty of gel and then I would walk around looking like a prat with this big hat on.

We all existed in two financial states: we either had money or we didn't. If we had money we would take the Shau Kei Wan Flyer bus down the hill into Stanley, pay a quick visit to the 7-Eleven for some 'green eggs' (Carlsberg) and then jump into two taxis to race into the Wan Chi. Occasionally, Dava Davidson and I would just nick a few bottles of San Miguel from the 7-Eleven, buy some travel sickness tablets and get off our faces sitting in the playground. Dava was one of the regular crew who would hit the Wan Chi on a regular basis. Like me, he was a private solider in Six Platoon. Dava was a bit of a Jack-the-lad. He had a wicked sense of humour and was always up for a laugh. If he wasn't out on the town, it either wasn't worth going out or he was ill. Despite being in the Wan Chi, which was effectively a huge playground, it was still the same format each time we went out. I think we nicked the San Mig because we were bored. Crazy, I know.

Camp was so big the Shau Kei Wan Flyer would come right up to turn around, just past the cookhouse. At the bottom guardroom (there were two) we had to get off again to book out. This was always a heart-in-the-mouth experience. If the Guard Commander didn't like what you had on, or just didn't like you, you were in trouble. A trip back to the block could put you back by thirty to forty minutes – it was a real pain in the arse!

When we didn't have money, we still got the Shaki Wan Flyer into Stanley more often than not, still visited the 7-Eleven for tins and then caught another bus to either take us over the hill or through the tunnel. Whichever way, we would eventually get to the Wan Chi as that's where it all happened.

The Wan Chi is a collection of bars, pubs, strip joints and clubs. It became synonymous with colourful nightlife in the 1960s, when US troops hit Hong Kong for rest and recuperation (R&R) from the Vietnam War and a lively red light district was spawned.

In fact, the Wan Chi's reputation was immortalised in the book and film versions of *The World Of Suzie Wong*. It was buzzing with life and rarely went quiet. Something I'm rather proud of is the fact that I spent fourteen months in Hong Kong and never once set foot inside a strip club – that is an achievement! The Inn Place, Makati Inn, Crossroads, the Horse & Groom and the most famous of them all, the Pussy Cat, were all within spitting distance of each other.

Beer was expensive in Hong Kong. My dad had talked a lot about Tiger before I got there, but the only place I found it served was HMS Tamar. In the bars it was either Carlsberg or San Miguel. A pint would set you back $18 (about £1.80), and this was a lot in 1985. However, there was salvation in the China Fleet Club, where servicemen could show ID to get in. The original site was next to the Wan Chi Stadium and I saw in the Chinese New Year on my eighteenth birthday watching the fireworks over the harbour. There was a hotel on top with ten-pin bowling and snooker, but what usually concerned us were the bars: two huge rooms which, every time I walked in, would be full of Cheshires. What I remember about the China Fleet was the waiter service. A pint was $7 or 70p and a rainbow cocktail was $10 (£1 back then), so we consumed these in vast quantities, along with big bags of chicken crisps that tasted nothing like chicken.

Things never really got going until about midnight, but the latest you could book out was 2200hrs. If you hit the town at seven or eight there was always the danger of not being able to stand up by midnight, so timing was everything. Usually, we would kill two hours in the Fleet then head to a club; either The Inn Place or Cross Roads. Going into a club would cost between $40 and $70 and the Triads controlled all of the clubs and pubs, but a deal must have been struck at some stage where the troops explained that unless we were allowed in for free, we wouldn't come in and drink their beer. As a result, the only nights I ever paid to get into a club were Christmas and New Year's Eve.

****

Tattoos were another big feature of life in Hong Kong, despite the fact that just setting foot in a tattoo parlour in Hong Kong was illegal for troops because of the dangers of contracting HIV or hepatitis C from dirty needles. A number of troops had tattoos of black dragons on their forearms, although the fine for doing so was high, around $2,000. However, this failed to put anybody off and lads who didn't have any tattoos before getting to the island went home with ten or sometimes twelve. The parlours were world-famous: Ricky & Pinkies is known across the world as one of the best and has been in the middle of the Wan Chi since 1975. In Hong Kong you don't pay for time, it's just down to the size of the work. If you wanted something small it would cost as little as $20.

I never bothered with tattoos. It's not that I wasn't tempted – I saw some beautiful work – but being of mixed heritage I was browner than most of the others, so the standout for colours was difficult and it always crossed my mind what they would look like when I was forty.

If we were still standing when the clubs shut at 0400hrs, it was off to the Horse & Groom (or House of Doom as we called it). This was one of those nightmare locations, full to the seams with drunken soldiers sitting in alcoves with equally drunken Filipino women they had picked up during the night. The regular dish was chicken and chips, which went down surprisingly well at that time in the morning. The ale was soaked up and this was an ideal way to start a working day. It was an initiation for all the lads: once you had been out all night, done a breakfast run to the House of Doom, got a taxi back, showered and then gone straight to work, you were accepted. We all did it back then, no problem. Today it would be a bit different.

A word on the taxis, though. Hong Kong is a twenty-four hour city and there were more taxis on the roads than anything else, so it was never that hard to get one, even if you couldn't stand up properly. The trouble came when we got in as the meters had two settlings. If the flag was to the side it was on the local rate, but if the flag was facing down, it was on the tourist rate, so of course the meter would tick over faster. The number of pissed up arguments we had with taxi drives about those meters! At least once a week some troop would get a cab all the way in to camp, get out outside B Coy lines and then run off without paying. This, of course, would not be a B Coy boy, but someone from A Coy who then ran through to their own lines.

When we went to the Wan Chi, we always went to eat at Johnny's (it's a dreadful admission, but I never once sat down and ate a proper meal at a Hong Kong restaurant. Off camp it was either the 7-Eleven, McDonald's or – more often than not – Johnny's beef noodles). Johnny did a 'special' for the troops, which he cooked in front of us in a huge wok. This was simple food, but it was just what you needed when you were going out drinking all night. Johnny always knew when the US military ships were coming to town, to the day. This was useful information as a battalion numbers six hundred and usually there were never more than three hundred out on the town. When the Seventh Fleet came in, however, two thousand or more US Marines descended on the Wan Chi.

Things usually started off on a good footing between us. We would drink and play 'quarters' – a US drinking game where a glass is filled with beer and left in the middle of the table – in the Fleet. Each person took a turn to bounce a quarter off the table into the drink. If you were successful, you nominated someone else to drink it down in one. Clearly the aim of the game was to get the US troops bladdered and, after six weeks at sea, none of them were particularly good drinkers. Things were normally great in the Fleet; it was down town that it tended to kick off. The US troops were invariably bigger than the Brits, so they would get hit with chairs, stools and all sorts. Often a British soldier would be flung across the room at high speed, but the Americans found it most unusual that the Brits just kept getting up for more! The US Shore Patrol and UK MPs would always be out in force trying to lock up whoever they could get hold of.

There was one occasion when George Bush, who was Vice President at the time (October 23, 1985), was in town accompanied by a number of Secret Service agents who decided to go out on the piss in the Wan Chi. When it went off, a number were filled in: I'm pleased to say by Cheshires.

When the French Navy came to town, their shore dress consisted of whites plus a white beret with a red 'nipple' on top. If you got back to camp with one of those berets you really were a player.

As mentioned, the Triads controlled everything in Hong Kong. All of the drugs were run through China via Hong Kong, and then into the European markets. The vast majority of crime was organised with and through them as fund-raising activities. There was at least one incident of two white kids found cut up in the Mid-Levels. This was believed to be a 'blooding'; an initiation for a new member of the group to prove himself. There was plenty of fighting in the Wan Chi: British troops, Royal Marines, German sailors and US Marines. You name it, everybody got involved. But if you ever got into a fight with a Chinese man with tattoos, it was time to walk away. These people would kill you rather than argue about it.

Chapter 10: Barrack room life

Living in a barrack room is like playing a game; the classic 'bullshit battles brains'. The idea was that if you showed people what they wanted to see, they were usually happy. The lines (or blocks) in Hong Kong were all interconnecting and followed the road around the outside of camp, offering great views of the South China Sea at the back, while to the front there was a square with football pitches behind. We were at the southernmost tip of the island and the barracks were built in a suitable position to defend. There was one road up the hill and the majority of the arc of vision behind the blocks was of the sea. Beautiful.

B Company block was at the end furthest from the cookhouse and the bus stop, next to the rugby clubhouse and gym. It was two storeys, with Four Platoon on the ground and us, Six Platoon, on top. If we walked through the connecting door it would lead us straight into C Company and to Nine Platoon lines.

It was, as you might expect, all shiny floors and wooden lockers. Unlike in training, each pit was made as homely as possible, with a TV, video player and pictures on the walls. But first thing in the morning it had to be regimental and 'squared away'. A rotation on the room jobs was posted each week to cover the washrooms, corridors, stairs, and so on. It was a pain in the arse, but it had to be done. Come night-time, it looked as if a grenade had gone off in most of the rooms: washing lines were made up of bungees and there were food wrappers all over the floors, but we all knew the drill. It didn't matter how bad it got, particularly at the weekends; it always looked on the ball when it had to.

As the battalion geared up to leaving in February, the inspections became more and more frequent. Posters had to be stripped from the walls and quilts put away. In fact, boxes of stuff were packed and shipped out long before it was time to leave, lending the block a real basic training feel.

Chapter 11: Our day in court

I was the only one who had a suit for the court case. I had it made for happier occasions by the tailor on camp, but that was just the way it turned out. We were as ready as we could be, having run over our story time and time again. All of the events of that evening were clear in our minds and we had been reassured: tell the truth, explain exactly what happened and everything will be OK. All we did in the end was defend ourselves.

But straightaway there was bad news. The magistrate who was hearing our case wasn't a friend of the Armed Forces. He was an expat who had an extremely poor reputation when it came to handling cases involving military personnel. In the past, he had put US sailors, Hong Kong Military Service personnel and Gurkhas away on separate occasions for fairly minor misdemeanours. It was too late to worry about it, though. We would just tell it how it was and hope it would work out.

To begin with, the prosecution got a chance to explain the events of that night in November. For the best part, Jacko and I sat in the dock in relative silence as most of the proceedings took place in Cantonese. Bruce and Bomber were there, of course, but our only chance to talk was during the recesses and the break for lunch. The Platoon Commander, Lieutenant Waltier, was there because when the time came he would be asked to provide character references.

There were plenty of security guards in court; I suppose all of those who were involved. I didn't recognise any of them as it had all happened very fast. The seven officers who had been taken to hospital were treated for cuts, bruises and a broken nose. It wasn't exactly the Somme; more the sort of thing you pick up in the NAAFI on a Saturday night! What became apparent was the way they referred to me when I was mentioned. It was always 'the negro'. Not defendant number one or number two, just 'the negro'. Jacko and I picked up on this and it became a point of amusement. On one occasion, when Jacko was referred to, I quietly whispered to him, "That's the white one," and we both creased up in laughter.

Whether he had it in for us from the beginning we'll never know, but the magistrate then asked both of us to stand up. What he said next, I remember word for word: "Mr Charles, your two defendants seem to find this case increasingly amusing. Perhaps the outcome may not be so." More nails had been added to the coffin!

The second day of the trial (Friday, February 21) was also my nineteenth birthday. Unfortunately, Jacko and I were both asked to take the stand so it wasn't a great birthday. When Mr Charles was asking the questions, he sort of led us in the right direction; no problems there. But when the prosecution lawyer's time came it was a different story.

The closest I had been to a court before was watching *Crown Court* on TV. I wouldn't wish the pressure we were under on the stand on anybody. The pace and precision of the questions was frightening and unless you're very careful, you end up saying what is in your head at the very moment you think it. On the stand I felt I was really under the cosh. The angling of the questions eventually came round to why I had broken a particular security guard's nose. Why, why, why did I do it? What I eventually said was another nail in the coffin: "Because I thought I ought to." Oh dear...

After me, Bruce and Bomber got up to say their bit. Perhaps it wasn't looking too bad, I thought. After all, we had all been involved, we had all hit somebody. Why had Jacko and I been singled out for the attention, for the charges? It was easy now to see why: we were the easiest to identify. I'm six feet tall and of mixed heritage. Jacko is about five-feet two and nearly as wide; he looks like a bulldog. We were easy to pick out and they were trying to pin it on us. It was OK as long as somebody got punished.

That night we ended up in the Wan Chi. It was my birthday and it was a Friday, so what else were we going to do? We had a quick beer with Squadron Leader Charles and then he left us to it.

I was feeling more depressed than ever before. What the hell was going on? When we were charged, I had had to phone my mum to tell her I wouldn't be coming home with the rest of the battalion. I made the call from the foyer of the China Fleet Club with a $50 phone card. She had already been through the wringer watching the tears and sweat I had produced during training, and this was too much. Our local paper back home, the *Chester Chronicle*, had been pumping up the story of our troubles for a month: the Cheshires are coming home. But not this one.

We got absolutely hammered that night: first at the China Fleet, then the Inn Place, where we dug in for the night. Somewhere along the way we had met up with an English girl I knew whose dad read the news on HBO at the weekends. She wanted to get my kit off and I knew it. The only trouble was that although she was a lovely girl, I just wasn't really attracted to her.

That night she ended up taking me home. I was in one of those bolshy drunken moods, the sort where you need your face smack- ing. All I wanted was to go home to Chester. I remember getting to the flat, sitting on the sofa and that was my lot. In fact, she was very good to me; better than I deserved. She lay me down on the sofa in my drunken state and slept on the floor beside me. She did this because when you wake up from that sort of session in a strange place, it always freaks you out – and it did. She explained where I was and calmed me down.

Sunday was one of those 'just try and stay calm' days. The camp was virtually empty of Cheshires and the Coldstream Guards had effectively taken control. Our lines looked like a ghost town, new and clean. The four of us that remained were just left there with a few suitcases. Jacko went on another real bender and could hardly stand up when he got back in. I couldn't face it, I was trying to stay calm. Lieutenant Waltier turned up waving our tickets about. We were booked to fly out the following Tuesday. Squadron Leader Charles said we would get a heavy fine, but that we should be OK. All we could do was wait and see.

Whatever happened, one way or the other, Monday was the last day. It didn't look that bad, but whether I really believed that or I was kidding myself, I don't really know. We had to believe it would be OK – we hadn't done anything. A punch-up? It goes off every weekend in Hong Kong. I'd lived there for a year and never, ever got involved. Yes, there was fighting, but nothing major. I suppose it was the sort of thing that people consider a regular occurrence where soldiers live, but this was never the case for me. It just hadn't happened.

I had proved myself in the boxing ring. Nobody thought I could do that, but I did. In fact, I did the business in front of the whole battalion, Commanding Officer, Regimental Sergeant Major and the second-in-command of the British Forces. I had always kept a low profile when out on the town; I was there for the crack, the music and the women. This one time I had got stuck in because I had always been taught not to let people shit on me, not to let people take the piss. I get stuck in once and that's it: ABH and assault. Just my fucking luck.

Summing up, Squadron Leader Charles did the business, as did Richard Waltier, who got up and said that we were both good lads. It wasn't enough, though; it was never going to be enough. In some respects, this was high profile. The Commander of the British Forces had been involved (the Governor) and they wanted this matter resolved. Even with that sort of interest, an example was about to be made. A Guard's regiment was arriving for two years and they wanted to send a message to them that if they misbehaved, this was what would happen to them.

The magistrate told us to stand up. I didn't catch all the finer points of his judgment, but I got the important bit: "I can't let this pass with a mere monetary sentence. Three months for common assault and three months for actual bodily harm, to run concurrently. Jacko had more charges against him, but our sentences were the same. He just wanted to send us down.

I really couldn't comprehend what was happening. It wasn't real… this couldn't be happening. I didn't know what to do, I couldn't speak. The shock was registering all around the court. Even the police were caught off-guard; there was a definite delay before they cuffed us. After what seemed like an age, we were led downstairs to the holding cells. Neither of us spoke, probably as the realisation of what it meant to receive a custodial sentence while serving in the Army hit home. All of our possessions were taken form us: wallets, belts and even our shoelaces. These were all signed for and then we were put in a small cell. Sitting together, alone for the first time, it began to feel all too real. Jacko was a tough lad – he was junior Army boxing finalist – but it was all too much and he began to cry.

Time felt irrelevant at this point, but it didn't seem long before we were on the move. Cuffed once again, we were put on a prison truck. It was one of those where the back section is split into two sides: one for guards and the other for prisoners. On boarding the truck, our ankles were cuffed, rather like being in a chain gang. We were joined by several Chinese lads who were also fresh from the Magistrates' Court, and we picked up a handful more on the way. In all there must have been eight of us, with five or six guards on the other side of the grill for company.

We were on our way to a youth correctional facility in Kowloon, which housed men between the ages of fifteen and twenty-five. We must have spent an hour in the truck, stopping at various police stations to pick up prisoners. By the time we arrived, it was dusk. Jacko and I said very little as we were both in our own little worlds. Neither of us was willing to admit to the other how much trouble we had got ourselves into.

There were big gates outside this place, standing tall at twenty feet high. As we stepped together from the truck, the lights trained on the gates were glaring. We went through the outer then the inner doors and we were in. We just followed the prisoners in front of us, as at this stage we were all in the same boat.

First we all had to strip off, and our clothes were bagged and taken away. Now we had no personal belongings at all. Standing around naked was degrading in itself as the prison guards, armed with revolvers, wandered around saying things and pointing here and there, and things didn't improve when we had our medicals. Basically they wanted to know if we had lice or were trying to carry anything into the prison, so we had to jump up and down then submit to them rummaging through our hair, followed by an internal search from a guard. As I queued up for my turn, I remember seeing a young lad of fifteen or perhaps sixteen who was obviously in distress as a guard shoved a hand up his backside. I looked at his colleague's sidearm and thought, 'I may as well get on with it.' Then I immediately thought, 'NO!'

Previously whenever I thought about internal searches, I remembered Chevy Chase in *Fletch* saying: "What are you using, doc, the full fist?" It wasn't that funny in real life. He stuck a bit of disinfectant on his finger and Bob's your uncle. Thank God he didn't find the six-pack of Carling! Haircuts were next. I came out shaved, carrying what was left of my hair in my hand. This actually got a laugh out of Jacko until he went in himself.

Then that was it; we were kitted out in the prison rig. This consisted of blue baggy trousers that finished at the shins, a blue denim shirt, a brown jumper and a quilted blue sleeveless top. It was very stylish. It must have been getting late, but neither Jacko nor I had a watch or knew how to ask the time, so it was all guesswork. As we were led off to the cells, the shock wore off and reality hit home. After that first night, and every morning after, Jacko and I were woken by the revolting sounds of young men coughing up phlegm, part of the daily routine for other inmates. Next, a young lad chosen for the job pushed a large bucket along the cells handing out a Kraft cheese slice and a piece of bread for breakfast. This turned out to be the best meal of the day, and it was accompanied by a cup of what could loosely be described as tea.

At the end of our first full day of incarceration, Jacko and I had a visitor: Lieutenant Waltier. Once again we were marched down past the football pitch, which resembled a building site, to the reception area. Looking at his face it was difficult to see what he was thinking; he was either going to start crying or burst out laughing. He came armed with words of reassurance, not only for us but also for himself before he got on the plane and went home. His initial stance had been that he wouldn't leave until he got us out, but three months was a long time and now the tack had changed. The regiment had appointed one of the top barristers in Hong Kong, mainly because they didn't take too kindly to the headlines in the *South China Morning Post* about the Cheshire Regiment's soldiers being jailed for assault. This meant it wasn't just me and Jacko who were in the shit; they had to get us out to save some face. It was good to see the boss, and although he didn't manage to fire us up, at least it was another English voice.

After that, we settled into the routine: Radio 2 played at night (about every fifth tune was an English one) and we were given hot milk. The hot milk was wonderful. During the evening, a huge bowl of it was pushed along the front of the cells. We would pass our mugs out to the lad and he filled them up. This was beautiful until a few days in when one of the prisoners, probably trying out his English, asked if we drank the milk. Our reply was probably standard: the milk was the best thing available to eat or drink. Or so we thought, until he explained that it contained bromide'(potassium bromide is used to suppress sexual desire). This drug is believed to have been used by the British Navy in days gone by. It apparently stops you getting an erection, but to be honest I had so much on my mind I hadn't noticed. Anyway, we stopped drinking the milk!

Chapter 12: Hong Kong and its importance to British forces

Hong Kong was the last occupied corner of China. The British famously had a ninety-nine year lease, or concession, to Hong Kong's New Territories from China, from June 9, 1898, to July 1, 1997. When people think about Hong Kong, they only think about one island, but there are actually two hundred and thirty-six dotted around. It is broken down into four regions: Kowloon, Hong Kong Island, the New Territories and the Outer Islands (Lantau, which is actually twice the size of Hong Kong, and the like). The port on the main island is one of the greatest trading ports in the world and, with more than six million people living on the 1,070 square-kilometre island at the time, space was, and still is, at a premium.

The first direct contact between British and Chinese came in 1637, when four heavily armed ships under Captain John Wendell arrived at Macao in an attempt to open trade between England and China. The English were not backed by the East India Company, but rather by a private group led by Sir William Courteen, including King Charles I's personal interest of £10,000. They were opposed by the Portuguese authorities in Macao and quickly enraged the Ming authorities. They sought help from the Portuguese to secure the release of hostages. They left the Pearl River on December 27; however it is unclear whether they returned home at this point.

The Chinese finally opened their doors to Europeans in 1685. The East India Company's ships began to arrive on regularly from then on and warehouses were established near Canton to export tea and silks. Everyone wanted to get involved; the British and French were followed by the Dutch, Danes, Swedes and the Americans in 1785.

The British Forces were based in the southern peninsula of the island. Stanley Fort (or 'cha chi ping fong' – the place where the soldiers live) was perched up on a hill above the village of Stanley. At the base of the hill – which we ran up on a regular basis – was a prison built by the British in 1937. Unfortunately, this was used by the Japanese to intern British expats during World War Two. After the war, and when returned to Hong Kong/UK hands, the prison became a maximum-security facility. In fact, two Scots Guards got drunk in 1982 and decided they wanted to go home. This attempt involved taking weapons from the camp, stealing a Land Rover and setting off for the airport. They were eventually surrounded in a tunnel on the way to the airport and arrested. Sentenced to time at Her Majesty's pleasure, one was placed in Stanley Prison, the other in the delightful establishment where Jacko and I had ended up.

Stanley Village offered plenty in the way of shopping. It is a busy market where people went to pick up clothes, fake designer goods, furniture and, of course, street food. The seafront had a number of memorable landmarks. These included the Smugglers Inn, which was frequented by the large expat community and soldiers alike; however, I am pleased to say that I didn't once step inside to buy a pint. It was also home to the Hong Kong Shanghai Bank, where the 'Crew' stood on many a warm, close evening waiting for Olly Almond to hand over his hard-earned cash so we could hit the town.

When we stood on the seafront in the evening the air was sweet and very humid. You could see the pads (married men's accommodation) jutting out on the side of the hill, but the Fort itself was completely out of sight. As you ran up from the prison at the base of the hill there were civvie flats on the right looking out towards the South China Sea. Unfortunately, the flats were very close to the Army pads and, while similar from the outside, these were filled with serving soldiers, their wives and kids.

The perks for married men were great, particularly in Hong Kong. The accommodation was of a good standard and they got extra money for having their families over. What could be better after you've had a shit day getting bollocked than to go home to your own pad? The single lads were over for two years, and for some the lure of the pads' perks was enough to convince them to marry their young girlfriends before long tours. So it came as no surprise that these marriages didn't always work out very well. This was quite evident when B Company were on the border and many of the B Company wives could be found in the Wan Chi getting pulled by American sailors. And people wondered why there was trouble!

The hill then seemed to get quite a bit steeper and finally it reached the bottom guard, which is where we booked out to leave camp. Soldiers had to be dressed in shoes, trousers and a collar to do so, but the lengths soldiers would go to to get out without a collar on! I saw plenty of shirts cut off at the chest so they could be worn out of the gates under a jumper and then discarded.

Beyond the guard room, the high wall on the left is actually part of the huge storm drainage ditches which weave along parallel to the road. The pads inside the camp were built up high on the left with balconies and veranda that are very reminiscent of colonial buildings. To the right the road dropped away quite sharply to the medical centre hidden in the trees. Battalion HQ was on the left of the road; a three-storey building in a similar style to the pads. The upper guard room was on the ground floor and the armouries for all companies were at the back of this building.

Just past Battalion HQ was the turnaround spot for the Shau Kei Wan Flyer. The road then split into two: the left fork led to the company offices and Colour Blokes' stores, where any kit you needed to sign out (torches, radios, etc) would be kept. Beyond this was the Officers' Mess. The right fork led to the cookhouse for ranks on the corner and then off towards the company blocks. Down this way, you could go in at one end (HQ Coy) and come out right at the other end (B Company). The alleys were all connected, but the bottom line was that if you weren't invited, you didn't go into another company's lines. B was next to C and the rivalry was fierce. Four Platoon on the ground floor could walk into Seven Platoon lines, then Five was in the middle, which led into Eight Platoon, and so on.

Once in front of Battalion HQ, you could look down through the trees to the square, which was huge, rolling down to the football pitches and then the sea. Past the end of the blocks was the rugby club, which sat on its own and looked a bit lonely, and then the gym. The road went right around the square and pitches, and it was used for all of our runs. Off to the left beyond the gym was some ground that still belonged to the military but was occupied by cable and wireless dishes. The track and very steep steps were used on the Pearson Run every Friday. Pearson was a battalion cyclist who was killed in an accident, and the Pearson Run was cross country in sports kit on a Friday as an intercompany race. When we finished the Pearson that was the start of our weekend; what fun it was.

The sea was heavily polluted as it was used by many Hong Kong inhabitants as an open sewer. On battle PT we often ran down the hill to the beach by the prison. Tommo (our PTI) would make us run up and down a bit and then swim out to the pontoon before running back up the hill in our wet kit. On one particular occasion I remember swimming hard. Then I met a human turd in the water, and that made me swim a little harder!

Also on the seafront was the 7-Eleven, which I first visited with Olly during my first week. We sat on the step and ate warm ham subs. This was the very same shop where Tosh Williams went bonkers and started attacking the staff. The incident was captured on CCTV and he received a few days in the big house to think about it.

You could always tell when the troops had money. For a few days

after payday the trip to the Wan Chi would be made in taxis, with
everybody racing each other to the China Fleet Club. Each trip
would be accompanied by green eggs, and the partly drunk cans
would be dispatched out of the taxi windows at high speed as we
passed local barbecue parties at Deep Water Bay and Repulse Bay.
After the tenth of the month, when we were all skint, the same trip
would be made on the bus. We would try to get the back two rows
upstairs, where we sat with our beers and put the world to rights,
but every time we passed the bays we would fling half-full cans out
of the windows. I don't know if we ever hit anyone, but I'm sure
the *South China Morning Post* would have got to hear about it if
we had. The taxi trip was a lot quicker, and as the cars swung off
the flyover and down into the Wan Chi we would always pass the
famous Shark's Fin Restaurant and then I knew we were almost
there; back into the thick of the action.

****

To give an indication of how much we were drinking, I once
went for a medical so I could take a parachuting course and failed
because I had blood in my urine. This all-night drinking almost got
me in a lot of trouble (other than fighting) on one occasion. Just two
days after competing in the intercompany boxing championships
(more on that later), I had been 'volunteered' to join A Company to
take part in the Gurkhas' field force march and shoot competition;
a gruelling one-day event on the New Territories, despite the fact
that boxers were meant to have a week off. It involved a combat
fitness test (CFT), which was eight miles with kit across country,
followed by an infantry combat fitness test (ICFT), two very quick
miles with kit weighing 35lbs for eighteen minutes, followed by
a field test involving NBC, first aid and map reading. On the day

75

of the competition, troops were dropping like flies: Gurkhas and Cheshires alike had to be 'cas evaced' to hospital by helicopter.

The training for this event was about as much fun and involved a lot of running around. I was most put out after boxing my socks off for B Coy that they had sent me to A Coy for this. Yes, I was fit, but I was also bloody knackered! This meant that I had one day off after the finals and then I was straight back into it. It was an important event and meant training at the weekend, but Friday night was sacrosanct, so I set out on the town regardless. When I got back at 0500hrs – only to get up at 0530hrs for an eight-mile bash around the drainage ditch around Repulse Bay – it didn't seem like such a great idea.

We set off from camp in full kit before the sun was properly up. I was in a sort of pissed daze, not really thinking and just following the man in front. Isn't that what soldiers are supposed to do, not think?! By the time we got up on the ditch the sun was up. I was bimbling along, talking to someone and putting my feet down without thinking. The next step I took was into thin air. The ditch follows the line of the bay and curves around; I, on the other hand, was walking in a straight line. As I began to fall it seemed like a long way down and I could feel the heavy kit bulking up around my shoulders. Around the point of no return, a kindly C Coy bloke called Evo gripped my Bergan. He was lying on the floor and holding me up by my kit. It was all over in a flash and Evo, with the help of a few others, hauled me up and we carried on. But if he hadn't been there it was a sheer drop of a hundred or so feet down to the building.

We jumped onto the four-tonne trucks back to camp and had breakfast before lessons. Staying out all night was starting to make me feel really ill and I desperately needed some sleep. Instead of going to breakfast, I lay on my bed for thirty minutes before first aid and NBC in the classrooms at Battalion HQ. The first aid class was taken by Lance Corporal Sheridan (Shez), a battalion boxer who was not a bloke to be fucked around. I didn't find first aid a particularly riveting subject, particularly as I'd had no sleep, so it wasn't long before I dozed off and began snoring loudly. I was woken by Shez who was bawling that I should stand up, so I duly did while he carried on with the tedium. Unfortunately, for the first and only time in my life, I fell asleep on my feet and started snoring again. The whole place erupted and the troops were crying with laughter. Shez wasn't pleased and had another go at me. I was, after all, a CROW, and me winning the intercompany boxing championships meant nothing to him. I just about managed to stay awake for the rest of the morning. The agony wasn't over, though; there was still the ICFT to come. This was a real strain, and by this stage I was making some very strange noises to try and keep up. How I got round I don't know, but I made it. I was so tired I didn't know what to do with myself. Somehow I got cleaned up and got a bus into the Wan Chi, at which point I went to Sonya's flat. Sonya was a beautiful Filipino girl I had met out on the town one night. She lived in town and often scooped me up and took me back to her flat when I had drunk too much beer, so fairly often. When I got there on this occasion she helped me undress and put me to bed.

****

As far as I could see, there were three types of women in Hong Kong:

1. Chinese. They very rarely fraternised with the troops. They knew us too well and didn't want to get involved.

2. Filipinos. There were hundreds of 'Flips' who were employed as domestic help or nannies by the middle classes. Their day out

was Sunday or 'Flip Day', when they all had twenty-four hours off. They loved the troops and some would look for a way out, hoping for an English passport. A few did marry lads from the regiment.

3. Gweilos. Most of these were teenage kids whose parents worked and lived in the middle-class apartments in the Mid-Levels. They were rich kids out playing, but the ones I met were good kids. They were out partying most nights and got to know the regular 'Wan Chi warriors' well. Nicky was one of the rich kids I met on one of our many jaunts to the Wan Chi on the ale. We never slept together, but I had a bit of a soft spot for her. She was blond and very pretty. More about her and her friends later.

Chapter 13: Boxing

'Milling' was still practised by infantry soldiers when I arrived in Hong Kong. This basically meant showing aggression and was a free-for-all marshalled by the PTIs. We wore 16oz gloves (big pillows) and one morning we were lined up and put into pairs by height. Unfortunately, I was tall but rather skinny and ended up being paired with a big lump called Brian Meredith. To put it mildly, he knocked the shit out of me: I ended up with a split lip, black eye and broken nose.

On the back of this I went see Davey Parsons, who was putting the boxing team together, and asked if I could join the team. He laughed and told me to go away. I then had six or seven weeks away on exercise in Fiji. It was a cracking tour but, as always on tour, I lost some weight. On getting back to Hong Kong I went to see him again and asked if I could box. This time he weighed me and asked if I was sure. I then had a choice: I could either stay as I was and go in at Middleweight (11st, 6lbs) or lose weight and go for Light Middleweight (11st). I opted to lose weight and the hard work started. Boxing was a high priority in the regiment and training was full time. I was on a liquid diet for two weeks and did most of my training with Macca (Welterweight) and Davy Young (Bantam). Macca was in the pit opposite me in our room in Five Platoon lines. He too had won the Gale Cup at Litchfield. He was extra fit and an excellent sports man. Davy was next door. We all arrived at the battalion during the Hong Kong tour and being nigs you seem to gravitate as a group and stick together.

At this time we ran and ran, mainly with black plastic bags layered inside our training kit. It got to the stage where the weight loss was slowing down so much we would run and then lie on the floor for thirty to forty-five minutes in the hope that we would sweat more off. One Friday night, Davy Young and I had had enough and we got chicken fried rice at the NAAFI. We sat on the steps outside looking at this beautiful food and the next minute Davey Parsons was standing in front of us. Neither of us managed a spoonful. I remember training with Davy Young in the drying room on a heavy bag and seeing a Lion Bar on the floor with ants all over it – and being tempted! We were that desperate.

We managed to get access to the medical centre scales the night before the weigh-in. This was a no-no. We legged it down there, stripped off and got on. I was dead on 69.5kg (11st), so Davey P sent me back to the block with no food or water. He told me to get my kit off and go to sleep. When I got up in the morning, I put my kit straight on and headed back down to the medical centre without a drink. I weighed in and boxing started later that day. First things first, once the weigh-in was over the most important thing was food. All I had been dreaming about was tomatoes on toast. The boxing squad was allowed to go into the cookhouse in tracksuits to eat after the weigh-in, which was an exception. I got in there and picked up about five slices of toast and a huge pile of tomatoes… and I managed about three mouthfuls; my stomach had shrunk.

In the semi-finals I boxed Si Humphries of C Coy and stopped him in the second round. It was a technical knockout. The final was against Paddy Gilmore from A Company. On finals night I was shitting myself. We sat in Four Platoon lines doing our wraps, listening to the Rocky theme music ("Gonna Fly Now", not "Eye of the Tiger") over and over. Then it was time to go over to the gym. As the squad went outside, B Coy was already formed up and the Sergeant Major brought the company to attention as we went past. It was quality!

In the gym changing room I warmed up and was immediately knackered; it was the fear of stepping into the ring. Mine was the first fight after the interval, so I was gloved up with my 10oz gloves and ready to go. Davy came to collect me and I remember my legs not being my own. Davey P had to pick me up and place my gloves on his shoulders. The bugler in the upper level of the gym blew and the noise started: I could hear the air horns and B Coy were out of their seats. I felt better with each step. I got a unanimous decision over three tough rounds against Paddy. I couldn't speak for about an hour afterwards and only managed two beers at the rugby club before I was pissed out of my mind. I woke up the next morning with my boxing kit still on.

****

Married men in the Army get a lot of stick, but the pads were quite kind to the old singles when it counted. Christmas was a good example. The battalion held Christmas Day celebrations around December 22-23. After the carol service, the ranks ate in the cookhouse and were served by the senior NCOs and officers. It was a joyous time, with decorations, fruit and beers laid out on the long cookhouse tables. The band set up in the corner of the cookhouse and played throughout the meal. The banter was great as the seniors gritted their teeth and had to be pleasant to the troops.

The band would rattle through a number of tunes, but each and every attempt to play The A-Team theme tune was met with roars from all the other companies and spoons were smashed down on the tables. The A-Team music was A Company's theme and therefore wasn't on at all. The culmination of the meal came when the youngest man in the battalion, Millie from B Coy, was forced to get up and conduct the band. This was a nightmare for him, as each time he moved the baton, some strange sound would emerge from one instrument or another.

Before we dispersed, the Commanding Office stood at the front and addressed the lads. It was the usual thing: we were doing well, but could still do better. Then the band cranked up the regiment tune: "Will You Dance, Charlie Boy?" This was the signal for everyone to get up on the tables and start dancing, but no one seemed to mind. We then all got a few days off, which if you were single meant you got on with it in the blocks, and if you were a pad you went home. It was traditional that the married lads from each platoon would invite the single blokes round for Christmas dinner. Jacko, Bomber, Davy Young, Scully and I were invited to Woody's (Corporal Woods' home).

Being my first Christmas away from home, it was bit of a shocker. My mum had sent a shoebox full of presents in October, which I had stashed away until Christmas Day. Inside was a blue shaving and wash bag, sports soap, a huge can of Foster's lager and a cigar. We all dragged ourselves out of bed as it had been a big night in the Wan Chi. After showering and arming ourselves with a case of green eggs, we headed over to Woody's house. The blocks are cold and lifeless, and it could have been any day of the year, but to see his kids open up their presents was magical. We all settled down for a few ales while his wife prepared the dinner. When it arrived it was the next best thing to home; none of that cookhouse stuff that totally lacks love and attention. After the food and several more beers, we all struggled to keep our eyes open for the Queen's speech. After that it was the standard kip followed by some sandwiches, then back to the Wan Chi once more.

Chapter 14: Entertainment away from the Wan Chi

The Wan Chi wasn't the only place to go out and play. Kowloon offered its own delightful spots. If we didn't have money, usually after the tenth of the month, we went over there via the Star Ferry. You could go upmarket for eight pence or downstairs with the peasants for five pence. One thing you did get on the ferry was a view of the island as you looked back; of the fantastic lights on all of the skyscrapers and up on the peak. This was the people ferry, but when we were moving across with the four-tonne trucks going to the ranges we would go on the car ferry, where you could pick up a blinding egg and noodle soup for about fifty pence.

Nathan Road, named after the thirteenth Governor, Sir Matthew Nathan, is pretty famous. Lieutenant-Colonel Sir Matthew Nathan (who was awarded The Most Distinguished Order of Saint Michael and Saint George) was a British soldier and civil servant who also served as Governor of Sierra Leone, the Gold Coast, Hong Kong, Natal and Queensland). Nathan Road was home to all of the electrical shops. Troops have a fascination with electrical kit, so this is where they would be on or around payday. In the blocks we had three or four TVs or stereos fighting for ears in the same room! The Sheraton Hotel – where all of our real trouble started – was at number 20 Nathan Road.

There were also the infamous night markets at Temple Street and Tsim Sha Tsui (TST). Here you could kit yourself out for about £10, including shoes! The life expectancy of the kit was about forty-eight hours, but that didn't matter; if you got into a fight and your shirt was ripped, that was where you went to by a replacement Le Shark, Lacoste, Adidas or Puma item. None of it was real, but it looked just about good enough, especially after a few pints. Everyone wore a Rolex in Hong Kong. About five percent were real and the rest came from the night markets. The air was thick and humid, with hundreds of stalls selling assorted noodles in the streets. These were dotted among the makeshift stalls, which would sell us anything we wanted. It was all there.

When the weekends came around, the last thing we wanted to do was have to book in and out of camp. One time I had forgotten to book out for the weekend and had a mad rush back to the bottom guardhouse, where Kev Taylor (B Coy) was waiting for me at 0700hrs on a Saturday morning. It was then a case of grabbing a quick shower and heading back out again. To avoid this, the thing to do was to book out with the Colour Sergeant at the end of play on Friday. He would be lurking around the company stores after the Pearson, and the only thing you needed was an address to book out to. But this wasn't easy if you didn't know anyone. Troops would go up and give the address of the Inn Place or Cross Roads or even the actual camp, just as long as there was an address in the book. No one ever noticed... or cared, for that matter.

Once we got into a routine of working, playing sport and then drinking at night in the Wan Chi, it became very boring. To liven things up one night, one of us (probably Dava) said that we should try taking travel sickness tablets and then drinking beer, so we did. I had never experienced anything like it in my life; I was off my head. This was never a regular occurrence, but when we got bored of the some old faces in the Inn Place and the Crossroads we would buy some large bottles of San Miguel in the 7-Eleven and then sit in the park on the swings and watch the world go by. At least it broke the time up a little.

RECRUIT SELECTION CENTRE
St George's Barracks Sutton Coldfield West Midlands B75 7FH

Telephone Sutton Coldfield Military } ext 344
021-378 1282

Mr D H Ivimey
22 Earlsway
Curzon Park
Chester

Your reference

Our reference RSC/43/5/1

Date 24 November 1983

Mr Ivimey

Dear Mr Ivimey

I am pleased to inform you that your son/~~ward~~ has been found suitable for
training as an Apprentice in the trade of Radio Telegraphist in the Royal Signals
                    at the Army Apprentice College, Uniacke Barracks, Harrogate,
Yorks   commencing on 6 January 1984

This vacancy is conditional on your son/~~ward~~ maintaining satisfactory Medical
and Character standards. These have been very carefully and concisely explained
to him.

Full details of enlistment procedure will be forwarded to you by the Army Careers
Information Office.

May I conclude by wishing your son/~~ward~~ every success in his future.

Since he is still at school, we would   Yours sincerely
be grateful for approval for him to
have in time for this intake.   B A C

Lieutenant Colonel
Commanding
Recruit Selection Centre

Copy to: ACIO Chester

Letter from the Army Selection Centre, Sutton Coldfield, confirming my apprenticeship

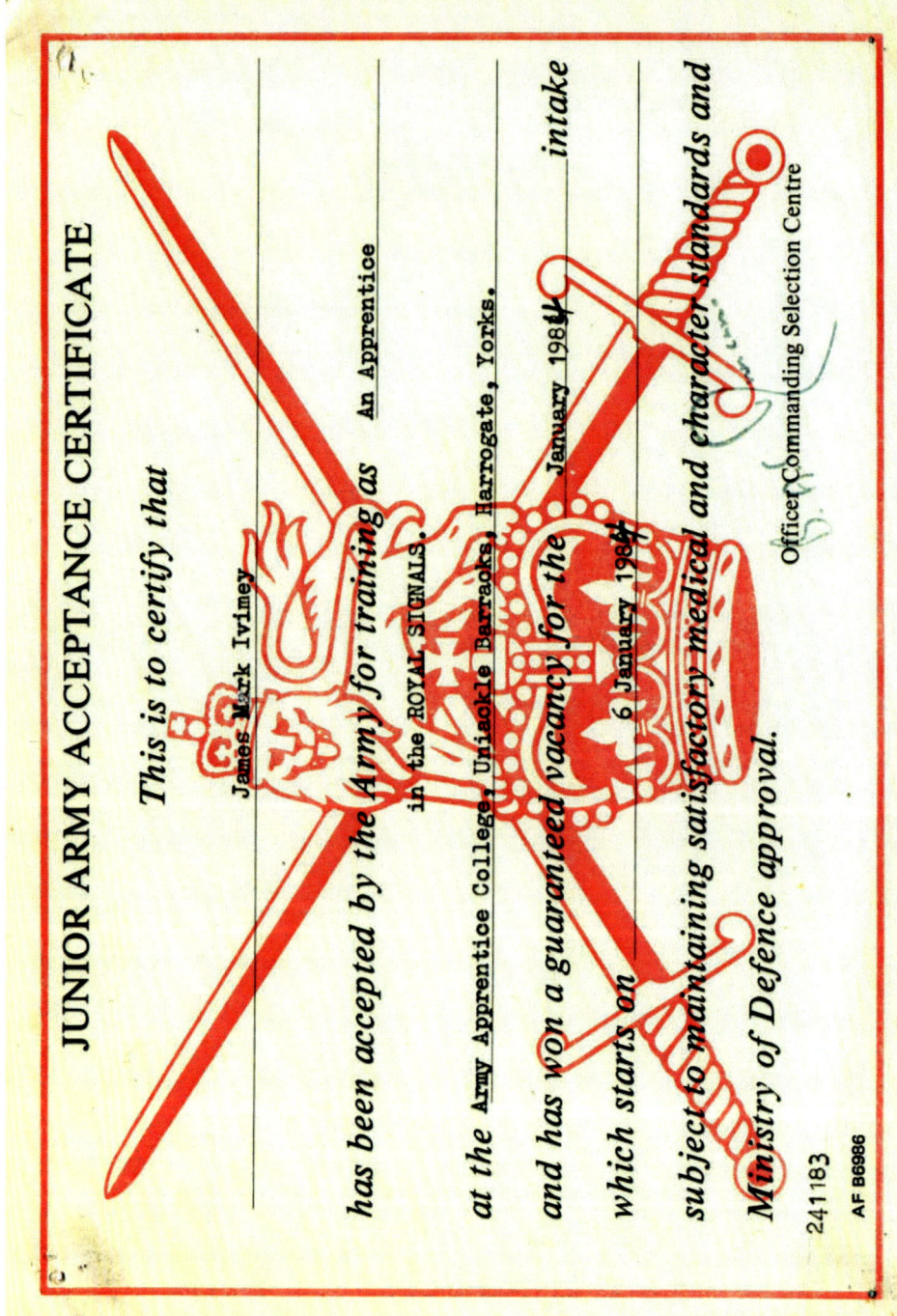

My Army Acceptance Certificate, issued by the Army Apprentice College, Harrogate

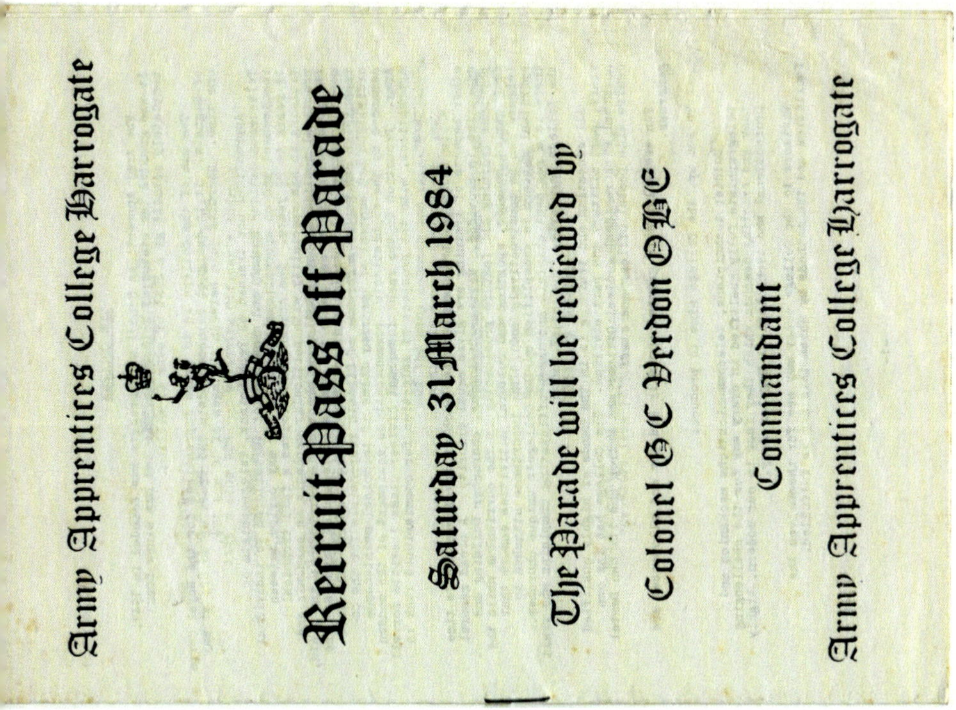

Recruit Pass off Parade

Saturday 31 March 1984

The Parade will be reviewed by

Colonel G C Verdon OBE

Commandant

Army Apprentices College Harrogate

Invitation to the Recruit Pass Off parade, Harrogate Army Apprentice College

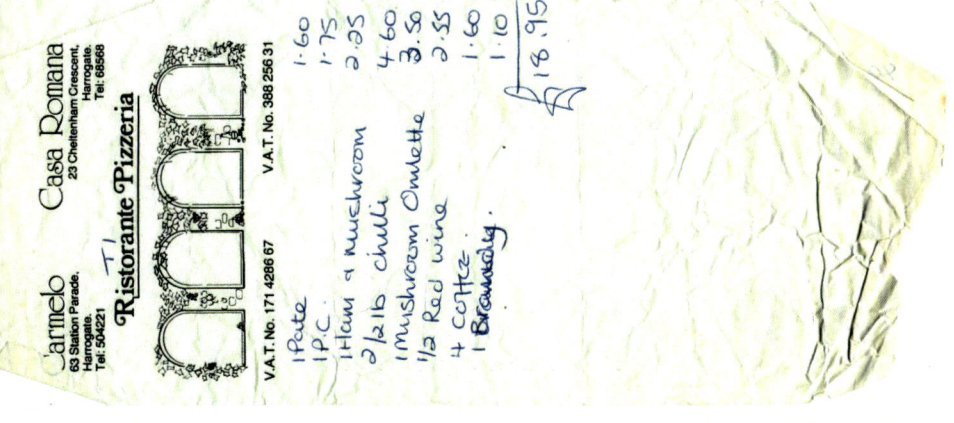

Carmelo   Casa Romana
63 Station Parade.   23 Cheltenham Crescent,
Harrogate.   Harrogate.
Tel: 504221   Tel: 68568

Ristorante Pizzeria

V.A.T. No. 171 4286 67   V.A.T. No. 388 256 31

1 Pate   1·60
1 P.C.   1·75
1 Ham & mushroom   2·05
2/2lb chilli   4·60
1 Mushroom Omlette   3·50
1/2 Red wine   2·55
4 coffee.   1·60
1 Brandy.   1·10
                              £18·95

Receipt from the family meal to celebrate

City of Chester
The Roman Fortress of Deva.

The Right Worshipful The Mayor
Councillor Cecil M. Eimerl.

21st December 1984.

Dear Mr and Mrs Ivimey,

                  I cannot let
the occasion of your sons success at
Litchfield in winning the Gale Cup,
pass without saying how delighted my
wife and I were at being at the passing
out parade of the Gheluvelt Platoon on
Thursday last.

                  Mrs Ivimey and
yourself will be justly proud of this
outstanding achievement,and I hope that
as Mayor of Chester I may also be allowed
to feel pride at your sons performance,as
will all those in our city who take an
interest in the successes of our younger
generation.

                  With every best
wish for the coming year.

                Yours Sincerely.

                Mayor.

Mr and Mrs D.H.Ivimey.
22 Earlsway.
Curzon Park.
Chester.

The Mayor's Parlour,
Town Hall, Chester CH1 2HJ
Telephone Chester 41441

Letter to Mum and Dad from the Mayor of Chester following the passing out parade at Wittington Barracks

ollecting the Gale Cup (Best recruit) from Brigadier Michael Donald Keen Dauncey DSO, DL

1e with the Gale Cup and (on my left) my sister Tilly, Dad, Mum and Brigadier Dauncey.
o my right are The Mayor of Chester, Lt. Col. Lockhart and my girlfriend Helen

№ 063776

SUPREME COURT, HONG KONG
香港高等法院

M. A. Action No. 309/86   Date 14.4.86
案號   日期

Received from James Marc Fromley   交來
茲收到由

the sum of Dollars Two Thousand Only   元
款項港幣

being Compensation paid onto Court
該款為

$2,000.**

Cheque 支票 ....
Cash 現金 ✓

for *Registrar.*

經歷司   (代行)

S.C. 115

HONG KONG GOVERNMENT
MISCELLANEOUS RECEIPT

香港政府收據

H 976385

Received from 茲收到	in respect of 有關下列事項	the sum of dollars (in words) 交來金額	
James Marc Fromley	Fines M A 309/86	One Thousand Only	$1,000 ** 港幣
14.4.198 6			

日期:
Try. 44a

for Head of Department 機關首長   Name of Department 機關名稱.
(   ) 代行

Receipts from the Supreme Court after our successful appeal

After the weigh-in for the boxing finals. I came in at 11 stone – result!

My semi-final bout versus Si Humphries (C Coy). I won with a TKO stoppage in the second round

FRIDAY, APRIL 11, 1986

Soldiers' careers saved by court's 'act of mercy'

Two British Army privates' appeal against sentence for assaulting hotel security guards was granted by a High Court judge yesterday as "an act of mercy."

Mr Justice Wong reminded Simon Jackson and James Ivimey, however, that army personnel do not enjoy greater privileges than civilians and in fact face double punishment, under the law and through disciplinary action.

He replaced their jail terms with fines and orders to pay compensation to the victims.

Jackson, 17, was fined $1,500 and must pay $1,000 compensation to each of the three people he assaulted, while Ivimey, 18, was fined $1,000 and ordered to pay $1,000 compensation to each of his two victims.

Jackson had been convicted on three counts of assault occasioning actual bodily harm and Ivimey of one count of assault occasioning actual bodily harm and one of common assault.

A magistrate sent them both to jail for three months.

The Crown case was that Jackson and Ivimey had an argument over split beer while drinking with three fellow soldiers in a bar in the Sheraton Hotel in the early hours of November 12 and the five ended up fighting.

When security guards intervened, Jackson and Ivimey assaulted them.

Their counsel, Mr Michael Lunn, submitted that the injuries the security guards sustained were confined to swellings and small bruises and there was no evidence that any weapon was used.

Mr Lunn said the appellants were young men with previous good characters and any form of custodial sentence would terminate their army careers.

The court was dealing with young men just past their boyhood, he added.

He submitted the magistrate erred in thinking a custodial sentence was the only way to deal with the pair and said the magistrate also failed to seek reports on them as required by the Criminal Procedure Ordinance for young offenders.

Counsel submitted to Mr Justice Wong reports on Jackson and Ivimey written by their superiors and by a social worker.

The reports on Jackson described him as a professional and disciplined soldier, a sincere and congenial man who had a bright future in the army.

Jackson, a young man of humble origin, had made a considerable success of his life, one report said. He bitterly regretted what he had done and it would be a tragedy if he forfeited his career in the army as a result.

Ivimey was described as a capable, hardworking soldier with the prospect of quick promotion and a successful army career.

Mr Lunn said Jackson and Ivimey were aware that their behaviour was boorish, loutish and that they had brought disgrace on themselves and their regiment.

Mr Lunn said this was an isolated incident and he asked the court to treat the appellants' conduct as wholly contrary to their characters.

Perhaps they were affected by alcohol and got carried away on their first night out after six weeks work on the border, he suggested, noting they had been in prison for nine days.

Senior Crown counsel Mr Gerard McCoy supported the sentence imposed by the magistrate and submitted a financial penalty was inappropriate.

It would be regrettable if the appellants lost their careers but this was a risk all soldiers were aware of when they joined the army, Mr McCoy said.

In his judgment, Mr Justice Wong said the sentence was not improper under the circumstances. Offences of this type were rightly called unforgivable behaviour and would normally call for a deterrent, custodial sentence.

The judge agreed, however, it might be better if the magistrate had had more information before him when sentencing the two soldiers.

The information now before him was useful and helpful, he said.

The judge said the appellants had served nine days in custody and he assumed they had learned a lesson.

Both appellants were young men and, according to the reports, had good prospects in the army which would not be forthcoming if the custodial sentence remained, Mr Justice Wong said.

Fortunately, he said, the victims were not seriously injured.

Society was not vengeful, he said, and the interests of justice would be served if he exercised an act of mercy and gave the appellants a chance, although he might be erring on the side of leniency.

Mr Lunn was instructed by the Army Legal Services.

Fishy case leads to fine

Seventy-eight Asiatic boney-tongued fish left Wong Shu-kan $20,780 poorer yesterday.

Wong, 39, a fish-shop owner, admitted possession of the unlicensed fish and was fined $10 per tail.

Causeway Bay Court was told that Agriculture and Fisheries Department officers arrested Wong for possession of live Asiatic boney-tongued fish without a licence at his shop in Cannon Street.

Wong said he paid $20,000 for the fish.

Wong's request to have the fish returned to him was refused by the magistrate, Mr Edward Yanne, who said confiscation was mandatory.

Article in the South China Morning Post after our appeal

Coach Davey Parsons leads me out to take my place in the Light Middle Weight final

win the title with a unanimous decision against Paddy Gilmore (A coy)

Brawlers shown mercy

REMARKING that society is not vengeful. a judge yesterday set aside prison sentences in favour of fines for two teenaged soldiers whose careers in the British Army would have been in jeopardy.

The soldiers. D S Jackson and James Ivimey. had both appealed their three-month prison sentences to the High Court.

Jackson. 17. and Ivimey. 18. were convicted on February 24 of assaulting uniformed hotel security guards when the guards tried to split up an argument among other soldiers inside a bar in the Sheraton-Hongkong Hotel.

Mr Justice Wong said there was nothing unjust with the trial magistrate's decision to send the two to prison.

But after hearing reports of the soldiers' background and how their military careers would end if they were sent to prison. the judge said he was in a better position to decide upon appropriate sentences.

He said he was prepared to give them another chance.

"Society is not vengeful. I'm in a position to temper the justice of mercy." Justice Wong said. "But let it be remembered that members of Her Majesty's Armed Forces do not enjoy any privileges."

He quashed the prison sentences and fined Jackson $1.500 and Ivimey $1.000. which. if not paid within seven days will result in immediate terms of 14 days in prison.

Jackson was convicted of three counts of assault for striking three guards and Ivimey of two counts for punching two guards.

The judge ordered the soldiers to pay $1.000 in compensation to each of the victims.

Newspaper clipping reporting on our appeal

On internal security detail with Griff (left) and Dave Gynane

Bomber and me in a tower on the Chinese border

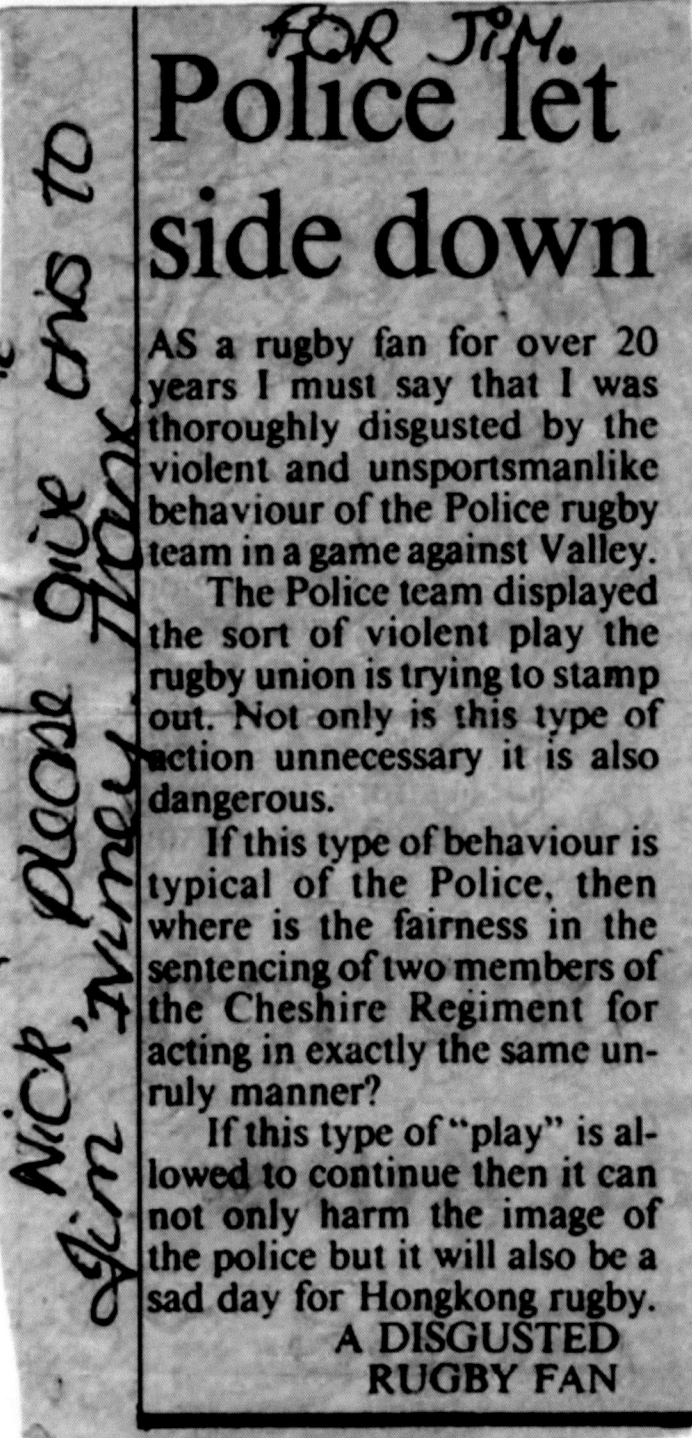

FOR JIM.

Police let side down

AS a rugby fan for over 20 years I must say that I was thoroughly disgusted by the violent and unsportsmanlike behaviour of the Police rugby team in a game against Valley.

The Police team displayed the sort of violent play the rugby union is trying to stamp out. Not only is this type of action unnecessary it is also dangerous.

If this type of behaviour is typical of the Police, then where is the fairness in the sentencing of two members of the Cheshire Regiment for acting in exactly the same unruly manner?

If this type of "play" is allowed to continue then it can not only harm the image of the police but it will also be a sad day for Hongkong rugby.

A DISGUSTED RUGBY FAN

Nick please give this to Jim. many thanks

A letter in the Hong Kong press following our conviction

Hitting the bars in Thailand with Dava

Me and Spud at a hotel in Pattaya

The Wrecking Crew before the incident (from left): me, Jacko, Bruce and Bomber

The Wrecking Crew face their first court appearance (left to right): Jacko, Bomber, Scully, Bruce (complete with bruised face) and me

acko and me on our way to court for an appeal hearing

n Stonecutters Island waiting for our appeal

Jacko and I are joined by a couple of girls from the Mid-Levels to celebrate winning our appeal –
Charlie Tapp had promised us the weekend off if we won

Chapter 15: What about us?

At this stage, I still thought that we would get out of this trouble in time to go home with the rest of the battalion. The whole camp was in cleaning mode; everything was being scrubbed and scrubbed again. Rather than leaving any washing machines in the blocks for the Guards, these were thrown down the hill at the back of the blocks towards the sea. No one regiment has any affinity to another, so there was no chance we wanted to be seen helping out the Guards. Sort your own bloody washing machine out!

We all had to stay in and clean the place. Boxes were issued to all of the lads and most of their kit had to go in it, so for the last few weeks we had to live out of our kit bags. In our room, Olly, Macca and I decided to turn this endless cleaning into 'big nights in'. We bought room T-shirts, which had coloured dragons running down the front and over the shoulders, and we would go down to the 7-Eleven and buy ham, cheese, bread and drinks, then lock the door and stay in. We would carry on cleaning but have a feast with some tunes on while wearing our room T-shirts, of course. But sadly, I wouldn't get the chance to fly home with Olly and Macca.

****

After a few days of induction, we got into a bit of a routine in the nick. There were about twelve of us in our 'group' and we were tasked together. The mornings were spent in a workshop, the afternoons in classes. Very early on, Jacko and I had made the decision to stick as close to each other as possible when outside our cells. This probably had something to do with us being the only non-Chinese prisoners in the nick, which attracted attention from the other inmates. We were in there for a poxy three months for ABH and common assault, while most of the other lads were in for eight to ten years for dangerous drugs or some kind of serious assault. So we thought strength in numbers was best, combined with keeping our heads down. We went everywhere together: the showers, the cookhouse – everywhere. We attracted inquisitive attention, but generally people just wanted to try their English out on us. They didn't cause trouble and that was good. We had had enough of that for a while.

Jacko and I decided to go into the bookbinding workshop as it sounded the most interesting. However, it turned out to be about as interesting as watching paint dry. It was like a school crafts lesson. The teacher, a Chinese bloke in a lab coat, tried to enthuse us about the art of bookbinding, but it just wasn't happening. We managed to get a few classes in, but to this day I still couldn't tell you how to bind a book.

Lunch in the prison canteen wasn't too dissimilar to eating lunch in your cell. The food was crap and I didn't like the look of most of it. It was like being on survival training, but worse as the food had a mass-produced, synthetic smell to it. When we were out on the town in the Wan Chi, some of the open stalls would have a repulsive smell to them. I could never understand what the cooks did to those chickens with third-degree burns that they would hang upside down on display. This was a step on from that, but at least we had the advantage of being out of the cells; at least we could hear and see other people. In the cell, sitting all alone, there was a real danger I was going to flip out. You can only tell yourself so many times that things are going to be all right. Anyway, Jacko and I made each other laugh. Despite all the shit we were in, we still had a laugh.

The afternoons were spent in English classes. Jacko and I sat at the back and tried to look busy. It was usually total chaos, so after the teacher had attempted and failed at the basics of the English language, he would put the TV on and walk out. Cartoons seemed to soothe the violent mind, because all of a sudden there would be calm. It's also a universal language, because you don't need words for Tom and Jerry. Then it would be back to the cells for Radio 2 and rejecting the warm milk.

We did get visitors one day. Bruce had left Hong Kong in tears because of our predicament and had told his Filipino girlfriend to visit us in the clink. She turned up on a Sunday afternoon, which was not surprising as this is the only day of the week the Filipino maids and nannies get off. Jacko and I were in our cells and were just getting down to our delicious meal when the guards turned up and said we had to come with them. Only when Jacko and I marched together, without anyone else, could we get into a proper military stride. It was our thing for 'don't let the bastards grind you down', and we would march with pride through the prison. Never mind that we both looked like idiots in our brown and blue uniforms, we were still Cheshires. When we reached the reception area, we sat and waited until Jacko and I were directed into separate rooms. Bruce's girlfriend was in my room, separated from me by a thick piece of glass. The only way I could speak to her was via a telephone. There was a guard sitting behind me and another behind her. I could feel the tears welling up in my eyes; we were in a right fucking state. She explained that she had been to the market and bought books, underpants, socks, fruit and sweets, and that all of this had been left with the guards. The kindness hurt and made me feel very uncomfortable. She didn't even know me and probably didn't know Bruce that well either, but she knew Jacko and I needed some support and had gone out of her way to help on her only day off. I spent a while looking at the young girl in front of me who was bubbly but nervous. After a while, the guards made noises and gestured that it was time to go and I was led away. I never

saw her again. Nor did I see any of the food and presents she had
brought, save for a box of tissues.

We did have one other visitor: an American priest on Jacko's
birthday. My birthday had taken place in court and Jacko's
happened while we were inside, so these were ones to remember.
This priest was doing the rounds and walking past the cells
speaking to whoever was interested about anything that was on
their minds. He was probably taken aback by the fact that there
were two non-Chinese prisoners, but the small talk about how we
felt provided a welcome change from our endless conversations
about the pieces of bread and cheese we got for our dinner.

It did cross my mind that we had had it in the British Army. Even
if you receive a suspended prison sentence you're on your way. So
I was starting to think that the only way to carry on soldiering was
to join the French Foreign Legion. Learning to speak French would
be the biggest stumbling block.

The only time we were out of the cells that I had to leave Jacko
was during sports in the afternoon. In the middle of the blocks there
was a floodlit area that resembled a building site. It was covered in
dirt and rocks and was surrounded by a twelve-foot fence. This was
the football pitch. There had been a few problems trying to fit me
into the prison uniform and my sandals had to be ordered specially,
so the pumps and sports kit were too much of an ask. None of it
would fit. Perhaps they didn't like the idea of a big centre-half
anyway, so I had to stand on the sidelines and watch. Jacko got
stuck in and ran around a lot, but I was thankful that he didn't
tackle with his usual disregard for the other players' legs. We could
do without another incident. I was allowed to have a shower, and
this was the only time in my life I ever had dandruff as a result of
using soap instead of shampoo.

As we adapted to prison life, huge efforts were being made on the outside to get us out. The name of the regiment had been brought into disrepute and this had to be rectified. After eight days they cracked it and we were released into military custody on bail. There had been another meeting with Lieutenant Waltier, who had said that this was on the cards, but it still came as a shock when we were told we were on our way out. Our civvies had been packed into cardboard boxes and stored in a room where the boxes stretched up to the ceiling. Our names and prisoner numbers – mine was YP (young prisoner) 68345 – had been written on the outside, and once found we could get changed. We were met by two Lance Sergeants from the Coldstream Guards in No.2 dress and they were to be our escort. The Cheshires had already gone, so it wasn't our posting any more. The Guards had taken over and had their own way of doing things. There was plenty of bullshit. It was wonderful to get outside – it even smelt different – but the escort was an indication that we were out on licence and would be kept on a tight rein. The Army had been embarrassed enough by us.

We were transported via the tunnel back to Hong Kong Island and HMS Tamar. There we were marched in front of some twat who said that we had let the Army down, blah, blah. Jacko and I were just pleased to be out and gave it plenty of "yes sir, no sir". At lunch in the cookhouse, Jacko and I were once again the centre of attention; this time because we had an escort in No. 2 dress. As we walked around there was a distinct rumble of disquiet and disapproval. The Cheshires had gone and we were the only two irritants left, so they felt they could be as unpleasant as they liked to us. We did bump into another Cheshire, a major (quite possibly Nigel Hine) in a lift at Tamar who acknowledged the fact that we existed, asked how we were and then went on his way. It could have been worse.

Chapter 16: Serving time on Stonecutters Island

Stonecutters Island in Hong Kong Harbour was basically a huge ammunitions dump; the actual piece of rock is no more than a mile and a half long. During the Second World War, the Japanese used it as a rest and recuperation location for officers. When Hong Kong Island was about to be retaken by the Allies, the Japanese released hundreds of snakes onto the island. It was not known how many were left by 1984. The ferry to the island left the jetty from Tamar and took about twenty minutes; not because of its distance, but because it had to dodge all the other sea craft, Hong Kong Harbour being one of the busiest in the world. The island is square on to Hong Kong Island and offered the most spectacular views of the skyscrapers and the peak.

Jacko and I were put there purely to keep us out of trouble. The Guards were now the resident battalion, and two Cheshires out on bail were only going to attract the wrong sort of attention. There wasn't really anywhere else to put us, so by confining us to the island it was decided that we couldn't cause much damage.

Stonecutters was a working location, with ammunition kept underground and the Royal Hong Kong Constabulary's training centre above. Chinese volunteers would come in and use the facilities at the weekends and on weekly courses. There was an assault course, a twenty-five metre range, accommodation and classrooms. There was also a pool, but this had been taken over by the pads. The island was run by an adjutant from the Hussars who smelt a little funny and was rather pompous, but in the end turned out to be a good friend to me and Jacko. There was also a contingent of Royal Engineers on the island: some in married accommodation, others single. However, the man who really ran the island was Charlie Tapp, the Regimental Quartermaster Sergeant (RQMS) from the Anglian Regiment. We reported to him. Tapp was a big man, broad with a chiselled jaw. He was, I suppose, what people call firm but fair. He was a little miffed at the prospect of having two scrapping Cheshires on his island, but as he laid down the law while Jacko and I stood at attention, it became clear that if we played ball he would do the same. We would get jobs such as landscape gardening and clearing storm drains (watch the snakes!) in the morning and in the afternoons we could play sport.

The initial reception Jacko and I got from the lads and their families on Stonecutters was frosty. During the Cheshires' tour, one of the regiment had been caught stealing women's underwear from the pads' washing lines. To stop him from getting lynched in the camp, he had been sent to Stonecutters. Jacko and I were the only other Cheshires they had come across, so we sort of got painted with the same brush. But after a few days the barriers were broken down, we exchanged a few words and eventually we became good friends with all of the lads and their families. They lived out there, but Jacko and I were merely confined to the island, so we had to make the most of whatever space was available. We were put in one of the training barrack rooms, which was pretty basic, but we had beds, mattresses and proper bedding. When we were sent down, what was left of our kit back at camp had been packed away and sent to Tamar and it was waiting for us when we arrived.

It wouldn't have been good for anyone if there had been a bad feeling about us being on the island. They gave us a chance to tell our side of the story and took us into the group. It was odd that they were the first people we had had a chance to explain ourselves to since we had been sent down. We were rushed in and out of Tamar as the Guards wanted nothing to do us.

We soon settled into a nice routine. We would report to Charlie first thing in working dress and he would task us for the day: Officer's Mess garden or storm drains. We would go off and collect the kit from the stores and just get on with it. The girls in the cookhouse were lovely. They only had a handful of people to look after, so they knew us by sight and greeted us each time we walked in. We were even allowed to choose what we wanted to eat; that's unheard of in an Army cookhouse! Jacko and I were putting on weight like no one's business.

We would strip down to our vests or take our shirts off while working to catch some rays. At around 1100hrs we would have a brew break at the NAAFI, which had breathtaking views. The NAAFI was right by the sea looking out to Hong Kong Island, so we would order tea or coffee and egg banjos and sit reading the *South China Morning Post*. I do remember one morning reading a story that made us both laugh. There had been all this bollocks about the Guards being more disciplined than the Cheshires; that they knew how to behave on tour. But the story on this occasion was of a fight in the Horse & Groom (that place again) involving several Guards. There had been a number of arrests and at least one had been glassed. Yes, we enjoyed that story.

Although we worked hard for Charlie Tapp, we did have to fit in some skiving, too. Who knew how many snakes were in the storm drains?!

Jacko and I became friendly with a group of Engineers. Two were single lads, and because this was their permanent posting, they had a flat. It was fitted out with all the mod-cons (fridge, TV, video and so on), so after we had been seen in a location putting our backs into it, working hard in the sun, we would thin out and sit in their pad and watch videos. In the afternoons we would occasionally go for a run. Sometimes we swam, other times we would throw around an American football. Some of the blokes were married and had

93

families out there, so we would sit by the pool in a big group and chew the fat. It took a few days to get over the shock of what had happened at the court and in jail, but we were one hundred percent better off on Stonecutters. Things had turned out well.

The regiment now wanted to get our case heard in the appeals court. For this to happen, Jacko and I were told we needed to sign papers to the effect that we would contribute to the costs of our legal team. In later years, I would perhaps have questioned why we had to sign this paperwork, but at nineteen and just out of a Chinese prison, I would pretty much have signed anything. The barrister assigned to our case was Mr Lamb, and we were told he was in the top ten in the country. The only occasion I got to leave the island during our stay was in uniform to visit Mr Lamb at his offices on Hong Kong Island. (Jacko got off on another occasion to visit the dentist at Tamar. While in surgery, the door was left open so Jacko's escort, an MP, could watch the action. I think the Guards thought he might do a runner.)

We were allowed visitors, and one Sunday Olly, Macca and Evo's girlfriends turned up together armed with bottles of wine and food. We had a lovely time sitting outside, talking and playing a bit of football, but there was a dark cloud hanging over me and Jacko as we got closer to the appeal date. If anything, we gradually began to prepare ourselves for how we would cope if we had to go back. It was a terrible thought, but it was one we had to consider.

There was little to do in the evening besides drink green eggs and watch TV in the NAAFI. We must have done wonders for the takings; it was only the two of us in there! When recruits or a course was in from the Hong Kong Volunteer Force (HKVF) they would usually be in and out after a quick beer as they had work to do. They would never sit with us anyway; they had probably been warned off.

94

One night we had a few too many green eggs and began to argue, who knows what about. The shutters had come down and the lights were off. Jacko and I were sitting in the dark with a table full of cans – some full, most empty. The full ones had been bought in a panic as last orders were called. Anyway, we started fighting. We had never had a fight before, partly because we were friends, but also out of mutual respect. We were both fairly handy and we both knew it. The emotion of how we had been treated and what could happen to us came out and Jacko got filled in: I smacked him in the head several times before he fell on the floor.

The next day we walked into the cookhouse as usual and the girls shouted hello. Then they saw the bruising on Jacko's face and knew by the embarrassment on mine that I had done it. We were mates again, we were straight away – as soon as it had finished. It was just because we were scared of what could happen to us. Charlie Tapp wasn't so happy and bawled for a while as he explained that we were in enough trouble as it was. No shit!

One day there was a bit of excitement away from the storm drains and gardening. There was a truck engine that had to be moved back to the mainland to be repaired. The RAF was sending a Wessex to pick it up, so the engine was going to be slung in a net and lifted. Jacko and I probably looked pretty stupid, and sure enough Charlie asked us to 'volunteer'. We were briefed on the fact that we could get a shock from the winch, so we were urged to hook it on without any prolonged contact. We were each given a pair of gloves and then we were off.

The engine was on a stretch of concrete down by the docks. I remember standing there with my arm up, guiding this chopper in. He knew where he was going without my arms in the air, but it made me feel better. He came in low enough for us to clip the engine in the net. It was a piece of piss, or so we thought. Then we realised this wasn't quite the case as he gradually lifted up and the engine rolled, then fell onto the floor. It was probably fucked by then anyway and there was no point in moving it, but with Charlie egging us on from a safe distance we had another go. After being blown around for a few minutes and coaxing the loadmaster to get a bit closer, we got a result and the engine was winched off Stonecutters, spewing oil into the South China Sea as it went.

We sneaked back into Charlie Tapp's office that night and each phoned home. It was soul-destroying to hear my mum on the phone and not be able to give her a hug. I hadn't been home for a year and was possibly going to be staying a bit longer. I tried to put a brave face on it, but she could hear how unhappy I was.

The appeal was getting closer and Jacko and I had become a little withdrawn, spending more time alone to get our heads together. The Army had started to put together reports on both of us for the appeal: references from school headmasters, Platoon Commanders from training, the Platoon Commander from the regiment and also a social worker's report. This one was compiled by a huge round woman from the Women's Royal Voluntary Service (WRVS) who came to visit us on Stonecutters. We both spent time with her, individually answering questions on our upbringing and how we enjoyed military life.

Chapter 17: The appeal

The day finally dawned and we had to go to court with Mr Lamb
and Squadron Leader Charles. What we had heard in the days
running up to the appeal hadn't been very reassuring. There were
four possible judges who could have heard our case, one of whom
– Lord Wong – was anti-military. Guess who we got?

Our group assembled at the offices near the ferry: the adjutant,
Charlie Tapp, Jacko and me. Once off the ferry at Tamar we picked
up a few more, including Squadron Leader Charles and the WRVS
social worker. We had quite a posse. It was only when we got to the
court house that the horrible discovery was made that Jacko didn't
have a jacket with him. In normal circumstances this would have
been fine, but standing in front of Lord Wong probably wasn't the
time to show off your tattoos. The adjutant very kindly said Jacko
could wear his jacket in court. Problem solved.

Our actual time in court was all a bit of a blur. Everything was
going on around us and it was all out of our control; we were
merely spectators. When the judge came in and we all stood up,
I realised how big the courtroom was and the vast distance between
us and him. Jacko and I were in the dock with a police officer on
either side. We sat and listened to the references people had given
about us, it was all quite emotional. Whether it was all true or not,
people had understood that we were in trouble and gone out of
their way to help us. The kind words flowed from Mr Lamb,
but they seemed to have little effect on Lord Wong. When Mr
Charles finally finished, it was time for the state to reply. The most
significant thing was the amount the prosecution said: very little.
I'm sure the lawyer had the opportunity to stand up and repeat
how many security guards had been in hospital and then list their
injuries or talk about the damage caused in the Someplace Else Bar,

but he didn't. He stood up and asked for the original sentences to be upheld, that was all. The judge then left to consider his verdict. We seemed to be waiting hours, but it was actually about twenty-five minutes, and then we were back in.

Jacko and I were asked to stand up in the dock and Lord Wong set about summing up. The fear had clearly made me deaf, because I heard the first line, "Society isn't spiteful", and that was it. He apparently rambled on about these two young men who still had something to contribute to society and then he said we were free to go. The police officer opened the dock but we both just stood there, dumbstruck. After a few seconds he ushered us out, probably happy to see the back of us.

We were both in a daze. What we hadn't really heard was that we would be fined $1,000 per offence and $500 in compensation for each security guard injured, and that we had just twenty-eight days to pay. But that didn't matter; we weren't going back to jail!

As we got outside, the press swooped and there was so much noise I couldn't hear anything. I remembered back to when we'd been sent down and Jacko had cried in the cell below court. Now it was my turn, so I asked the WRVS woman if she had a handkerchief and set off for the toilets, where I cried for about ten minutes. It was all over and we were going home – that's all that mattered.

The celebrations could now begin and we were taken for a beer at the Bull & Bear on the way back to Tamar. It was a breath of fresh air, but neither of us could really relax. We were suited and booted and, not wishing to be rude, the posse we had with the adjutant and social worker on board was not the normal crowd we would drink with. But they had all been brilliant and played a part in getting us out of trouble.

The next stop was Tamar and the WRVS offices. There was a determined air about the social worker. Once she had a line to the operator, she said she needed to make two calls to England; a chance to let our mums know we were coming home. As the phone rang in Mum's house on the other side of the world, I had in my mind exactly how long it would take her to get to the phone. It was about 0400hrs in England, so she would hear it from the bedroom. Now she would be putting her dressing gown on, now she would be walking carefully down the stairs, and bingo! She picked the phone up. All I said was "I'm coming home," and she started to cry. At last I could put her mind at rest. The remainder of the battalion had got back in February. We were still in Hong Kong and it was April.

Before we knew it the day was almost gone. We went back to Stonecutters and had a beer by the pool with the Engineers and their families, but the partying couldn't really start because Jacko and I were skint and needed to get to a pay office. So that night we had a few green eggs and watched TV. It was the same old, same old.

Charlie Tapp had promised that if we got off, Jacko and I could take the Friday off and celebrate. At 0830hrs we were stood in working dress at his door with a copy of the *South China Morning Post*. The headline on Friday, April 11, was "Soldiers' careers saved by court's act of mercy". He said "fair dos" and sent us on our way. Our first port of call was the pay office at Gun Club Hill Barracks where, after a call from Charlie, we were allowed to withdraw $2,000 each (about £200) to keep us out of trouble for the weekend.

Jacko and I partied hard. There were plenty of people we needed to say goodbye to. All the English girls from the Mid-Levels were pleased to see us and we spent most of the weekend out with them, either in the Wan Chi or at their apartments. We visited the China Fleet Club to say goodbye and, as expected, it was full of Guards, but there were no bad feelings and someone recognised us and said hello. The regiment was keen to get us home, so we flew out of Hong Kong the following Tuesday. Leaving was sad, despite the events of the previous few months. The girls came along to cheer us off and there were tears all round. Privates Jackson and Ivimey were the last Cheshires to leave Hong Kong on Tuesday, April 15, 1986.

Unlike the rest of the regiment, who had flown home via 'Crab Air' (RAF), we flew with a civvie airline, which meant less time in the air, good food and comfy seats. We were met at Gatwick by Billy Flynn (ex-B Coy, who was in the motor pool and provided transportation for the battalion) in a Land Rover. It was more than twelve months since I had been in the UK and it was bloody freezing. We knew the Cheshires had been posted to Caterham in Surrey to take up ceremonial duties, but neither of us had been to the camp or knew what it looked like. As we swung in through the gates, the cold grey stone blocks could be seen beyond the square. This was a far cry from Stanley Fort.

Once we got our bearings, we found B Company lines and the offices. B Coy were dismounting from Buckingham House (or Buckingham Palace) duties that morning and were due back after 1400hrs. We twiddled our thumbs waiting for them to get back, but this was going to be the real acid test. Yes, we had finally got away with it, but how would we be received by the battalion? And, closer to home, how would we be received by B Company? Eventually, the white coach turned in through the gates and rolled towards the block. As it got closer I started to make out familiar faces. Jacko and I stood and waited. The first man off was Company Sergeant Major Eddie Cook. He had his grey coat on with a peaked cap and white gloves. I tensed as he stepped towards us, not really knowing what to expect. He stuck out his hand and said: "Welcome back, lads." It felt good to be home.

The final test would be a reunion with the Company Commander, Major David Colbourn. Jacko and I stood outside his office and were finally called in. As ever, he played it straight, but underneath we could see he was smiling and pleased to see us. After the standard questions (What was it like? How were you treated?), he asked us how much leave we would like. We were stunned by his generosity and, after an age, said that two weeks would be nice. He said that was fine and that we should get away. We came to attention (no salute, no uniform), turned to our right and went home. It seemed there'd still be plenty of soldiering for Jacko and me yet.

Chapter 18: Politics and music in 1985

Hitting the headlines

In the UK, the Tories and Margaret Thatcher are in the chair.
The first British mobile phone call is made by Ernie Wise to
Vodafone.
Civil servant Clive Ponting resigns from the MoD after his
acquittal for breaching Section 2 of the 1911 Official Secrets Act
concerning the leaking of documents about the sinking of Argentine
navy warship General Belgrano during the Falklands War.
The miners' strike is ongoing.
Hundreds of football fans are injured and thirty-nine die in the
Heysel Stadium disaster at the European Cup final in Brussels.
Despite the tragedy, the match is played and Juventus beat
Liverpool one nil.
May 31: The Football Association bans all English football clubs
from playing in Europe until further notice in response to the
Heysel riots. Thatcher supports the ban and calls for judges to hand
out stiffer sentences to convicted football hooligans.
June 25: Police arrest thirteen suspects in connection with the IRA
Brighton hotel bombing of 1984.
September 11: The rioting in Handsworth ends, with the final
casualty toll standing at thirty-five injuries and two deaths. A
further two people are unaccounted for.
October 1: Neil Kinnock makes a speech at the Labour Party
Conference in Bournemouth attacking the Militant Tendency
(originally the Revolutionary Socialist League) in Liverpool. Lord
Scarman's report on the riots in Toxteth and Peckham blames
economic deprivation and racial discrimination.
Economists predict that unemployment will remain above the three
million mark for the rest of the decade.

What was I listening to in the bars, clubs and NAAFI in Hong Kong:

19 by Paul Hardcastle

Easy Lover by Phil Bailey and Phil Collins

I Want To Know What Love Is by Foreigner

You Spin Me Round (Like a Record) by Dead or Alive

There Must Be an Angel (Playing with My Heart) by Eurythmics

Everybody Wants to Rule the World by Tears For Fears

Solid (As a Rock) by Ashford & Simpson

Welcome to the Pleasuredome by Frankie Goes to Hollywood

Something About You By Level 42

Say I'm Your Number One by Princess

The Word Girl by Scritti Politti

Alive and Kicking by Simple Minds

Things Can Only Get Better by Howard Jones

Ghostbusters by Ray Parker Junior

Chapter 19: Standing on ceremony

Caterham was a ceremonial posting and meant the 22nd Cheshire Regiment would be the first non-Guards regiment to take on a two-year posting on duties in London. For sixty years the old brick barracks had been home to the Guards. The easy access to London meant that it was a fitting location to prepare for Buck House, St James's Palace and the Tower of London. The old blocks were originally constructed in 1850 and it felt as if little had changed between then and our arrival.

Ceremonial duties were a huge pain in the arse. To the outside world you look like a solider; however, you spend a disproportionate amount of time either drilling or 'bulling' kit/ironing. The pub down the road was called the Caterham Arms, renamed in gallows humour as the Arms & Legs after a bomb went off in the dance floor area of the pub on Aug 27, 1975, causing severe injuries and extensive damage. The venue was frequented by soldiers from the barracks. At the time it was troops from the 1st Battalion Welsh Guards who had just returned from duty in Northern Ireland. No warning was given. Among the casualties was a man who lost his right leg and a soldier who lost both legs and an arm.

It wasn't my favourite posting during my ten years in the Army, but there were some highlights. I was a Lance Jack in Five Platoon at the time and my boss was Lieutenant Bede Etherington. He was from just outside Chester and, being a commissioned officer, he saw the world through different eyes compared with an NCO like me. Saying that, what a great platoon commander; he led from the front. He was fair and comfortable in command because his delegation was first class. He was also a good laugh. There is always talk in the military that fraternising between the ranks is not a good idea, but during this posting Bede and I sank a few beers together on several occasions. I suppose this shows that underneath the rank anyone wears, we're all very similar. He was the boss, but ultimately this was just two blokes out on the sauce. We managed to sink a few more during a six-month tour in Belize (more on that later). He was also Guard Commander at Windsor Castle, and one night he invited two young ladies who were touring the grounds for a drink in his chambers. Let's just say we both got a result!

****

While in residence at Caterham, the regiment also toured Canada in 1988. This was dismounted infantry based in Wainwright. There are no training areas in Britain big enough to carry out a live battalion attack with all of the support, air support, artillery and mortars, which is why thousands of troops end up out in Canada. Not much happened. The anticipation built up over the weeks until we got to the actual attack, which was a bit of a damp squib. The best bit was sitting in a lie-up position before the attack, listening to the target position getting battered by some serious ordnance.

The rations we got in camp were Canadian and they were far superior to the British slops. I could have got fat on them very easily. Even so, we still had to supplement this by calling the local pizza delivery man, who would arrive on his scooter with enormous pizzas. We cottoned on pretty quickly that A and C Company were doing the same, so when he got off his scooter to recce the drop in their lines, we would despatch a fast CROW to snatch the pizza from his box – result!

Adventure training was in the Jasper National Park. This is the only place I've ever visited where I had to get dressed to go to bed; it was bloody freezing and we were living in tents. As soon as we got off the coaches it was trunks on for a swimming test across a small stretch of water. Cold? My nuts were in my throat for the next twenty-four hours. Then a ranger came and gave us a brief about bears and we spent the next week looking for them.

Civvies would pay thousands of pounds to be in these mountains as the view looked like the front of a box of chocolates. It was fantastic and we tried it all: white water rafting, rock climbing, abseiling, horse riding and cycling. The latter was interesting. They drove us up the ice fields on the back of a four-tonner with the bikes on another, then dropped us off and told us to ride the ninety-six kilometres back. Some, like Tosh Williams, really went for it and got home in around two hours. I took it nice and easy with Carl Fin. It took us about five hours, but the scenery was spectacular.

R&R was in Edmonton and most of the time was spent on the piss in the West Edmonton Mall, which was about the size of Chester.

Before all of this fun, and not long after Jacko and I got back to the real world, I took part in the NCOs promotion cadre. Major Colebourn, Officer Commanding B Coy, had visited me at a stagging on location on the Hong Kong border when I was eighteen and asked me to do one then. I had declined, explaining that I wanted to get it right but needed a bit more time. It was a shocker; run by Lieutenant Garlic with a programme designed to fuck us all up. Fifty-two did the assessment, thirty started the course and we finished off in Brecon, where eleven completed the course. The one-man tents were taken down one at a time and only seven passed. I was in the top three, after Andy Jackson and another Andy, who was the son of a former SAS soldier and went on to serve with the SAS himself. Our promotion took immediate effect and this got me and Tony Harris into a bit of trouble. On the Monday the regiment started a week-long march through Cheshire; the last march being in Chester, where the CO was to award our

107

stripes on the square in front of the battalion. The only problem
was, Tony and I had been wearing them on our blues for a week!

****

Overall, I don't think the locals liked the Cheshires being in
Caterham. I'm not sure why; perhaps it was because we weren't
Guards. And there were a few unfortunate incidents. On one
occasion Mickey Fields (last located in the Gulf of Oman as a
contractor) filled in a few locals. One had tried to run him over on
a motorbike, but he had mistakenly identified the wrong person,
who happened to be wearing a similar helmet. In another incident,
Jimmy Baker got glassed and the local lad got sent down for it.
There was a sexual assault on a local girl by a Cheshire who later
hanged himself. In addition, one of the arms store men was splitting
up with his wife. He signed out his keys, placed his wedding ring
on his chest and blew the top of his head off by putting an SLR
in his mouth. Finally, a member of Support Company had a heart
attack and died on exercise.

Chapter 20: Politics and Music in 1986

January 9: Michael Heseltine resigns as Defence Secretary over the Westland Affair.

February 15: Fifty-eight people are arrested by police at a demonstration connected to the Wapping dispute.

March 13: *The Sun* newspaper alleges that comedian Freddie Starr ate a live hamster.

April 17: Journalist John McCarthy is kidnapped in Beirut. The Revolutionary Cells (RZ) claims responsibility in revenge for the American bombing of Libya.

June 10: Patrick Joseph Magee is found guilty of the Brighton hotel bombing and sentenced to life imprisonment.

July 23: Prince Andrew, Duke of York, marries Sarah Ferguson at Westminster Abbey in London.

August 22: John Stalker, Deputy Chief Constable of Greater Manchester Police, is cleared of misconduct over allegations that he associated with criminals.

October 26: Jeffrey Archer resigns as Deputy Leader of the Conservative Party over allegations connecting him with prostitutes.

October 27: "Big Bang" day arrives: the London Stock Exchange is computerised and opens to foreign companies.

October 28: Jeremy Bamber is found guilty of the murder of his parents, sister and twin nephews. He is sentenced to life imprisonment with a recommended minimum term of twenty-five years, which is likely to keep him behind bars until at least 2011. (He remains behind bars at the time of writing.)

October 29: Margaret Thatcher opens London's completed M25 orbital motorway.

November 18: Ian Brady and Myra Hindley, who are both still behind bars some twenty years after their Moors murders convictions, confess to the murders of two missing children. They admit their responsibility for the deaths of Pauline Reade, who vanished in July 1963 at the age of sixteen, and Keith Bennett, who was last seen in June 1964 at the age of twelve.

December 17: The world's first heart, lung and liver transplant is carried out at Papworth Hospital in Cambridgeshire.

What I was listening to at this time:
Walk Like An Egyptian by The Bangles
On My Own by Patti LaBelle and Michael McDonald
The Way It Is by Bruce Hornsby and the Range
Kyrie by Mr. Mister
West End Girls by Pet Shop Boys
Sledgehammer by Peter Gabriel
Everybody Have Fun Tonight by Wang Chung
Addicted To Love by Robert Palmer
I Can't Wait by Nu Shooz
What Have You Done for Me Lately by Janet Jackson
Word Up! by Cameo
Something About You by Level 42
We Don't Have to Take Our Clothes Off by Jermaine Stewart
Living In America by James Brown
Sweet Love by Anita Baker

Part Two – Belize

Now that I had my first overseas posting under my belt after Hong Kong, as well as ceremonial duties in London, it was time to get stuck into my second tour; this time in Central America. And it couldn't have been more different from Hong Kong.

Belize

Contents

Chapter 1: Rideau Camp

Belize, formally British Honduras, was a British colony that gained full independence from the UK in 1981. It is bordered to the north by Mexico, south and west by Guatemala, and to the east by the Caribbean Sea. The official language is English, but Belizean Kriol and Spanish are more commonly spoken. British forces were there to protect Belize against invasion from Guatemala, which failed to recognise the border.

While there, the British forces consisted of an infantry battalion, RAF Harrier and Rapier support at Airport Camp. The county was split into two battle groups: one north, the other south; and four camps: Airport, Holdfast, Rideau and Salamanca. B Company was based in Battle Group South at Rideau. The nearest town was Punta Gorda, some five miles away (population 6,000). There were various bars in the town – Bobby's being the most popular – many of which switched between being in and out of bounds for British soldiers (more on this later).

There had long been talk of another tour to Belize for the Cheshires. This was a place some people (old sweats) never thought they would see again. Old sweats are long-term career soldiers who seem as if they've been around the regiment forever. Well, here we were. On paper, this probably looked like a good option for a six-month posting, but it turned out to be the posting from hell. The regiment hadn't long finished a two-year posting in Hong Kong, where it was hot and there was a lot to look at, including women and plenty of good bars and clubs. Belize was hot, but it was completely lacking in any kind of infrastructure. Compared with the Hong Kong posting, the swap out and change in personnel was staggering; the battalion had a completely different and rather new feel to it. In a military context, this isn't always a

115

good thing. There was little to do other than bitch, drink and fight – mainly each other – because we were in the middle of nowhere and there was nothing better to do.

I flew out as part of the 1 Cheshire advance party in October '86. On arrival at Airport Camp we had a quick familiarisation brief from an officer before they chucked the B Coy contingent plus all our kit on to a ramped powered lighter (RPL) for an overnight trip around the coast to Punta Gorda. It was blowing a gale and any thoughts of staying dry were soon dampened, literally. We hadn't been there twenty-four hours and I was already feeling sorry for myself.

There was no rest for the wicked. It was kit off the RPL and on to a luxurious four-tonne truck. The dusty road up to Rideau Camp was a trip I would get to know well. The camp wasn't particularly impressive, but it was going to be home for the next six months. Like something out of *It Ain't Half Hot Mum* would be the best way to describe it. It was full of Nissen huts with fans, very big storm drains and lots of attaps (traditional houses). We were met by a load of gloaters from the Queen's Regiment who were just about to ro-tate back to the real world. One of them showed me a tarantula that he kept in a container near his pit.

There was no real advantage to getting out there early, other than the fact that when the main party arrived you had a 'beer steer' on where stuff was. The shape of things to come was apparent when I met a beetle on one of the paths between the accommodation blocks: it was the size of half a cricket ball. It was me or him, so I stepped on him, but I didn't even make a dent. It seemed to shrug its back and walk off – shit! Is all the wildlife here armour-plated?

The rest of the company arrived en masse, by which point everyone in the advance party knew the craic, so we got among them quickly to instil a sense of urgency. It may seem rather unkind to get in their faces the minute they arrive, but it's what an advance

116

party is supposed to do: get all the kit signed over and ensure
that when the main body arrives everyone gets into their routines
as quickly as possible. We sorted bed spaces and a camp tour –
all the important bits such as the cookhouse and NAAFI – and
it wasn't long before we started ten days of familiarisation
training in the jungle.

As no one (other than the old sweats and the SNCOs, who had
been on the jungle training course) knew what supplies to take
out, we took everything. When we landed in the middle of bloody
nowhere – a football pitch in a village – we were each carrying
a ten-man ration pack (about the size of a set of golf clubs) plus
a full load of kit weighing about 40lbs. As soon as we landed,
everyone ditched about a third of their ten-man ration pack, mostly
offloading it to the local kids in the village. At this point we realised
that every time we would see a child for the next six months, the
standard line would be: "Give me biscuit", accompanied by big doe
eyes. And regarding the kit, nobody ever took that much out again.

We got the idea pretty quickly: it was very hot and once you were
wet you stayed wet. At night you found somewhere to lie up, put
the hammocks up, had your food and changed your socks before it
got dark. As soon as the sun set, that was it, it was absolutely pitch
black until dawn. I've never had so much sleep anywhere in the
world. The idea was that you carried a dry kit to put on at night,
but I never did. The prospect of changing back into wet kit again
in the morning was too hideous. Instead, each night I dried and
powered my feet, put on my desert wellies, got under my blanket
and dried off – lovely. You don't wash or shave in the jungle, partly
because of the giveaway smell of the soap and partly because if
you cut yourself you're fucked because you'll develop an infection
very quickly and have to be cas evaced. You do always brush your
teeth, however, because it doesn't matter how hard you are, if you

get toothache you're buggered. The result of being out in the jungle was that by the time we got back in after anything more than three or four days we were in a real mess and it took a day or so and several showers to get cleaned up.

On this first patrol we had had enough after about six days. The lads started running out of food after eight days and, to cap it off, A Coy got lost over the border, thereby postponing our extraction. There was one lift, which took out Bede and a handful of troops, leaving Sergeant Baldwin and the rest of a rather sorry-looking platoon. We were desperate; so much so that when they called and said we wouldn't get a lift, Steve Baldwin, our Platoon Sergeant, got out the TACBE, an electronic distress beacon, and was ready to send out a distress signal.

In the end we got a call: either you wait until the morning for a lift or you tab. It was an easy decision: we would tab. Now I've already explained how dark it is at night, but the desire to get in for a shower and a bed was overwhelming. We picked up our kit, got close, dug in and tabbed hard. There was only a bit of grumbling and we finally got to the pick-up point and waited. It started raining and I was about ready to top myself when we saw the lights of a four-tonner. When it stopped, Bede jumped out and produced a bottle of dark rum. We all had a good slug – first patrol done!

Chapter 2: Beer and fighting

By this time, B Company was well-established at Battle Group South after the timely departure of the Queen's Regiment. I only really started getting into writing down what was happening when it felt as though all the people who meant anything to me seemed to have deserted me. On the advance party, I managed to knock out letters to everyone. And on the nightmarish ten-day familiarisation training, one of the few things that kept me going was the thought that people at home were thinking about me. Pre-internet and mobile phone, a letter was the only way for them to demonstrate this.

On walking into the block when we got back after the initial ten-day patrol there was only one letter on my bed. It was from my mum, which was lovely, but what about all the other sods? It's not as if they were busy. What the fuck were they all doing back at home that was so important? It takes about ten minutes to write a letter; in fact, you could get a pen and write: "I HAD A CRACKING PINT AT THE WEEKEND – THERE'S ONE WITH YOUR NAME ON IT FOR WHEN YOU GET HOME." That would take about twenty seconds and at least it's an envelope to open. It was amazing how quickly depression set in when post didn't come your way. It felt as if everybody had forgotten about you.

I'm sure it's very difficult for people to understand what it really feels like to be thrust into Central America (basically the middle of nowhere) for six months, but there it is. I wasn't happy, so I decided to keep a diary in Belize to stop me from going bonkers. This account is based on those diary entries.

The first port of call for us all was the guard room, which I soon got to know like the back of my hand. It was hot and dusty, and it felt rather shitty ending up sitting in a brick box while what little life there was in and around the camp seemed to be going on without you. Usually this was in the form of a town patrol. We would do anything to avoid looking at the same four walls. Pretty often if we were on guard we missed a great night. It's the same all around the world and not just for soldiers; like the night you didn't go out clubbing. In this mode you regularly found the lads in high spirits, but at this point of the tour there was very little trouble. Sadly, that wasn't to last.

Early on in the tour it became clear that many of the lads couldn't resist the local girls. I just did lots of wanking! I'd had so much shit going on with G over the previous few years that getting involved, even for a quick roll around, wasn't on the cards for me. I just wanted to get the tour cracked and to get home. The early talk of the platoon and town centred around the self-confessed virgin of the platoon, Rambo. He was introduced to the fine art of swordsmanship by 'Rosie'. Rosie was a local prostitute, perhaps better known as 'Gobbling Jenny's sister'. I suppose after that there was no going back for him and the bar had been set pretty low.

It was already dawning on us that all we had to look forward to for the foreseeable was the company of local hookers, the baking sun and piss-poor beer. With this in mind, a lot of the lads were already focused on where they would go when R&R came round at some point mid-tour. I was already thinking about visiting Cancun in Mexico, but there was plenty of time to make up my mind. Dave Dunning and I had our hearts set on a week in France after the tour finished. This was probably down to all the pictures of beautiful models – mainly French – on everyone's lockers.

As I mentioned, when the mail arrived and there was a letter for you, it could make or break your week. Either the postie would turn up in the NAAFI and call out names, or the Platoon Sergeants would get our allocation and put them on the lucky troops' beds. To see one waiting on your pit was fantastic, but occasionally it was an anti-climax, like the time the longed-for letter I received turned out to be my lifelong membership to the Regimental Association.

I earned some stitches and a new scar while on a boat patrol pretty early on in the tour. It was a bit of a cabbie (a bit of fun) to go out in the Rigid Raiders (fast assault boats). With our personal vibes (PVs) on, we got to fly up and down a few waterways. We would go firm at night, get some snap and then get some kip in a hammock. No one sleeps on the floor in the jungle as there are too many insects, so our choices are either an A-frame – which was not easy to construct – or a hammock. I opted for the latter, and it was as we were breaking location to come back to camp after two days that I sustained the injury.

The nylon tie on my hammock was tight, too tight to get off, so I decided to cut it off. I said to Fred: "I'll hold the tie and you cut it." The standard British Army machete that he was using was pretty useless; it was heavy but rather blunt, unlike the parangs (knives) the locals used. As Fred did the honours, my positioning was all wrong as I was facing him. He couldn't cut because the blade wasn't sharp enough, so he began to saw. When it went through, the tension on the nylon meant that the machete came forward at speed and hit me in the face. It caught me on the cheek and across my eyebrow – very luckily not in the eye. First things first, we needed some photos of the impressive injury, and next we needed to get back to camp. The patrol commander was my Platoon Sergeant, Steve Baldwin. We were carrying the standard first aid kit, including morphine, and Steve kindly offered to stitch the cut for me. I thanked him, but declined.

When we got back in I reported to the medical centre. Usually they only saw us when someone had had a good hiding fighting or we needed to soak our feet after they had started to rot on patrol (they gave us a purple solution that seemed to do the trick). They took one look at me and struggled to decide who was going to do the job. The lucky medic then had a practice on an orange before he turned his attention to me, and what a cracking job! In fact, the scar has been virtually invisible for many years – unlike the scar on my chin caused by a civvie hospital doctor who made a terrible job of stitching a cut after I was kicked in the face playing rugby. He pulled the skin up and over, causing a ridge, but my wife finds it sexy so it's not all bad!

After exactly a month in Rideau, Friday night celebrations were in order. Yozzer, a long-standing and rather tough member of the platoon, Colo, a fresh-faced young CROW not long out of basic training (he was very blond and had a bit of a Hitler youth look about him!) and I proceeded to Bobby's Bar, where a bottle of Caribbean rum was consumed – each! Colo was very ill.

Bobby's was a standard pit stop for the troops and the Miramar was an occasional back-up. The number of troops out, the amount drunk and the general feeling – how much people felt they were being fucked around – dictated how bolshie the mood would be. You could never really gauge this until you got out and there were times when I wished I hadn't bothered. However, the amount of beer and rum put way was fairly constant: it was always a lot. We got absolutely bladdered at night, staggered back to camp and then attempted some kind of physical exercise in the morning.

Reveille was usually at 0600hrs, and at this point there would usually be a mad dash to the toilet blocks in shorts and flip-flops. This was due to the overnight fermentation of the beer and dark rum. Most of the time the majority of troops made it in time, but this wasn't always the case. Despite this, we would run, do battle PT and play volleyball looking like sacks of shit. Whatever it might be, there was no getting out of some kind of exercise to clear out the system. It was kill or cure.

122

In camp we were on the rotation to carry out guards and duties. Being a Lance Jack meant I didn't have to stag on in terms of walking around the ammunition dump, which was great. The flip side was that all of the kit was on my flick, including the ammunition. Nightmare! With the numbing boredom of stagging on, troops would take it upon themselves to mess around with the magazines, which were charged with live rounds. Occasionally when I was carrying out a check or getting ready to hand over, the odd round would go missing. I would go ballistic (pardon the pun), but it still came down to the fact that this was part of the kit I had signed for. I would do the usual: check the lads' pockets, webbing and kit. On one occasion, after what seemed like an hour of me flapping around, a round was found on the track near the compound. Was it the actual round from the official stock? Or was it a 'buckshe' (spare) round? I didn't care, it was 5.56 standard issue and that was good enough.

The other main aspect of the Lance Jack job was to act as a glorified nanny to scoop up, collect, pick up, carry and tuck in to bed troops who would be in various states of undress and consciousness in the NAAFI or down town.

But actually, it didn't matter how well or badly behaved they were, the uniform we wore made us an instant target for abuse. Some evenings I would do two or three runs into town with the transport to get them all back in. Fucking brilliant! Closer to home, when the phone went in the guard room and the message came through that they wanted me to attend the NAAFI my heart would sink. The guard room's front desk had an open window, so I would already be immersed in the thick hot air, but as you got closer to the NAAFI complex the noise levels rose, as did the feeling that it wasn't going to be an easy ride.

The abuse varied. Now and again as you stepped through the

door it would suddenly go quiet again. Then I would hear giggling troops like Rosie and Jim from the old children's show. Of course, there were other notches of escalation (verbals), but now and again if it was really going off they would throw whatever was nearby; usually empty cans of Schlitz (beer made by the Joseph Schlitz Brewing Company, an American brewery). One indication of how good a night it had been was the size of the pyramid of beer cans on a table. Whoever was causing the trouble had a choice: either shut the fuck up immediately or get locked up. Further to this, those with rank (Lance Jack or Full Screw) would get it back in spades when they were next on duty.

When we were in camp, the 'swing fog' would come into play as the sun began to set. I have no idea what chemicals they put in that thing: it was supposed to keep the mozzies at bay. Whoever was in charge of the contraption would have a mask on (which wasn't a good sign) and the smoke would find its way across the whole camp: starting at one end of each of the billets and out the other. Anyway, once it had cleared we would clean ourselves up and sometimes head to the NAAFI for a change.

It would be great to know the percentage of time a solider actually spends on NAAFI soil. If you're in camp, you go there at least once a day for a stimm and a growler during the official NAAFI break at 1100hrs. We often headed up there in the evening to get pissed. Occasionally they would put on a film, which gave us something different to look at for a few hours but, as you can imagine, the projector kit wasn't exactly state-of-the-art. If the equipment died it was back to plan A: get the beers in.

Many of the platoons also had their own attap bars. The RHA had their own because no one wanted to drink with them. The Engineers had a great one with their resident snake, a very long python called Lance Corporal Fluff. Pretty early in the tour when I had waved the lads off on ops duties, I had six days when I wasn't exactly pushed for work. With this in mind, I therefore took it upon myself, and anyone else I could drag in, to start building our own platoon bar: The Pits. When the camp was constructed, the old Nissen huts – the ones that were like a corrugated tube sliced in half lengthways – were laid out with space left at one end, which was where the attap hut was. It was pretty minging, with a stone floor and wooden supports holding up a brush/leaf roof; hence the name for the bar.

In our Nissen hut I slept at the attap end, opposite Jimmy Baker. The glass-slatted windows were missing a few pieces of glass as it was probably built in the 1950s, so they leaked. Put it this way, I got wet when it rained. There were big-bladed fans which, when at full speed, sounded as though you were too close to a chopper. When we were getting briefed in there it was too noisy, so we needed a better hut.

There wasn't a great deal I could do. Perhaps if I had been more forward-thinking I would have looked at it in terms of what I could leave behind for the next set of mugs who were coming out here to be bored out of their tiny minds. Sod that, we were off in approximately four-and-a-half months. I did, however, paint a sign for The Pits, give it a sweep, put in some seats, and Bob was our uncle! That said, going into the attap building business was like keeping up with the Joneses. Every man and his dog passing through would come and take a look at what such and such a platoon had knocked up… or not, as the case may have been. Six Platoon's bar was called The Mushroom Club: kept in the dark and fed on shit. Beat that!

In early November, a letter from the folks confirmed that they hadn't moved house since I had been away, which was previously on the cards. They sent photos, too, which was a real bonus and made me feel a little closer to them all. The homesickness was really kicking in and I was craving some female company. It made me think about past relationships. I suppose this made sense as there was nothing going on out there.

G was flavour of the month; obviously we had some history and suddenly I was preoccupied with the idea that you never seem to realise how good something is until it's gone. I tried to get my point across in a letter, but it wasn't easy. Never mind that, when I did actually get a letter back it invariably never related to what I had written anyway. It's like they had missed the point or decided to ignore it. Mum and Dad don't really understand how I feel about her or the things that have happened, but my feelings for her didn't just come from that. They stretched way back. I suppose the abortion and what might have been would always be at the back of her mind as well as my own. It was a difficult one to talk about when we were on opposite sides of the world.

Bonfire Night came and went and it didn't feel right at all when we were sweltering in forty-degree heat. Soon after that I got a letter from G, one I didn't really want. It was always difficult for me to get any feelings out of G; she played her cards very close to her chest. When she did finally let slip what she was thinking or wanted to happen with me, it invariably wasn't what I wanted to hear. I wished she hadn't fucking bothered. You can't win sometimes and I had to revert to Plan A again: try not to think about G and get bladdered again in the speak-easy.

Chapter 3: Foot patrol and football

We moved out by Puma a few days later. It was a day later than the battlegroup had originally planned. The top brass visited on what's called a 'Terrain Tour', so he had priority. We were dropped at an L2 (observation post) in a village called San Benito. The kids are there as always ("Give me biscuit!"). Some things never change. After the two lifts arrived we quickly moved away from the swarms of children.

The rain was plentiful and the mud made me think about what the soldiers of World War I must have gone through. The river we had intended to cross was much wider and faster than anybody expected. We'll stay here tonight then, hey?!

In the following hours of darkness, I had a very strange dream. Firstly, about my boxing exploits being in the newspaper. (I wasn't that good!) Secondly, the front page news being: "Is Gwen Guthrie Dead?" I think the bacon grill must have been having an effect on my subconscious!

The following morning, once everybody was fed and watered, we began to cross the river. A large fallen tree bridged the gap over the first part (the river was broken into three sections by small islands). To begin with, people began to walk over the log. Then, after Martin and Fred fell in, the troops began to use a less conventional method. This involved sitting on the log and 'humping' our way across; straight from the textbook! The magical moment was even captured on film.

At last everybody was across, and as a platoon we moved up the hill into the primary jungle. After several hundred metres, everybody had had enough. "Find yourself two trees," came the command. Most people, including me, chose to use hammocks instead of A-frames. There was far less work involved.

The rain can really hammer down in Belize, and despite having an Aussie poncho, the position of the trees I had used meant that the rain trickled along the ties of the hammock. That's why I had a wet backside for the next four days. The next day we practised navigation. To tell the truth, it wasn't my strongest subject in the Army, and this was no exception in the jungle. You really have to trust your compass. The vegetation and the thickness of the secondary jungle means it all looks the same. The ground and terrain is undulating and unforgiving. God help anyone who has had to fight and live in this stuff. Bede, Professor Broomhall and I, along with several of the lads, set off full of enthusiasm. But after attacking a few 'little' hills, heads began to drop. I'm sure it's all to do with orientation. Despite what my compass said, I felt as if I was going in the wrong direction. But base location hadn't moved and we did eventually find it.

With all this relentless shit, the days rolled on and the routine was set: drills, work and tasks during the day, then come 1600hrs we would get some food, powder our feet, jump into the hammock and tell stories into the night. Then we would go again.

The next day it was contact drills, something everybody was interested in because this is supposed to be bread and butter for infantry soldiers. It's our job to carry the kit we need, get there, occasionally under our own steam, and fight; to secure and hold ground. Having said that, it's very difficult trying to get blokes to switch on and carry out correct drills when there's no enemy there. Blanks were issued, we went again and the section all worked very hard; the three actions we carried out were the best in the platoon.

At this point I should mention the mental state of the team: mainly 1 Section. By 1800hrs it was very dark but too early to go to sleep, so we usually sat under the light of a burning candle and talked. This patrol's topics consisted of the golden oldies: the

Clangers, Crystal Tipps and Alistair, The Herbs and Fireball XL5, but particular attention went to The Beverly Hillbillies. I think it was Mac and Animal who started off singing the theme tune – mainly around 12 bells – that's once they had had a nap and woken up again. This spread like wildfire and I'm sure that by the end of the patrol there weren't many people who hadn't had a go, or at least hummed along. By the Saturday, everybody was thinking hard about things to do. We were reduced to tracking and traps.

When Sunday came, that was it. After a few quick ambush drills, we hastily packed our kit and moved back to the river. By this time it was a Standard Operational Procedure (SOP), and of course we crossed the same way; 'humping' the fallen tree.

As we tramped through the mud up the hill it was beautiful to see the sunshine as we neared the top. The main man, or 'alcalde', at the summit of the village kindly let us use the spare attap. It was just right for hammocks. Once the connor had been cooked there was still time for a quick round of kangaroo court before people began to settle down. A few hundred awful jokes were told, mainly by Mickey Fields, before I fell asleep.

Monday finally came and the last day of our patrol was upon us. Weapons had been cleaned and everybody peered towards the sky waiting for the most amazing sight. "Look, there it is!" The RAF had decided to play and Five Platoon was the first foot patrol to be lifted in and out. What would we do without the reliable RAF?!

Despite what the boss said about work priorities, ammo, War Office Controlled Stores (WOCS) and so on, I think everybody had to have a little look to see if there was any mail on their beds. My luck was in: there were seven including my long-awaited shorts from home. There was also one from the daughter of one of my sister Tilly's friends. I think I'd gone for the sob story that none of my mates had written to me, so Tilly had come up trumps and I had

129

a letter and a photo from Funmi, who was quite pretty. The Royal Mail is a wonderful organisation.

After coming in from foot patrol, we found the training programme had changed, which meant that Five Platoon would be on guards and duties from the Tuesday. But first things first, we tried to get as many hot showers as we could in the first twenty-four hours to try to 'get our skin out'. We were desperate to get some sun on our backs and relieved not to have to walk around with dirty, sweaty kit on all the time. Working dress in camp was shorts and boots; T-shirts were optional when we were actually grafting. Camp was an absolute shithole, but it was a hundred percent better than being on the ground. There was electricity and stuff to eat that hadn't come out of a tin!

The new OC, Major Walters, and Sergeant Major ('Dog') Lydon had taken over. From what I had seen, I didn't think B Company would change that much. Anyway, Dog Lydon had arranged that each NCO in camp would perform an equal number of stags. As it turned out, I hadn't done one guard during Five Platoon's turn that week.

On Tuesday night, probably against my better judgement, I went downtown with Colo. After visiting Bobby's Bar we moved on to the Miramar. I had intended to drink only Coke but, perhaps predictably, this idea quickly changed and beer became my main priority. The reason it had been against my better judgement was that a dreaded BFT was scheduled for the following morning. I didn't set out to break any records, which was lucky, because I didn't. I recorded a time of just under ten minutes for the mile-and-a-half in boots and lightweights.

On Thursday I had the opportunity to go on the Cadernis Op with the Colour Bloke. He went to take up kit, while I was there just for a look. Actually, I think it was a driving lesson (in a Puma) for the RSO. He was at the controls most of the way and he must have done OK because we got there!

Punta Gorda was a very popular place with me at this time. That Thursday night I went downtown again with Mickey and Colo. As usual, Bobby's was the first port of call. It seemed different because it contained a large number of white women, who weren't usually seen in these parts. For a short while we visited the Miramar, which was pretty dead, and then it was back to Bobby's. By this time the rum had begun to take effect. Now there was no stopping us, and we moved on to the hard stuff. First it was the Green Strips, next the One Barrel (these were Caribbean rum brands made by Cuello's Distillery Limited). Here I must warn you that twenty-four hours after trying these drinks your body begins to decompose from the inside out. By the end of the evening, Mickey had tried several chat-up lines to no avail. On reaching camp, I realised he was totally incapable of controlling his body or his mouth. Until the next morning he wasn't able to speak English. I was fairly out of it myself. It was at this point that the Sergeant informed me I would be going to Hunting Caye the next morning for the takeover. This was the reason I had done no duties.

I cracked on with my kit and when it was boxed off the next morning I deployed (by Puma of course), first to L2. The first time I tried to board the chopper I had to get off as the loadmaster was having none of it. The Engineers had loaded several cases of beer and obviously that took priority. On the second lift I had more joy.

Chapter 4: Desert islands and stagging on

I never thought I would see the day that I would be stagging on on a desert island. Hunting Caye really is like something off the old Bounty adverts. It's part of the southern group of islands that run in a loose line heading towards Honduras. The boundary for the Sapodilla Cayes Marine Reserve encompasses the southernmost section of the barrier reef. We were here mainly to watch the shipping, but at the weekends we watched the tourists too. Not long after I arrived, around seventy visitors from Guatemala landed with, might I add, a lot of beer.

The sun was gently setting and I was stagging on, in uniform. Never mind, it's never perfect, is it? Saying that, stagging on was sitting in a hut about ten metres away from the water's edge. Plus stagging on in uniform actually involves sitting around in your shorts, flip-flops and a combat shirt, so it's not that bad. You would sit there while the rest of the lads swam on the reef, fished, slept or wrote, and then it was your turn. Some bright spark had built the wooden dining table and benches in front of the stagging on position, so when the lads were eating and I was pulling a shift I couldn't see a bloody thing anyway. The weather was beautiful and in the mornings we could tell by 0700hrs whether the sun was going to be hot or not. When it was like that it was hot all day and long into the evening.

One morning the Puma came in. The flight in was spectacular and seemed to be reserved for the tourists. The pilot dropped in very low to the sea, probably about five metres above it, which made the sea water rip up in the air behind the chopper as it ran in towards the beach. Fifty metres off the shore he brought it up almost vertical in a climb. I was pleased I wasn't on that one! The landing was gentle as always and the lads – Sergeant, Prof, Yozzer,

Huggis, Red Dog and Mickey Fields – debussed with surprisingly big smiles. The prospect of spending the next week on a desert island wasn't so bad. I greeted them, along with the 2 i/c Coy, in my shorts and then waved off the recce party, which was heading off towards the jungle again. A few hours earlier I had swum out to the reef in search of big fish. My luck was in; I saw a four-foot stingray that I had first spotted on my swim the day before.

What a jacked-up bunch of lads. They'd brought a boogie box and a few tunes in the sun did us nicely. There was the customary 'horse trading' about stags, but I decided to stick to my 1600-1800hrs stag. That gave me time to think and watch the sunset.

That Wednesday was probably the hottest day we'd had on Hunting Caye up to that point. I pushed out my stag as the sun came up between 0400hrs and 0600hrs. It wasn't quite a dog stag, but it wasn't brilliant. It didn't seem like long before I was on again for an hour to push through until midnight. The next day, just as the sun reached its hottest point, an RPL arrived at 'the Caye', and with it, building materials for the 'new' op accommodation (after eleven years they had finally decided to build a brick one). The stagging on position and accommodation were in two separate huts; timber and corrugated sheeting with some pretty leaves on the roof for effect. We all got a bit hot and bothered, but the materials were eventually unloaded. Phew! The fresh rations were looking sparse to say the least, but it's amazing what you can do with a bacon grill when you're hungry.

I pushed out another stag later on and it was still surprisingly hot for the time of night. I had the choice of whether to take off my Six Platoon sweatshirt, which of course would have made me a little cooler, but I would undoubtedly have looked like a teabag by the time the mozzies had finished with me. I decided against it.

Eventually our break in paradise was disrupted and we had to

134

rotate back to Rideau. The routine continued, but it switched up a gear as preparations were made for the company exercise. It was kit and drills, over and over again. When it finally came, the exercise passed by without too many problems. We spent three days in the field, but it was nothing to shout about really. Then came a weekend off, which included the Combined Services Entertainment show, which proved to be a good night out. The stand-up was 'Mooey' from Channel 4 programme *Scully*, and despite getting a fair amount of stick and barracking, he soon put people in their place. Then three white women pranced about the stage and certainly received the most applause. Plenty of ale was consumed by all, including me, and we all felt it the next morning. Thank goodness there was no run.

It was at this point that the stomach bugs and beer got the better of me. My backside was being constantly sick and I was no good to anybody. I missed the majority of the CO's exercise because of this, but I did take part in the attack on Snake Cayes, which was brilliant. The waifs and strays that were left in camp were rounded up and split into four-man teams to man a number of Rigid Raiders. At full tilt these boats can really shift (30 knots when loaded), so it didn't take long before we were in position, 150 metres or so off the Cayes, just before first light.

Troops from A Coy were dug in on the beach and I suppose they had received the nod that there would be an attack. Noel Brookes was our Commander and it was worth being with him to see what happened to him when we hit the beach. When we got the go-ahead, the coxswain went full-throttle and we all had to get down low and hold on for dear life. Noel had opted for a spec forward in the boat, but there was no slowing down as we got to the edge of the water. We just kept going, running up the sand onto the beach. As it came to rest, Noel was launched from the boat and landed next to the gun position. The expression of shock and abject fear on his face was a fucking picture.

A week of guards and duties followed and then, during Christmas week, it was ops. I really had banked on going adventure training that week, but once everything was arranged I found out that the centre on St George's Caye was shut. I was gutted. With all of the places on the ops taken, I began to prepare myself for Christmas in camp. It was by no means my preferred option – a company of Cheshires, Engineers and Royal Horse Artillery (RHA) was a recipe for disaster.

Just before Christmas I found myself stagging on in the guard room... again. I had just taken over (signed my life way) and sat down, and I was feeling quite pleased with myself because there was a witch hunt on about kit going missing from the flicks. I checked it all and took no chances. Then, just as I began to get settled in, a message came over from Gaz Mac, a Full Screw in our platoon. The OC had grilled him about letting a private soldier take over an op (which he had done because Bede was on R&R in New York and Sergeant Baldwin had gone back to England for Christmas and Senior Brecon). Anyway, the bubble burst and Gaz Mac said it had been the boss' idea. The OC wasn't having any of it and demanded that an NCO take over, so that meant it was down to me. With very little time available, I managed to pack my Bergan and get on the 44 call sign. My kit included my two cases of beer!

This was it; I was back on Hunting Caye for Christmas. It was a cracking spot and I knew if I had been stuck in Chester I would have been dreaming of somewhere like this, but it still wasn't right for Christmas. I was half a case of beer down within a day – just practising!

On my first stag, as I watched the sun set, people at home were deep in my thoughts. Almost half of the tour had gone, so quickly

136

as well. I hoped that the second half would fly by as quickly. I still hadn't heard from some people, which was a fucking disgrace. I suppose I could blame the Royal Mail but my brother, a postie, would fill me in; and anyway, I know it isn't true.

Chapter 5: Christmas on tour

Christmas Eve 1986 was preceded by a major downpour. The weather had finally broken and suddenly it was looking rather like Rhyl. The sea was still beautiful and warm, but the place seemed to lose its sparkle once the sun had gone in. It must have been the most un-festive place in the world! Imagining what people were doing back home was preoccupying the troops.

Gaz handed me a large chunk of coconut, part of the staple diet in Belize. This was Colo's first Christmas away from home and, despite putting a brave face on it, I don't think he was very impressed. If the truth be known, I don't think any of us were.

I was almost halfway through the book *Legionnaire*. Reading about Simon Murray's exploits in Algeria, where terrorists' heads were being cut off and 2 REP (the 2nd Foreign Parachute Regiment) were being lined up for an airlift to support De Gaulle, made all of this seem rather lame and unimportant. Yeah, 1 Cheshire – we came, we saw, we cleaned… and then we got bladdered. Speaking of which, plenty of beer had to be consumed that afternoon and evening as the fridge had to be cleared for the OC's visit the next day. I wondered whether he would be dressing up as Santa Claus!

Christmas Day was amazing. We started it all off as everybody should – the night before. Everybody drank far too much beer sitting around the fire. We listened to a festive tape and minds drifted once again towards home. I wasn't feeling too clever on my stag between 0400hrs and 0600hrs. By the time I had finished it was light and I couldn't go back to bed, not on Christmas Day. I opened my presents at 0900hrs, choosing that time because I knew the Queen's speech would be on around then at home. Mum and Dad's gift was fantastic: a shoebox full of goodies including a bottle of ten-year-old whisky and a King Eddie's cigar! Tilly sent some expensive skin lotion, which looked rather good. There were also the ubiquitous socks from Sarah, who also sent crackers and party hats. Rob had already sent some adult mags, which would soon be in circulation around camp.

Next, there was the mouth-watering prospect of a chicken Christmas dinner, something all the lads had been salivating over for the previous few days. However, all hopes were cruelly dashed when the bird was discovered to have gone off. In fact, when we went to have a look at it, it was practically walking around the kitchen on its own, so alive was it with maggots. Spirits plummeted as it was looking very much like compo rations for Christmas dinner. But then the CO came to the rescue by putting in an unscheduled appearance, flying in on a Puma. He brought individually packed Christmas dinners with him, complete with mince pies, Christmas pudding, beer and a bottle of champagne. What a hero! We all sat down to the wonderful food with party hats on; the ones supplied by my sister Sarah. We ate at our dinner table in front of the stagging-on position on the beach, which shows just how far down the order of importance it was to look at the shipping. Sat at the table we completely obscured the view!

There was a lot of mail that day, including a letter from G. It was a nice touch from her, so I sent a little note thanking her; I hoped it was the right thing to do. That afternoon we went over to Lime Caye with Monty, the boat OP. The main reason for this was to look at the German tourists. We sat in the sea and on the beach and drank lots more beer. That evening we finished off the beer and washed it down with half a bottle of Guatemalan rum. Good stuff! Every subject was touched upon as we put the world to rights. After that I felt rather pissed, but my 2200-2359hrs stag had almost finished. Thank goodness; it was time for a sleep.

New Year's Eve soon rolled around. The platoon's day started off on the range, after the customary run that is. It was quite good fun really, first on the AR15 shoot and then we had a go on the Light Machine Gun (LMG). There were team races with the 84mm – Gleavies and me being the fastest – and things were rounded off with a 'cabbie' (a fun shoot, if there is such a thing) on the 9mm pistol. Being in a tropical setting, it didn't really feel like New Year's Eve at all. Still, celebrations got underway at 1500hrs. The RHA had set up a 105mm gun outside the cookhouse. Most of the camp gathered around and bidding got underway for the brass casing shell. It eventually went for $330 to a cook, which was wonderful as all of the money went to charity. Not only did he get the case, he got to fire the round as well. On the stroke of 1800hrs, the roar of the 105mm could be heard around camp. Happy New Year, England! I knew then that it was time for a beer, so I headed straight up to the NAAFI to stock up. A lot of the lads I bumped into around camp seemed very upset and mentioned how depressed they were feeling. I didn't see it like that. Sure, everybody would have preferred to be at home, given the chance, but didn't they think the people who cared for us would be missing us as much as we were missing them? I bet a few of them wouldn't have minded swapping cold, rainy Britain for a stint in the sun, either.

Anyway, after sinking a few in the NAAFI, most of us moved back to the attap. The radio was on and we listened to the requests for troops all over Belize. One came up for us from the RHA, but nobody was very impressed. I could sense the mood was turning and that trouble was brewing.

It was fortuitous, then, that Corporal Ray Beth from Six Platoon came over at that point to wish us all the best and asked if we would like to join them. What a great idea that was. All of the chairs and beers were carried over to their attap. Most of the company seemed to be there, and the party really got underway.

I must admit that by this stage I was pissed out of my mind, which made me rather talkative, and most of it was directed at the boss. I wonder what I said! I'm told that by around 2230hrs I needed a little sleep, but I left Yozzer with strict instructions to get me up before midnight. Thankfully I was up in time and Macca gave me a cigar, which I chewed like Columbo. Everybody shook hands, gave out big hugs and danced; 1987 was upon us.

At some point in the evening, Noel Brookes was carried around camp. He was tied up, and for a dollar a word we could write what we liked on him. I couldn't let the chance slip by for $1, it was well worth it! I scribbled a large 'knob' on his forehead. Noel looked terrified, and who wouldn't be with hundreds of pissed-up squaddies writing on you? But all the money went to charity.

The mood was still unsettled, though. Some lads just couldn't be told that it was now New Year's Day and that the party was over. It all looked set to go off and before long it did. Yozzer hit Dave Dunning before Tate could, which was a wise move, and arguing broke out all over. I couldn't be doing with it, so I headed for the Engineers' bar. Spirits were sky high there since most of them only had a few more days to do. I wished the ones I knew all the very best of luck and bought them a beer.

I think one of the Paras there thought I would be a soft touch to crease as there weren't many Cheshires there to back me up. He stoked up the longstanding argument about who was better. It was all handbags, however. I felt the red mist descend for a few seconds, but neither of us was really in the mood for aggro. Soon it was all drowned in whisky and beer.

Later on, Tate and I struck up an amazing dancing partnership and showed everybody how it's done. I lasted until almost 0300hrs, when my tired eyes got the better of me. It was time for bed.

On reaching the block, I stumbled into a big slanging match between our lads and – you guessed it – RHA. Yozzer and 'Hubby' seemed ready to take them all on, and Yozzer probably would have done quite a bit of damage with the six-foot picket he had in his hand, but we needed more support. A big effort was made to get the rest of the company up, but most of the lads were incapable of lifting their heads from the pillows. The ale had taken its toll and, thankfully on this occasion, it turned out to be little more than squabbling, so I retired to bed. There's always another day.

Hangovers and dogs' heads were in abundance on New Year's Day, although most people were still unconscious. The officers and Senior NCOs woke us up the traditional way: with gunfire. Then we all had tea with rum, which was a treat. A barbecue had been planned for all units, and as the RHA had promised trouble, I had to show my face. My head was spinning and I don't think anybody else was up to it, so the fight was forgotten, steak quickly disappeared and sleep was the order of the day.

Early January was the start of patrol week for our platoon. I went out on foot with the boss and six lads: Colo, Hoggie, Red Dog, Fred, Smudge and Schoi. We were dropped by the 44 call sign at Otoxha village (R910). At one stage, I thought we would have to get out and push. The pilot was a bit 'niggi' (new) and didn't exactly put his foot down. The weather was beautiful, though; I hoped it would stay like that. As we were being dropped off for a foot patrol, the Puma had to find somewhere to land. As usual, the village football pitch was the best place.

The noise of the helicopter could be heard for miles around, and minutes before we actually landed the local children would gather to watch us debus. There was always a chance there was someone important on the Puma, so we always made sure our drills were good as the chopper lifted off on leaving. Once it was out of

143

sight, we would drop our kit, strip down to our boots and combat bottoms and, as was customary, start a game of international football against the locals. This match turned out to be a brilliant one for us: we creased it 8-2. More often than not, we would recognise the kids from a previous patrol: Pablo, Masakal and all the others. I wonder whether they remembered us or whether we were just another set of combats.

The next day, still at R910, Colo had a temperature and didn't move all day. Schoi stayed with him while the remainder of the team, led by the boss, did a patrol heading northwest, eventually hitting Freshwater Creek. We went past the site of the original base location, where all of our tins had been dug up. Bloody kids! Burying our rubbish was standard stuff; we either had to carry everything in and out of the jungle, or we buried what we had to leave or couldn't be bothered to carry.

It's now early January, so we were on the home stretch and the weather was still lovely. What a thing it was to go back to camp with a better tan than we started with! Colo was feeling better by this point. We patrolled west to Guatemala, leaving Fred and Red Dog with the kit. The aim was to show a presence in the area and to gather intelligence as we needed to know whether other troops (Guatemalan) had been over the border. It was just over 2kms to the then disused R912, which had been revamped as a marijuana plantation! It was everywhere! The boss kept a leaf just to check (sure!). Hundreds of thousands of pounds' worth of cannabis plants were all around us on a helicopter landing site. If confirmed as such, the police would no doubt have wanted us to come back and burn the whole crop.

We carried on for another 2kms to the border, where Bede took a photo of us on the Guatemalan side. We stopped for a brew just on the Belize side, feeling rather pleased with ourselves, but it could have proved sticky for us if we had run into any recce troops from Guatemala. British Forces carried live ammunition, so our patrols were classified as operational postings. However, the ammunition was carried in magazines and in our webbing pouches, not on our weapons, so Northern Ireland it was not. For its part, Guatemala didn't recognise the border with Belize, so their troops probably wouldn't have taken kindly to seeing British troops in what they considered to be their region. The British Army in Belize was a token force; Guatemala, on the other hand, had in excess of 20,000 troops in the border area. They were probably a fair bit more battle-ready then we were, too.

Anyway, it's a moot point as we didn't run into any hostile foreign troops. Back at R910, a 44 call sign arrived to take us back, catching out Fred who was sunbathing and had to scramble to get his combats on.

The football was found and we played another game to finish off. At first we were being diplomatic, giving them a chance, but then our competitive natures took over and we eventually won 6-4! The following day we said our goodbyes to the children of Otoxha and set off north towards the Moho River and the village of San Benito Poite. We had covered 6kms and I think everybody's feet and shoulders were sore. We had had enough for that day, so we broke track with a large hill range in front. Standard operational procedures kicked in, so it was hammocks up, feet powdered and food eaten. We would crack on in the morning.

When the sun went down in Belize, it went down fast. There was no dusk; everything was just suddenly plunged into pitch blackness from about 1830hrs. For this reason we had to be timely about finding a place to set up camp and preparing before night fell. Then we got a chance to rest in our hammocks to tell and listen to a few old tales. I had never had so much sleep on a tour.

The following day we were still in the same location by the river. It was lovely to hear the fast-flowing water after being in the jungle, so it was difficult to leave at this point. We kicked back and took turns stagging on the radio, chewing the fat and drinking brews. In the afternoon I did a recce into San Benito, accompanied by Fred, Colo and Red Dog. Tracks were going off in all directions, but at last we found some huts and confirmed that we were at the right village. It didn't take much to persuade the shopkeeper to open up and we all chipped in and bought a feast. After almost a week on compo, freshly baked bread and luncheon meat was beautiful, and it was all polished off with crisps and biscuits. We all trod carefully on the rocks in the river on the way back to the troops with the goodies,. To lose a rifle would be bad, but the food – that would have been a disaster!

It was clear that there was no Guatemalan activity in the village, so the following morning we took down our hammocks and moved into San Benito. The alcalde was away on business, so we asked his second-in-command for permission to move into the spare attap, which he granted. The week had started to drag, so I think we were all pleased that the last tab was over.

That evening, one of the local lads came in to see us, and he brought his boogie box with him. We put the sounds straight on and sat by the light of a candle talking about movies. This had been the main topic of the week. Colo really got into his part and gave us his own, very special impersonation of Freddie Krueger, which was pretty good considering he was blond and five-foot-eight.

The next day, the 44 call sign wasn't expected at our location until 1450hrs, which was quite a long time to wait considering we had been up since 0630hrs. Everybody milled around, finishing off brews and listening to PVs with rundown batteries. I think it was the boss who suggested playing charades. Within minutes everybody was crawling around on the floor going blue in the face trying to get their message across. The local children crowded around the gaps in the attap looking quite amazed. "What's up with him?!"

Time drew on and at last it was time to walk up to the football pitch. After a few moments the familiar and welcome drone of the chopper's engine could be heard – and it was on time! Once on board, the boss thrust a piece of paper in front of the loadmaster's face requesting a demo of combat flying. What a ride! My stomach only returned to its correct position five minutes after we got back on the ground.

After being filthy and eating poor food (and no beer) for days, we needed to have something to look forward to.

SQUADRON COMMANDER'S
INITIAL REPORT

Squadron	Number	Rank	Name
BRADLEY	24686150	RCT	IVIMEY J M

Trade	Term/Class	Intake
RADIO TELEGRAPHIST	1	84A

PERSONAL QUALITIES

Appearance and Bearing	B	Common Sense		C+
Co-operation and loyalty	C+	Enthusiasm		B
Conduct	B	Reliability		C+
Initiative	B	Self-confidence		B
Determination	B	Ability to command respect		C+

MILITARY TRAINING

Drill	B	External Leadership exercises		
Physical Training	C+	Military Training exercises		C

SPORTS AND HOBBIES

Potentially good Ivimey has shown some flair in squash and contributes well in all other sports.

Comments:

Ivimey is a determined young man, fit and an actice participant in all troop activities. His standards of drill and turnout are good. Ivimey had an average first field exercise report which was disappointing. He gives the impression of not working to his full capacity which is something he needs to improve.

Date 7-4-84

Signed A J WILSON

Officer Commanding Recruit Squadron
Troop

Subjects with Grades
A Excellent
B Good
C Satisfactory
E Minimum acceptable standard
F Fail

Subjects not Graded
P Pass
F Fail

AA Coll/RF 1

tial report –Army Apprentice College

TELEGRAPHIST WING
INITIAL REPORT

Squadron	Number	Rank	Name
BRADLEY	24686150	AT	IVIMEY J M

Trade	Term/Class	Intake
Radio Telegraphist	1RTA	84A

Subject	Attainment	Effort	Remarks
Principles and Safety	P	B	
Radio Equipments (CLANSMAN)	P	E	Some improvement towards the end of term. Must be prepared to work hard.
Morse Receiving	F	C	Finds morse fairly difficult and will have to work hard on this subject.
Keyboard	F	C	Gradually overcoming problems, could be a long struggle.
Voice Procedure	C	C	Good student. Must not be afraid of making mistakes.

Comments:

Ivimey must convince himself that he is capable of learning this trade. He must put all thoughts of transfer behind him and get stuck in. He has the potential to be successful and I believe will be when he has settled down more.

Date: 5 April 1984

Signed [signature]
Officer Commanding Telegraphist Wing

Subjects with Grades
A   Excellent
B   Good
C   Satisfactory
E   Minimum Acceptable Standard
F   Fail

Subjects Not Graded
P   Pass
F   Fail

AA Coll/RF 13

Initial report on my performance, Army Apprentice College

Jen with Dad at a
street party in King
Charles Street in
London to celebrate
the 50th anniversary of
VJ Day

Mum, Dad, Jen and I watch the flypast and fireworks, 50th anniversary of VJ Day

INITIAL REPORT

Squadron	Number	Rank	Name
BRADLEY	150	AT	IVIMEY J M

Trade	Term/Class	Intake
RADIO TELEGRAPHIST	1 A	84 A

Subject	Attainment	Effort	Head of Department's Remarks
ENGLISH and GENERAL STUDIES	B	B	Interested and a cheerful contributor; competent allround.
MATHEMATICS	B-	B-	The slowest of the group. However is making progress and works well most of the time.
SCIENCE H & H	B	B	A very good terms work resulting in a good H & H result.
MAP READING	B+	B+	He has worked well throughout the term and achieved a very satisfactory score in the final assessment.

Comments: AT Ivimey has done well so far and should be able to cope with the work ahead of him.

Date 4 Apr 84

Signed

Senior Education Officer   Major
E N GOLDTHORP

Subjects with Grades
A   Excellent
B   Good
C   Satisfactory
E   Minimum acceptable standard
F   Fail

Subjects not Graded
P   Pass
F   Fail

AA Coll/RF 5

Report from the Army Apprentice College

THE SCHOOL OF INFANTRY
NCOs TACTICAL WING

272/88

SECTION COMMANDERS BATTLE COURSE

COURSE: 88/8   PHASE 2 4/88 TACTICS 5/88

(ADP Code 0172)

P/ARMY NUMBER: 24686150

UNIT: 1 CHESHIRE

RANK: LCPL

REGT/CORPS: CHESHIRE

NAME: IVIMEY

DIV of INF: PRINCE OF WALES

QUALIFICATIONS

COURSE/GRADING: PASS

INSTRUCTOR RECOMMENDATION:

AWARDED SPECIALIST QUALIFICATIONS

ADP CODE

SECT COMD

D44

recon- Section Commanders Battle Course report

LCpl Ivimey arrived initially lacking in motivation but otherwise prepared for the course. Initially he adopted an argumentative attitude to the instructors, but this soon changed and he became a popular member of his section who was willing to work hard and apply himself to the course. His assimilation of the classroom instruction was sound, and he passed the mid course and final written tests with good results. His other written work was neat and well presented but lacked detail. He presented a very poor set of written formal orders during an indoors exercise. His practical application of knowledge was generally sound.

He understood the principles of Battle Procedure and could apply the drills sensibly in the field. He worked hard to keep his section fully briefed and organised for future tasks. He had an adequate understanding of the appreciation process at section level. He could apply the sequence of an appreciation at this level to all phases of war, although he needs to take more time to arrive at sensible deductions. His plans were generally unworkable, due to his rushed appreciation. Nevertheless he had a good basic working knowledge of appreciations at this level and showed conviction in his plans.

He understood the orders process and his orders followed the normal sequence for all phases of war. However he must work harder to include more detail in his orders in order to ensure the success of his mission. Otherwise, he had a good, confident delivery. He must however make more use of confirmation by phases in his orders.

He showed enthusiasm as a section commander, and worked hard at his command and control ability. Although he was not afraid to discipline his section, he needs more practise in establishing his authority as his section were occasionally slow to react to his commands. However he led from the front and showed initiative during changing events in the field. However he must overcome his tendency to become flustered under pressure. He must slow down and consider a sensible, quick appreciation in reaction to a minor tactical problem, rather than react impulsively. Despite this, he did show potential as a section commander.

His personal skills improved throughout the course. His navigational ability was sound and he passed the practical NAVEX's with good results. He met the Fit to Fight requirements and could march with operational scales of equipment in the field, although his stamina did appear suspect on occasions. His personal and section administration were sound, and he delegated sensibly to his 2IC to ensure concurrent activity.

His Battle Lesson achieved the aim although it lacked imagination and interest. However his instructional manner was clear and confident. He shows potential as an instructor, given more detailed planning and preparation.

LCpl Ivimey had a satisfactory course. After a poor start he improved noticeably in all aspects of the course. He still requires some guidance on establishing his authority quickly and effectively over the section, and he needs to pay more attention to the planning and preparation of his tasks, particularly his patrol tasks. Given these improvements, he has the potential to become a successful section commander.

He is able to command and train a rifle section with more than normal supervision.

Grade C-

J H EASTON
Major
OC Junior NCO Company

J C F HUNT
Lieutenant Colonel
Commandant
NCOs Tactical Wing

Brecon - Section Commanders Battle Course report

Christmas Day 1986, Hunting Caye

Live-firing exercise, Cyprus 1987

Advanced Certificate for Bupsie (a local dance), Belize Adventure Training

River crossing Belize

Macca and me, firing SMG on the ranges

On patrol in Belize-
notice my dry desert
boots and brew nearby
- a bit of reading
before it goes dark

Sorting out the Pits Bar – 5 Platoon Lines, Rideau Camp, Belize

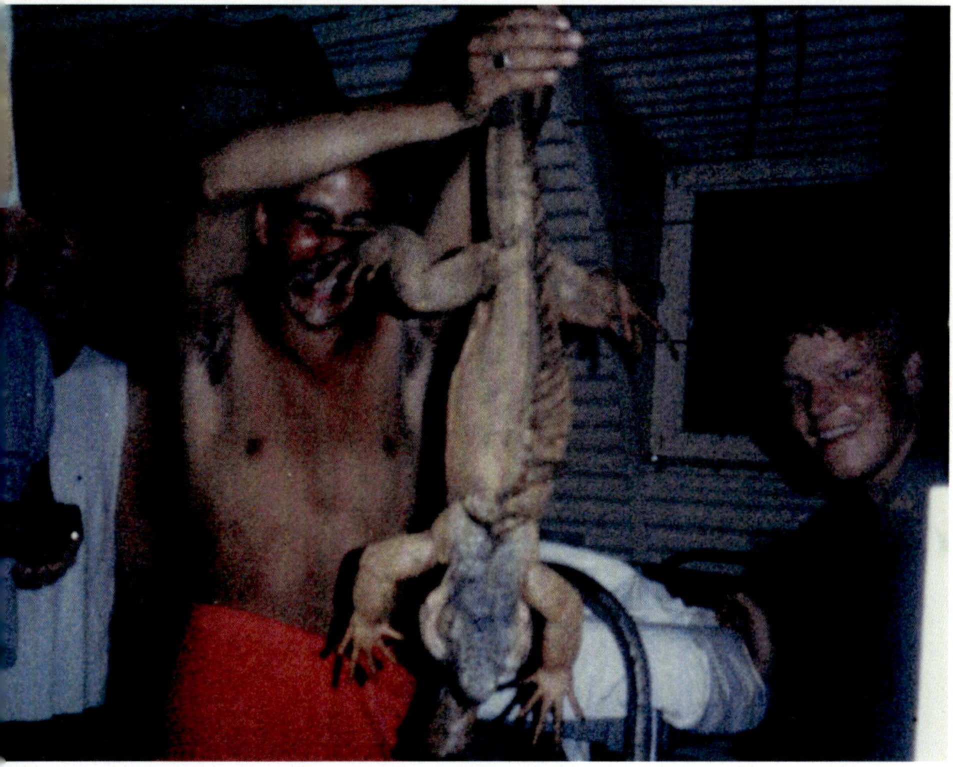

Platoon lines in Belize – I'm holding up an iguana found on patrol

Showing off my stiches after the machete accident

Fred (left) me and Andy Hogg on boat patrol

Judge Bede presides over a kangeroo court, with Prof Broomhall in the dock – on patrol in Belize

Mum, Dad and me at home in Chester before a regiment event

Swede, the boys and me on patrol – Belize 86/7

Dad, Jen and me – Remembrance Sunday Chester Castle, 1992

Mum and me before my first Sergeants' Mess dinner at the Dale, Chester

Top: Mum and Dad enjoy a drink at the Burma Star Social Club on Regimental race day in Chester. My Dad won the Burma Star

Regimental race day – Mum and Dad in The Cheshires' enclosure

From: Lieutenant Colonel R A Stewart

Commanding
1st Battalion
The 22nd (Cheshire) Regiment
St Barbara's Barracks
Fallingbostel
British Forces Post Office 38

Fallingbostel Military Extension 301
Civil code from UK 01049 5162 43301

Sgt J M Ivimey
Army Careers Information Office
177 Nantwich Road
Crewe CW2 6DF

30 August 1992

Dear Sergeant Ivimey,

Many thanks for your letter and for volunteering your services. Of course I know how you feel but I cannot agree to your request. I'm sorry. As things stand I suppose it may be some small compensation to you to discover that no decisions on our deployment have actually been taken.

Thanks again but No; I'm sorry.

Yours ever

Robert Stewart

Letter from Col Bob Stewart turning down my request to deploy to Bosnia

Chapter 6: Stagging on, guards and duties

Back in, cleaned up and rotated back to guards and duties, I got my first crack at being a Guard Commander. Not only did I have that job, but all of the kit was on my flick! Hubby was my second-in-command, and seeing as we had trained together, it was quite a good combination. Things were fairly quiet until it was time for the troops to come back to town. First to round the corner into camp was Tommo, closely followed by Rover, who was hobbling somewhat (he had jumped off the tailgate of the wagon). This gave me some indication of how drunk they all were: very. Tom Adams could hardly stand up and had what looked like a pretty nasty cut on his hand; in fact, most of them had blood on them. One explanation offered up was that a girl in Punta Gorda had cut Tom, but it seemed more likely that he had come by the wound fighting. I thought seriously about locking him up for his own safety, but everybody assured me they would take care of him, so I relented (against my better judgement).

Taff Jones was duty medic, so he got the duff job of bandaging Adams up, and he got attacked for his trouble. I had no choice but to intervene, reverting to Plan A and locking Tom up for his own and everyone else's safety. I couldn't have been that worried as at one stage I left Hubby with the problem and sneaked off to BHQ to ring my mum. After getting cut off twice, I finally got to wish her a happy birthday, which was lovely.

The next morning I was just out of my combats when the dog stag struck again. My bed was looking like a good bet when I was told I would have to appear on OC's orders. I think I was more nervous than those that were being charged for being drunk and disorderly. It was a formal process and one that was conducted at a million miles an hour. The CSM got to bark at everyone, and because he barked quickly it made everyone involved move just a bit faster. Oh yes, the cooks came in the early hours of the morning and they got to stand in front of the man as well. Your kit needs to be in decent shape and you need to tab in front of the OC and present the evidence to him in a clear and succinct manner. It was all rather stressful considering I was only acting on what I had seen.

"Wham bam, thank you ma'am!" They got charged £50 each by the OC and Tom got referred to Commanding Officers Orders, which is a whole different level of shit. I was knackered. "Where's my pit?!"

It was Hubby's birthday, so the celebrations got underway in the afternoon. When I went up to the stimms shop to get some liquid refreshment, the girl I had seen at the CSE show was there and we got talking. Her name was Yvette and her mother worked in the NAAFI. She invited me round to see her that evening. So first it was a few beers with the lads, then we had a bit of a barbecue next to our attap. Everybody seemed to be having a good time, so I sneaked off for a shower and put on a pair of jeans to book out. This was a golden opportunity to spend some time in female company. In fact, any company other than the troops I lived and worked with day in, day out was welcome. Over the tour I saw her a few times. It was no great love affair, but she was a nice girl who didn't wear combats and provided a bit of company.

Before long it was time for another Cayes fishing trip, and this time it was organised by Tommo. First we had to get some bait, which seemed to involve a lot of faffing around without much of a result. Eventually, it was decided the few tiddlers we had would do for starters and we headed for Moho Caye. Over the six-month tour there were a few chances to go on Cayes trips, and we would take the old, long canoes with outboard motors that the locals used. These would be loaded up with as much beer as we could fit in: a

150

few stimms, snacks and of course some fishing kit. It was usually a cracking day out with some glorious scenery, but you had to make sure you had plenty of sun cream on. Once at the Cayes, the natural cover was fairly sparse, plus we were out for most of the day. Tourists paid a fair few quid for this kind of day trip, but we just had to cover the cost of the beer. We borrowed Bobby's boat, and because we bought so much beer from his bar, he let us have the boat gratis.

Of course, there is always some sort of payback. After one of these trips, the next day we would need to spend most of the morning in our pits. Heads throbbing, we would be good for nothing. There is only one way out of that one: get out on the piss again.

Yet, despite this, we seemed to lurch from one extreme to another on tour. I think at the back of our minds we were always aware that we needed to maintain a certain level of fitness. Sometimes after lying in bed all morning unable to lift our heads off our pillows, we would take on a nine-mile circuit against the clock later that day. I usually managed a time of around seventy-five minutes, mainly thanks to the locals, who would spur me on by giving me a bit of stick for 'monging'.

There was a point to the nine-mile circuit: It was part of the platoon competition and in preparation we would run it as a platoon. By this stage of the tour we had all done the circuit a few times and I knew what I had to do to get round without biffing it. We all set off together, but after about three miles it split into two groups. The boss and I seemed to be going quite well together, but at one stage he left me. I wasn't put off by this and just kept plodding along. Actually, I probably went faster during the second half of the course! I eventually caught him up and we got in at 1hr 6mins, magic! The whole platoon – Smudge being the last – got in at 1hr 12mins. We were in the final, so we had to go out to celebrate. Bobby's Bar, here we come! We were on the piss again.

It seemed strange celebrating a fitness test with a session on the beer/rum, but this was the way of the world, as per the military.

It wasn't often that I was asked for advice, but Johnno, one of the chefs, wanted to try the selection to become an officer and had enquired about doing an infantry cadre. This level of training would give an indication of what would be required during officer cadet training. His eyes positively bulged with the news he would have to wear 35lbs of webbing and the like. Yeah, good luck with that one!

But that's a positive thing about the military: if you're good and you want to get on, you can. It doesn't matter who your dad was and where he worked, it's about your ability to play the game, get stuck in and move forward. The rank structure means you always aspired to fill someone's shoes, and the person you looked up to had done what you need to do: a cadre, or Junior or Senior Brecon. You could even skip up the ladder and make a leap to a different set of steps and become an officer, as Johnno was thinking of doing. That said, there are always obstacles that can put the kibosh on your dreams. Try moving away from the Cheshire Regiment, for example, and it could prove to be a challenge (more on that later).

I had a week working out of Airport Camp, which meant only one thing: a weekend in Belize City abusing my body. After this I was pleased to get on the 'mini' RPL heading for St George's Caye. During the tour, everybody gets the chance to visit the British Forces Adventure Training Centre. Almost as soon as we arrived there was a swimming test; something I didn't really look forward to as I wasn't exactly Olympic standard. It turned out not to be too bad and we all made it.

I put my name down for wind surfing, probably because I thought it was all to do with the hips and at the time I considered myself to be fairly flexible. I found out very quickly that it wasn't and I spent most of the first three days in the water. The good thing about the centre was that there was no pressure to make you do anything at all. If you wanted to sit around all day drinking brews and playing Trivial Pursuits in the sun, that was fine. So that's what we did, the boss, Burnsie and me. Now I'm not too bad at that.

The Caye was a beautiful place to look at, but it fell down on its total lack of facilities, including fresh water. Practically everything had to be brought from Airport Camp. As a result, there were no showers, and by the end of the five days I was feeling distinctly grubby. Sand flies were also a big problem and they certainly made a good meal out of me. At the end of the course there was the customary barbecue, which was a nice way to finish. The special guest of honour was the resident parrot, called Jabba, who had clearly learned some choice language from the many troops who had visited over the years. I'm not sure who was more pissed, but Jabba seemed to get stuck in like the rest of us. Have you ever seen a pissed parrot fall over? I'm not sure the RSPCA would approve, but Jabba was having a great time.

On the Friday morning, certificates were awarded for the various courses. Not having not properly completed wind surfing, I didn't really deserve one. Instead I got one for the 'Bupsie', a dance I learned in Belize City, at which I was definitely an expert.

Chapter 7: Road trip!

One Saturday in early February, Bede had arranged to use the long wheelbase Land Rover so we could go and see the Mayan temples. Our departure was delayed, mainly because we all felt pretty rough after another night on the piss, but eventually the boss, Assistant Adjutant, Ronnie Capper and I set off. The female Assistant Adjutant was a redhead and she was pretty fit as well. She was one of the few white women I had seen in Belize. I've no idea what it must have been like for her, but like the rest of the lads who came into contact with her, I found it pretty difficult not to stare. Our first stop was Belize Zoo, which was a bit of an eye-opener. I never realised there were so many animals wandering around the jungle. Fortunately, we only ever heard them in the wild.

It was a drive of another hour or so before we reached Holdfast Camp. The reason for the stop was to get petrol and to pick up Sergeant Baldwin. He had just come back from Senior Brecon and to say he had dropped a few pounds would be an understatement.

Eventually we arrived at the temples, and after looking at one on the front of a Belikin Beer T-shirt for so long it was nice to see the real thing. The whole trip turned out to be a great idea as normally I didn't get the chance to soak up the local culture. Despite bitching until the cows came home about life in camp, routine was set and it was easy to do the same things every day; we didn't have to think about it. Anyway, this was a cracking day out.

On the way back we stopped at the famous JB's, a bar run by an American and full of plaques from regiments that had served there. We dined on fat, juicy burgers washed down with ice-cold beer. I had it on good authority that our plaque was already being made.

Chapter 8: Airport Camp

Later that month, I did the All Arms Air Defence course at Airport Camp. Colo and Smudge had flown up from Rideau to take part as well. It was run by the RAF Regiment and the first thing that struck me was the poor organisation. None of the lectures ran the full course and the subtext seemed to be: "You're flogging a dead horse if you think you're going to shoot it down."

I also felt as if I was a grandma being taught how to suck eggs when they tried to teach us general purpose machine gun (GPMG); but then it was all arms, including non-teeth arms, and it wasn't just 1 Cheshire taking part. The firing was good from the louch poles and we used Harriers from the RAF detachment at Airport Camp as dummy targets. It's true that you have virtually no chance of shooting down a fast jet; at best the tracker might distract the pilot. You would probably need to bring in some ground-to-air missiles, but they weren't teaching that during the week. Anyway, at least it meant I had a few days away from the routine of camp and, of course, there was the obligatory end-of-course piss-up!

On Saturday February 14, I somehow managed to avoid rejoining the company on field firing for a little longer. I think there was a problem with the transport, which suited me fine. With it being St Valentine's Day, I eventually caught up with the Paymaster and decided to go out. The 'pub' had a special party on and the place was packed. As usual, we danced the night away. I met an interesting girl, Caroline, who was studying ballet. We walked and talked for a while, but soon it was time for me to go. I could feel that it wouldn't be long before the sun started coming up, so it was back to camp for me.

****

We had an early call booked for 0515hrs on the Sunday morning. The Ordnance Corps were on guard and had the honour of walking around camp checking the perimeter. Part of their morning tasking was to get different troops out of their pits at the correct time. They gave us a shout at 0615hrs; which was slack, but I suppose it was better late than never. Luckily the transport for Holdfast didn't arrive until 0700hrs. Next we were on our way to field firing, and late on Sunday afternoon we arrived at Baldy Beacon.

Wow, what a bleak place: it reminded me of Sennybridge, the area we trained in while we were in Wales, and it didn't feel like Belize at all. The camp had been set up by the Engineers, all tented like in *M*A*S*H*. Just for field firing, I had been given authority to range supervise, which meant that on the section attack I had a chance to watch somebody else sweat while I was running around behind the troops live firing. The range team's job was to check the firing arcs of sections and occasionally individuals to make sure they didn't shoot a member of their own team.

I enjoyed the company attack; it was hard work, but it was exciting. Harriers were supposed to fire us in to the target, but the weather was bad so they didn't come. However, we did have mortars, 105mm guns, SF GPMG and Light Tanks firing into the target position. It's the first live company attack I've done, so there was plenty of ordnance onto the positions. The aim was to destroy and take over a number of enemy positions (trenches/bunkers).

Back at camp, the other members of the range team and I had a debrief with the OC, who seemed fairly pleased with how the attack had gone, and then it was time to go. He would take advice from the range supervising team to gauge the fire and movement of the troops and the momentum of attack, and this in turn would

158

be passed on to the commanders and their subsequent teams. I had great fun trying to read my mail at the back of a four-tonner by torchlight! We had a quick barbecue at Holdfast, and then it was onto the bus for Rideau. The recce team was in high spirits. They had been on the beer and the singing was terrible. Between them and the bumpy roads it was impossible to sleep.

Chapter 9: Aggro downtown

On Friday February 20, most of the company decided to go out and town was buzzing. Late on in the evening, I was in Bobby's Bar when Pete came bursting in, saying that Deck had been shot. It took a moment for the meaning of the words he was saying to sink in; it's not the sort of thing you expect to hear. My first thought was, 'Yeah, sure he has.' But you could see the fear in Pete's face, so we thought we had better check it out. First, Bruce and I began to walk up the road, then it turned into a run and soon we were sprinting as we realised this could actually be a life-or-death situation. I found Deck lying in the gutter beside the path leading to the Venus bar. This venue was regularly declared out-of-bounds to troops, as it was considered to be a risk to Army personnel. It turned out the risk was real enough.

Deck was curled up in the foetal position and had blood all round his face. There was a lot of blood on the ground around him too. He was very drunk and didn't seem to be feeling his injuries as much as he should have. At first we thought the shot had been to his chest, but it turned out that the entry wound was in his chin and the exit wound was in his back. We used cigarette lighters to give us a clearer picture of his injuries. Considering he had been shot at point-blank range, he didn't seem too seriously injured, although he was drifting in and out of consciousness. It had been so quiet in Punta Gorda for five months, then this had to go and happen. Transport was called and Deck was moved quickly by the medics. First he was moved back to camp and then he was flown to Airport Camp and finally to Miami for specialist treatment. All the troops were extracted back to camp.

He was eventually taken back to England and was expected to make a full recovery. It turned out he was actually outside Venus when an off-duty copper came up to him and Paddington and asked Deck to give him his watch. When he wouldn't hand it over, he was shot. The policeman was captured, but they locked him up in his own nick, which he managed to escape from. You couldn't make it up.

That Saturday was my birthday; it was my fourth in the Army. There was a sombre mood in camp because of what had happened the night before, but despite this the lads still helped me to celebrate. Tucker, one of the cooks, made me a big chocolate cake, it was great! Everybody in the block tried a piece. During the afternoon we had a barbecue. This was halted for a few hours while we swept the area where the shooting took place, but nobody minded. It was accompanied by a few beers, which went on into the early hours.

Chapter 10: Rest and recuperation

My R&R took place between February 24 and March 11, and this
was something I had waited for for a long time. Mark and Dave
Dunning, Jacko, Colo and I had decided to go to Cancun, as we had
heard a lot of good things about the city. First we had to get there
and this meant a flight to Airport Camp, then we were on a bus for
eleven hours though the night. This wasn't a coach with air con and
nice seats; it was a bloody bus with chickens and crap everywhere.
It started raining at one point and we had these plastic sheets that
rolled down over the windows. Class! We arrived early in the
morning and went to the hotel, but they knocked us back as the
rooms weren't ready, so we went straight to the beach and ran into
the sea. The waves were massive! I spent about £500 during our
time there. I really enjoyed it and it's a trip that will remain with
me for a long time.

Cancun won't forget us in a hurry, either. With our Union Jack
shorts we were quickly recognised, and we could usually be found
in bars such as Aquarius, Blackbeard's and especially Coco's.
By the end of the two weeks, they knew us well. The owner of
Coco's commented that we were the best beer drinkers he had seen.
Everybody spent too much money, drank too much and didn't eat
enough, but it was good. We managed to squeeze in a trip on a pirate
ship, which sailed to Isla Mujeres (Island for Women). We bumped
into a group of US Army officers who managed to beat us in a
drinking game (the shame!). Oh yes… As is standard, we managed a
few fights. The Dunning brothers took on some locals and then Colo
and I had words and it finished with me filling him in and buckling
my ring in the process. He got a black eye for his trouble. After
fourteen days it was time to go back to work for a rest!

Chapter 11: Final push and moonies

In mid-March it was the RHA fun run. What a fucking nightmare after two weeks on the piss. It all started off as: "Have a go if you like", but then B Company quickly got hold of this and it turned into: "You will take part!" That morning I found out just how much the Cancun leave had done to damage my fitness. I don't think I've ever sweated so much.

It wasn't going to be the same sort of run as the inter platoon. The same course was used with a bit added in, making it 10.1 miles. I'm pleased to say I got round without stopping in 1hr 20mins. (I wasn't after any records and I didn't get any!)

The general routine of life in camp continued and by this stage the guard room and I were inseparable. Well, I spent my time either in there or scrubbing the block. By this point the block looked like it did on day one, week one, in the depot. The lockers and beds were in perfectly straight lines. This was all part of the 1 Cheshire handover. When I arrived, the place really was a mess. I'm sure the Queen's Regiment just got up that morning and left. We made sure the camp was spotless and we knew it would be even better by the time we left on April 6. We were back to the monotony of cleaning everything in sight. What we said in the Army was: "Bullshit battles brains." The paint had come out as well. Nothing was safe!

What a time to be on guard as the tour drew to an end. Troops were getting pissed every night (for a change), but 'fall down drunk' came into play at the weekends. Either the Commander or 2 i/c had to sit in the NAAFI at night: one, to keep order; and two, the guard room was being scrubbed! I just hoped I wouldn't get canned when it was my turn.

There was no mail again. People at home must have thought the wind-down was a piece of cake. That couldn't have been further from the truth.

On March 26, the pre-advance from the Highlanders flew into Rideau. I got to see one of those silly hats with mess tins on the front (their headdress). Our time was nearly up.

The heat was unbearable and Belize wasn't expecting rain until July! Some of the camps were having severe water problems, but thankfully Rideau was still operating as normal.

Each morning that week, the company took part in a drill. I could hardly believe it when Loz said: "Go through mounting the guard at the Tower of London, will you?" I was resigned to the fact that we might as well just get used to it. The programme for London made for interesting reading. 1 Cheshire would be posted to Caterham in Surrey and would become the first line non-Guards regiment, cavalry or infantry to take up a two-year ceremonial duties posting.

Despite all of this, spirits were very high. And seeing those Jocks reminded me just how pale people in the UK were!

The drill continued and appeared more and more on our remaining camp programme. That said, we still had a laugh. On one particular day it was drill in the morning, which was great fun (honestly!) and a volleyball competition, but the most action-packed event of the day was the company barbecue. Things kicked off just after 1800hrs, and with the amount of beer purchased I could see it wouldn't be long before the fun began. Just as we were trying to decide how to get rid of the steaks, the Engineers appeared; in togas, no less. There was an edge to the atmosphere when one of the lads mentioned that we had ten days to do. The different units' tour times are staggered; we just wanted to get home and it showed. The Engineers still had three months to do – never mind. The odd punch was noted here and there, but somehow it didn't manage to go full blown – it was just handbags really. The ale began to talk, though, and the night never regained its sparkle.

An important point to mention here was that I hadn't touched alcohol since R&R. It was very interesting to see how it changed people. I asked myself, 'Do I really act like that?' I'm sure I bloody well do and then some! The CSM wasn't just part of the action, he also threw up! Would he ever live it down? He soon did and respect was forthcoming. That's what I call leading from the front. Never ask anyone to do anything you're not prepared to do yourself.

One Saturday towards the end of March, after running around for days to set it up, our Cayes trip finally came around. After the kick-off the night before it was great fun getting a lot of people out of bed. A couple couldn't hack the pace and decided to stay in camp and a few others were on CO orders. The number that finally left was thirty-three.

Bobby's two boats chugged along and after about an hour and a half we arrived at Moho Caye. Towards midday the sun was really burning and some of the lads took shelter under the attap. The excitement generated didn't really match that of the usual Cayes trips. The previous night had burnt a lot of people out and sleep became a major concern.

On Friday April 3 I pushed my last guard. I finished as Guard Commander, which I suppose wasn't too bad as Macca was my second-in-command. A round went missing, which was a recurring theme, but this time somebody else could flap (being Commander, the kit wasn't on my flick). It turned up, as it had to, in the compound and all was forgotten. The advance party, consisting of almost thirty from the company, left, and Macca and I decided to sit on the desk and take the flack together. Actually, it was good to see them go because we knew our time would come.

On the Saturday it suddenly dawned on me that practice packing was a thing of the past; the real thing was almost finished. Boredom had set in and most of my time was spent either glued to the telly or to my bed. Wherever I went, camp troops were sprawled all over the floor trying to catch every last ray. Panic tanning was in session! The beer that wasn't drunk on the Cayes trip (a bin full) was finished off that evening. I didn't have any as I'd called it a day until I reached Chester, but I had a few stimms and got into the spirit.

Around 2300hrs I saw an amazing sight: a local coach that had been hired to transport the Highlanders up to the camp. Come on lads, what's six months?!

On Sunday April 5 there was a strong smell of burning flesh; the camp was full of moonies (new Belize-based troops)! In all honesty, people don't look all that well when they're so white. People had stopped asking me if they were brown and content smiles appeared on their faces – but still they didn't stop sunbathing, it had become an obsession. As long as the sun was out, they would lie in it. All of the tricks were coming in as well: lemon or baby lotion in the hair to bleach it in the sun. I didn't try it; I would probably have resembled a Guinness with blond hair!

Midnight came, and we knew that if all went to plan we would be out of there in twenty-four hours. Those that were left of our troops in the NAAFI were in a drunken stupor. No matter how I tried to be a part of the carnival atmosphere, it didn't feel right with me sitting there perfectly sober. As well as that, I was tired.

The tour was almost at its end, and by the time we flew out I had been there just over six months. I was so looking forward to being in Chester. Wherever you come from in the world, I think that will always be the place you love. There were so many people I wanted to see and there was so much I wanted to say to them. I knew I couldn't afford to waste this leave.

I was looking forward to meeting Funmi (the daughter of Tilly's mate) after writing for more than half the tour. We both had ideas about each other and I just hoped I could live up to her expectations. G had been in my thoughts for the best part of my teens and whatever my actions had been, nothing had brought us any closer. I felt it was finally time I stepped away from her and called it a day.

This tour had been a completely different kettle of fish from the Hong Kong tour. Yes it was hot, but the boredom was something to contend with. The jungle was hard work and as the 44 call sign left we knew we would be wet for the duration of that stay. Most of us had drunk our own body weight in beer and rum, which is something we all had to sort out when we got back to the UK. Using an ArmaLite as a personal weapon was interesting; it was better than an SLR as it involved less weight, smaller ammunition and was, up to a point, self-cleaning. It's a shame we couldn't stick with them when we got back.

When I had first arrived I couldn't see the end of the tour, and then suddenly it was upon us. I realised then that it wouldn't be long before we were in Cyprus. There had been talk about an arms plot, a big plan for troop deployments that the Ministry of Defence works to, and there were rumours that 1 Cheshire would spend six months there. This meant there was the prospect of getting a UN Peacekeeping gong for stagging on along the Green Line on the Cyprus border. The Green Line became impassable following the July 1974 invasion by Turkey, which intervened by air, sea, and land, capturing approximately eight percent of Cyprus.

Bloody typical, we didn't get the gig!

Chapter 12: Going home

We travelled to Airport Camp through the night on April 6-7 and arrived there in the morning. The anticipation was huge as this was the last trip we would make in this direction. The roads were poor; dusty and potholed. That, combined with the excitement, meant not many of us got a great deal of sleep. On arrival we had a wash and shave in the ablutions block. We had the radio on and it was announced that Sugar Ray Leonard had beaten Marvin Hagler after two years out of the ring – I couldn't believe it.

As always, the sun was out, so it would have been rude not to have a barbecue. As the Colour Bloke was flipping the burgers we watched our plane full of Highlanders come in to land. We knew it was ours as it was on time for a change and a huge roar went up as it came in low with the wheels down. It wouldn't be long now! After a refuel we picked up our kit and walked across the tarmac towards the VC10. We were piped aboard by one of their bagpipers and we were off to Blighty courtesy of Crab Airways.

Chapter 13: Girl trouble

Getting back home was fantastic. I gave my mum a big hug. She could have cooked anything she wanted for me and it would have tasted one hundred percent better than rations or the shit they served up in the cookhouse. I enjoyed all of the things most people take for granted: staying dry when you're in your pit; clean sheets; having different clothes to change into; not being bitten by lots of different big critters; and no swing fog blowing through the block every evening.

After getting letters from her for almost three months, I got to meet Funmi. She was pretty, like her photo, and very small. We went to see *Platoon* in Leicester Square. After spending six months in the jungle it seemed ironic watching a film about Oliver Stone's time in the Vietnamese jungle! I would have had a good time taking a plastic bag out for the night after six months away and we had a really good time, but nothing more.

It wasn't long before I met Clare B when I got back from Belize in the spring of '87. I had been in the scorching sun for six months and Paul had been freezing his nuts off with 3 Commando Brigade in Norway for three months. We decided we needed to go on the piss and we had eighteen consecutive days on it. I had pretty much been on the piss for the last six months, but not with Paul. We were out on a Sunday and we ended up in a basement bar in Watergate Street in Chester. I saw this girl and we started talking, but she couldn't understand how I could possibly want to be with her as she had a baby. My response was that we all have something that won't fit with everyone; I'm a black soldier. And that's how it started.

It was a whirlwind at first, and when I was in Chester I didn't want to be away from Clare. I went back to barracks in Caterham in Surrey, and she had just got a place studying at Goldsmiths in

Lewisham. That wasn't far away; in fact, jumping on the train and off at New Cross made it pretty quick on the bus into Lewisham. My Platoon Sergeant at the time, Tommo, was less than impressed as I often spent the night there and got an early train back in the morning. On more than one occasion I was just getting back to camp as Battle PT was starting – I wasn't flavour of the month.

Her little baby was called Francis (Frank) and I suppose in the end I probably went on to love him more than I loved her. However, when we started out she really was the love of my life and a breath of fresh air for me. She introduced me to lots of stuff that hadn't even been in scope for me: Miles Davis and Brian Eno, for example. In Chester we would go to High Society on a Thursday and listen to John Locke laying down funk classics as well as Earl Grant's *The House Of Bamboo* and *The Bottle* by Gil Scott-Heron. In London we would go to The Wag in Chinatown. She could dance, but she could also drink.

Clare asked me to marry her and I said yes, and at this point I decided to leave the Army. There was one consistent problem: my temper. I was very, very jealous of anyone around Clare and felt as time went on that a rift was appearing between me and a different class of friend she was socialising with at Goldsmiths. With a huge chip on my shoulder, I felt they were looking down their noses at me. Despite this, we pressed on and I left the Army.

It went pear-shaped almost straight away. The two of us were on the piss with her sister and her fella. We were in Borough and I had a disagreement with a group of lads, who filled me in. It was nothing serious, but a few of them got some digs in and that was sort of it. The next day I was pretty bruised and when Frank smacked me in the face I smacked the back of his legs. That was it, my relationship with Clare was over. I had never smacked him before, but I had had several blazing rows with her over one thing and another. I was good at punching things; I put holes in lots of things, mainly doors. I did one in an apartment in Spain with them once. It wasn't pretty.

Anyway, so I was out of the Army with no girlfriend, no baby and no bloody job. I was up shit creek. To be fair, I did think about topping myself on more than one occasion. Anyway, I did six months in adverting – telesales at VNU, a Dutch publishing house, working on *Micro Decision*, a computer magazine. I realised that if I didn't go back to the Army at this point I never would. I knew that if someone had been out for less than nine months they could assume their old rank, so I went back.

This happened after I went on a selection weekend at Lympstone in the hope of joining the Royal Marines. It was fine, but they said that I needed to go in and complete thirty-two weeks' basis training. At the time I was a fully qualified weapons instructor and a Brecon Section Commander. I said that all I needed to do was the All Arms Commando Course (eight weeks), and when they said no I told them to fuck off. Within weeks I was back in the Army, and over in South Armagh.

I went to meet Clare in London to tell her that I was heading to Ireland. We met in McDonald's in Lewisham and it didn't go well. She walked out and I chased after her and presented her with a blown-up picture of my team in Ripe Village training (at the Lydd base/FIBUA training facility) a few days earlier. Over the next few days I thought long and hard about what I felt she had done to me and I wrote a letter that was to be given to her if I died on tour. It explained that it was her fault I was dead and that she would have to live with that. This was my insurance and I gave it to Bomber Bailey, who was in a different multiple from me. If I did get snuffed out he had instructions to post it.

I remember writing to Clare on my first night at R14 in South

175

Armagh. I think I wrote a few times without getting any reply. About two-and-a-half months into the tour we got in off patrol and I went through the normal drills: kit check, batteries, rations, weapons cleaned and shower. When I opened the door to our room I saw two letters on my bed: one from Mum and Dad, the other from Clare.

When the lads were asleep and I was writing, I opened it up. The letter explained that she had met someone else. In the morning I saw Bomber and asked for the letter back – it really was over and I had to move on. The first step had to be getting home safely. When I got going in the Army, much was expected of me as Gale Cup winner and youngest Lance Jack and then Full Screw in the regiment. There had been talk of me being the first black RSM, but then I met Clare and I left all that behind me to be with her. It went tits up because I hadn't behaved well, but I still blamed her for dropping me like a stone.

Chapter 14: Politics and music in 1987

January 2: Golliwogs are banned from Enid Blyton books by the publisher and replaced by politically correct gnomes.

January 13: Prince Edward leaves the Royal Marines just three months after joining.

March 6: British ferry MS Herald of Free Enterprise capsizes while leaving the harbour of Zeebrugge, Belgium, killing one hundred and ninety-three on board.

The value of the pound is at a five-year high.

March 19: Winston Silcott, a twenty-eight-year-old black man, is sentenced to life imprisonment for the murder of PC Keith Blakelock in the Tottenham riots seventeen months earlier.

March 23: Thirty-one people are injured when a suspected IRA bomb explodes at a British army barracks in Rheindahlen, West Germany.

May 8: SAS soldiers kill eight members of the Provisional Irish Republican Army at Loughgall, County Antrim.

July 23: £60 million is stolen during the Knightsbridge Security Deposit robbery.

August 19: Michael Ryan shoots dead fourteen people in the Berkshire town of Hungerford before taking his own life with a rifle. Sixteen people are injured, some of them seriously.

September 9: Twenty-five Liverpool football fans are extradited to Belgium to face charges of manslaughter in connection with the Heysel Stadium disaster more than two years earlier.

November 8: Enniskillen bombing: eleven people are killed by a Provisional Irish Republican Army bomb at a Remembrance Day service at Enniskillen.

Late November: The first acid house raves are reported in the

UK, many of them held in derelict houses.
What I was listening to in Belize:
I Wanna Dance With Somebody (Who Loves Me) by
Whitney Houston
Control by Janet Jackson
Breakout by Swing Out Sister
La Isla Bonita by Madonna
The Rapture album by Anita Baker (we listened to this at the
block in Rideau Camp at night – most of us were crying!)

Part Three – Northern Ireland

The third part of my book is in diary format, almost exactly as it was written at the time, unlike Part 1, which was written longhand immediately after the events of Hong Kong, or Part 2 which was written in diary form in Belize, but was written up at a leisurely pace over a few beers. I have decided to leave it in this format because it conveys just how different this posting was in terms of the relentless pressure soldiers were under on operations in Ireland during the 1990s.

For me it felt like Groundhog Day. Yes, Ops Company had good lines (accommodation): beds with sheets on and TVs in the rooms, as well as a gym and a sauna, but the opportunities to actually use the facilities were few and far between. During our six months based out of Bessbrook Mill, we didn't spend more than thirty-six straight hours in barracks without some kind of movement.

There was also a bar, and Army rules state you can have two pints within a twenty-four-hour period. However, Ronnie and I had a chat about this before we arrived in South Armagh. For us, six months wasn't long to go without a beer. Yes, you could have a couple, but would it be worth it if your op went pear-shaped and the only way your team could be identified was by their dental records? What I mean is, you're no use to anyone when you can't think properly or move quickly because you've got two pints inside you and then been deployed. We got our multiple together at the start and said that if we smelt ale on any of them they were for the chop. That seemed to do the trick. When we did finally sink a few ales we were non-operational and test-firing on the coast.

The standard operational procedure for Ops Company was that we had to deploy the whole company within twenty minutes. That means we had to be in the air heading out to do something within that timeframe. This required the Air Reaction Force (ARF) to sit in the hut next to the helipad; unless the SAS were using it, in which case we were politely told to sod off somewhere else. Anyway, this meant the ARF team could take their helmets off, but that was about it. We kept our armour on as we watched videos on the box.

The ARF Commander, meanwhile, was required to sit in the Ops room in the main block, in a rather comfy chair in the corner, where he was able to watch all the operations being plotted on the big board. When it was time to go, the ARF Commander would be woken and a grid was pressed into his sweaty hand. As I or any of the other commanders can testify, it was then a mad dash with a sheep's head (having just been woken up) to the helipad. While this was going on, a call would be made to the ARF hut. The team would get their 'lids' (helmets) on and get on the Lynx (which was much faster than a Wessex) as the engines were fired up. The ARF Commander would jump on and show the grid to the loadmaster and we were off; it was exciting shit.

While this was going on, the rest of the company could be training, watching TV, spending time in the gym and sauna, or eating dinner, but when the call came in on the phone – which was manned twenty-four hours a day, all year round – the shout would go out and the clock was ticking. In fact, on a few occasions we were still in the air on our way back in when the chat on the net would be about our possible redeployment.

B Company had landed the 'plum job' under Major Rusby: Ops Company had involvement in all the planned Ops in the Tactical Area of Responsibility (TAOR). We caught up with the lads at Crossmaglen, Forkhill and Newtownhamilton and it was going OK, but how many times can you 'exit by Gate Three' before you're almost doing it in your sleep? We had the variety; we deployed pretty much everywhere in the air and half the time we

180

took off it was to somewhere new. It was fucking brilliant. But the downside was that the taskings came thick and fast. I've seen lads crying when the phone went because it meant we were off again; away from the TV and the sauna.

When we got in after a job – it may have been two or three hours or two or three days – we had to climb to the top floor of the mill where our digs were. When we entered the mill room it was huge; about the size of a football pitch. There would be lads standing waiting with binbags for our wet and dirty kit, along with piles of ration boxes and a selection of radio and Electronic Counter Measures (ECM) batteries. The IRA had a habit of booby-trapping kit that was left on the ground, including our water bottles. So when we got in, each multiple would line up and unpack everything.

We used plastic cuffs to dip the magazines to ensure that all the rounds were accounted for. The gunners had to show belts of 7.62 for the general-purpose machine guns (GPMGs) on the floor. (War Office Controlled Stores (WOCs) stored the important bits: binos, compasses, watches and everything else on an individual's 'flick'. Rations were replaced and kit was eventually repacked. It was then that Bergans were placed at the end of beds and the call would go out from the phone at the end of the corridor that ops were ready, if needed, to redeploy.

There was still stuff to do. We would sit on our Bergans, put on the TV or preferably some tunes and clean our rifles. If any mail had arrived when we were on the ground, this would be brought in. The team rooms were locked (each four-man team had its own room), but the keys were kept on the tops of our doorframes as standard. When we opened the door after an op it was lovely to see a letter, or sometimes two, on the bed. That said, I used to wait until I had finished my jobs before I allowed myself to open any envelopes.

Once the rifles were oiled we could then think about cleaning ourselves; washing, shaving, a shower and possibly even a sauna to get the grime out of our skin. When this was finally done, there would often be a commanders' debrief with Major Rusby. Sometimes team commanders were required to attend, but if it was just the boss he would let it filter down in time.

The cookhouse was open around the clock, so depending on the time we had, it would either be a proper meal or just egg banjos. Occasionally, we were too fucking tired to care. Then the lads would crawl between those crisp white sheets they had been dreaming of and as soon as their heads hit the pillows they would be out. It was then that I would sit on my bed at a small table and write my diary; this diary you're about to read. It was fresh and raw in my mind: what and who we had seen, where we had been and why. It detailed what I had done, hadn't done and should have done, and what we had got away with.

It was important to record the grind of the work in this kind of operational posting. On my table I had my dog tags with my morphine taped to the chain and my worry egg. This was a small smooth stone I found when we were on the Northern Ireland training ranges at Lydd before we deployed. I had just crossed a section of water and was drying out, i.e. with my combats around my ankles, when it caught my eye. After that, I never went out without it or the dog tags/morphine. Ops Company would be safe… until the phone went.

After a posting to Hong Kong and a tour of Belize, the pace was set to change again – dramatically. This time we were on our way to Northern Ireland and the all-too-real and present dangers of the IRA. It was time to put all those much-practised drills to the test.

Northern Ireland

Contents

Chapter 1: Chester 1998

We deployed to South Armagh from Chester, but this is only a sub-story. It was a local posting for me, and it was also the beginning of the end. As good as it may have sounded, being so close to home meant a loss of military focus. Like many others, I would pop home during the evening, see my mum and dad, have a meal and often sleep there. This was disastrous, as the camaraderie that builds up when lads only have each other when they're out of the country or miles away from Cheshire was lost.

I played rugby for B Coy in Hong Kong and then the regiment in Caterham, and this continued in Chester. I spent most of my time skipping around on the wing trying to keep out of trouble. We played the Cheshire Police when we were at the Dale Barracks in Chester and they won. We had a big drink in the NAAFI afterwards and we were all singing. At one stage there were thirty-plus players drinking and singing with their trousers around their ankles. Imagine the headline if a photographer from *The Sun* had got a snap!

I played football for B Company when I got to the battalion in Hong Kong and later for the regiment for a number of years. When we were in Caterham we topped the Guards Division League, which was nice. As with the rugby, I kept a place in the battalion side when we were at the Dale. I was a standard centre-half, nothing fancy, and although I always had aspirations of a role further up the field, I wasn't good enough.

Later, when I was at the Careers Office in Crewe, I had a chance to trial for the Infantry. This was after I had had an operation to put pins in my right ankle from an old injury, and the trial came too late. I played once but wasn't surprise not to be picked up again. After I left the Army I played rugby to a decent standard in London: first for the Old Blues and then Motspur Park, but once I had been under the knife my competitive sporting activity was coming to an end.

****

Before deploying to South Armagh, I took the Section Commanders' Battle Course, which enables Lance Jacks to become fully functioning Section Commanders. I did the first bit, which is six weeks of weapons instruction at Browning Barracks in Aldershot, and I did very well, narrowly missing out on a distinction. The problem came in the section piece, which was expected to be bread and butter for me. Clare was in the Philippines for three or four weeks seeing relatives. I was fretting and it reflected on my performance. I had a 'difference of opinion' with my team leader and that was difficult, so I passed, but not particularly well. In fact, this was noticed back at the battalion and I was told to attend an interview with the CO; without tea, which means without your belt and headdress. The aim was to try to get to the bottom of my crap scores. Hey ho.

It was during this posting that Clare asked me to marry her, and I thought that was it, that I was off. I left the Army but ended up in London with my tail between my legs after we split up. I then opted to go to Lympstone for selection for the Royal Marines; of course, I had tried this many years earlier. I did a few days and they said OK, but they wanted me to come in and do thirty-two weeks' basis training. I responded with the fact that I was a fully qualified weapons instructor and all I needed to do was the All Arms Commando Course (eight weeks). They said no, so I said they could stick it up their arse. I then turned to the Cheshires, who were still at the Dale in Chester. I want in to see the Chief Clerk, who said I should go to the Careers Office in Chester to complete my

186

paperwork. During my trip to camp I saw the lads were preparing for South Armagh. They all had to carry their Bergans as they walked around the camp to get them used to the weight.

The next day I went in to see Sergeant Docker Cubbins, an ex-Provo member of the regiment. We filled in the documents and he asked me when I wanted to go in. I said that I wanted to go back as soon as we could complete the re-join, and he asked, "How about tomorrow?!" Fuck me! I said I needed a few days to do my kit, which actually meant I wanted to go on the piss. I joined the regiment the following week, spending ten days in Brecon with a few days off. It was three weeks all told before I was in a one hundred-foot tower with call sign R14 in South Armagh, just five kilometres from Newry and about a thousand metres from the border. I had asked Lieutenant Waltier if I could join him. Waltier, my old boss from Six Platoon, was now the battalion's Command Observation Post (COP), but recce Platoon's teams and numbers were set, so I got knocked back.

Chapter 2: Northern Ireland 1990

Monday April 6 to Wednesday May 16

Ops Coy (B Company) was based at Bessbrook Mill; near the main Dublin to Belfast road and Dublin to Belfast railway line.

From this location we had a maximum of twenty minutes to move the whole company, either to operate independently or in support of A, C or Support Companies. The landing pads are extensive, so a number of helicopters can land on raised sections simultaneously. The only type that was unable to land inside the base was a Chinook; these had to come down just outside the main perimeter. This meant that the helipad was the busiest in Europe. Helicopters were used to move troops because of the large numbers, as green vehicle (Land Rover or truck) movement was banned due to the significant landmine threat. It was also used to supply other military outposts. The only other type of vehicle movement was unmarked cars used by Special Forces or a covert patrol van (CPVs); a van with a few boxes in the window used to move troops when the weather made it unsafe to fly.

It was thought that the IRA was organised into two battalions: one around Jonesborough and another around Crossmaglen. In the 1990s, the South Armagh Brigade was believed to consist of about forty members, many of whom lived south of the border. Thomas 'Slab' Murphy, who was also alleged to be a member of the IRA Army Council, was in charge (more about him later). The South Armagh Sniper was the generic name given to members of the South Armagh Brigade who carried out a campaign against British security forces using .50 BMG calibre Barrett M82 and M90 long-range rifles in some of their shootings. About 180 British soldiers, Royal Ulster Constabulary (RUC) and prison staff members were killed in this way between 1971 and 1991.

189

British personnel killed (South Armagh 92-97)

Name and rank	Date	Place	Rifle's calibre
Private Paul Turner	August 28,1992	Crossmaglen	.50
Constable Jonathan Reid	February 25, 1993	Crossmaglen	7.62 mm
Lance Corporal Lawrence Dickson	March 17, 1993	Forkhill	7.62 mm
Private John Randall	June 26, 1993	Newtown Hamilton	7.62 mm
Lance Corporal Kevin Pullin	July 17, 1993	Crossmaglen	.50
Reserve Constable Brian Woods	November 2, 1993	Newry	.50
Lance Bombardier Paul Garret	December 2, 1993	Keady	.50
Guardsman Daniel Blinco	December 30, 1993	Crossmaglen	.50
Lance Bombardier Stephen Restorick	February 12, 1997	Bessbrook	.50

(Source: Wikipedia)

190

Chapter 3: South Armagh

Wednesday May 16, 1990

Well, here we are. At last the talking can stop and we can finally get on with it.

Last night was a wonderful one, full of happiness and smiles; beer as well! I did lose several hours of my life and this morning my head was telling me to give up – it must have been good! The lads and girls from our Chester drinking crew were there to see me off in style.

By 0740hrs the next day the Regimental Sergeant Major's (RSM's) wife had obviously said something about my rather bald head to her husband (I had exchanged pleasantries with her the day before). He inspected my haircut and, to my surprise, even managed a smile when he saw how little hair I had. We had to hurry up and wait in traditional style, but we eventually got to Liverpool Airport. The flight over was a noisy one, as usual with the Hercules, but it only lasted forty-five minutes.

When we got off the plane, it instantly felt unfriendly with the rain pouring down, but somehow it looked quite normal. It really is strange to think that there are so many bad bastards out there who kill people.

From Aldergrave, we moved swiftly on to Bessbrook. The Chinook actually landed outside the Security Forces base, something none of us expected. Run!! The flight of a Chinook generates a certain distinctive noise and incoming troops, especially in number, provide a large target to fire at in a shoot. We were vulnerable until we got inside the base.

We only spent a few hours there, but it seemed like a great place for desk heads! Next, to our horror, we moved by CPV to the permanent vehicle checkpoint (PVCP) at Newry with no ammunition. Anyway we're here now and living conditions are tight. Saying that, we're out of the way. Tomorrow I'll move up to R14 (a tower at the top of a large hill).

Chapter 4: The one hundred-foot tower with a great view

Thursday May 17

What a walk up that hill! If I do that on a regular basis, I'll certainly stay fit. What a great place it is when you finally get up here. OK, it's all pretty basic, but you're left to do your own thing. The place is manned by four plus one to do all the cleaning and cooking. The toilet is X-rated and I haven't even considered using it. As well as this, you have to walk to the bottom of the hill for a shower... but I can put up with that.

The equipment at the top of the tower is good stuff, with distances of up to seven kilometres in range. There are dead spots and these will become more apparent when I get to do a patrol. There's a radio/tape deck up top, but things tend to get fairly busy during the day, with two radio sets, helicopters, roads and houses to watch. Night time is a different story, as we have limited night viewing equipment. Only Newry itself is visible from here.

I have a feeling that the first three weeks will be good up here; that there will be time to settle in gently. The Light Infantry (LI) lads are a good bunch and I think the handover will go well.

We had a brisk walk down the hill this evening for a shower. Unfortunately, United won the FA Cup. Never mind, I'm sure Chrissy (the brother of my ex, Clare Barlow) is celebrating.

The letter writing has started; two each night. I wonder when I'll get one back?!

Friday May 18

Today, the Colour Sergeant came out of the tower and I ended up signing my life away. It's now all on my flick (signature). This includes Sustained Fire (SF) GPMG, ammunition, 20/120 Nikon binos, Claymore in the wire… the lot. (Claymore is a directional anti-personnel mine; it is fired by remote-control and shoots a pattern of metal balls into the kill zone like a shotgun.)

We did twelve hours on stag and all was quiet until we were due to come off (2100hrs). A coach was stopped on the Dublin Road by about fifteen police. It turned out to be full of major players on their way to a Sinn Féin meeting. There was also a strange incident at The Newry Golf Inn involving a yellow van and four youths.

About an hour ago it was reported that a patrol near border checkpoint five had a car drive up in front of their location. A number of men got out, set the car alight and then drove off in another car. They also left a package inside a derelict building.

Is this the shape of things to come, or is it just the weekend?!

Sunday May 20
This afternoon I had a stroll down the hill to the permanent vehicle check point, call sign R15 for a shower; I'm now two shades lighter. I've swapped stags now, so I'm on until 0600hrs. It should be nice and quiet...

Monday May 21
We were stagging on from 2100hrs yesterday until 0900hrs today, and what a stag it was. Within thirty minutes of starting, a message came over from GO (control on the radio network). It stated that Special Branch believed a mortar attack on R15 was imminent via a yellow Toyota Hiace van, which had been stolen in the South. Well, that was it; we were in headless chicken mode. I think during that stage we must have sent traces on at least thirty Hiace vans, one of which was yellow. Thankfully, nothing came up on Vengeful, a system that was linked with the DVLA in Northern Ireland and was used by the British Army to identify vehicles of interest.

194

The night viewing kit is fairly limited up in the tower. During the early hours, the mist begins to come in and visibility is down to zero. That's when we began ranging. Picture the scene: Janet Jackson was playing fairly mellow sounds, and even with my eyes open I couldn't see outside the tower. Between 0400hrs and 0600hrs it was extremely quiet on the net and I had trouble keeping my eyes open. Oh yes, and at one point we lost comms. This was the same time as a green convoy was heading past our location. It all sounds fairly normal, except that there's no green vehicle movement in this area. We had to keep an eye on it and keep in touch with 0 (control). I found myself rolling around on the floor for about ten minutes trying to fix it. I don't know what I did, but eventually people started talking to us again.

Just as it began to get light, I realised I had lost the St Christopher Mum had bought me. I was upset, but there was nothing I could do. As I got into bed I found it on the floor. It was a good sign.

Tuesday May 22
It was reported that the enemy was test-firing weapons in Silverbridge last night; what a good start to the day. Oh yes, the 'Borucki Sanger' (Security Force base) in Crossmaglen also reported automatic gunfire. Things could be warming up.

In the morning I took a stroll down the hill to R15 and, after what seemed like a lot of fuss over nothing, I finally jumped into a Royal Ulster Constabulary (RUC) mobile and went to Corry Square. The cars they use are armour-plated Sierras: the panels, glass, the lot. I felt like Robocop inside!

Corry Square is the main police station in Newry. Three years ago it got mortared and nine died, but it's been altered since then. In fact, they say that the roof on the main building of the police station is so heavy that if it did get mortared all of the floors would fall on top of each other. Watch this space.

Anyway, Dava and I met up with some of the lads we flew out with when we got inside the station. They seem to be enjoying themselves. The accommodation is good and the food is excellent. Never mind that, women work inside the building, and outside the walls in Newry itself. I don't think I've ever seen so many beautiful women in such a small area.

During the afternoon I went out on a police mobile. It was a great opportunity to see some of the streets I'm observing from up here. There were lots of attractive women – none of whom would speak to us – and some fairly rough-looking areas. The Derrybeg is a nasty-looking place. Lots of players live there and their houses were pointed out to me. Not long ago a one thousand-pound bomb was found in the Begs and everybody was pleased until Special Branch pointed out that it wasn't the main hide where large quantities of explosives and weapons would be stored, so it was thought that more explosives were almost certainly in the area.

Now the police are restricted to about a quarter of their normal patrol area because of the landmine threat. While driving around we were called to the scene of a crime. Two lads were caught stealing from a local shop and they got a ride with us; the RUC and 1 Cheshire! The two RUC blokes I'd gone out with both seemed like interesting fellas. They gave the impression they enjoyed their work plus the risk of their job. I'm not sure it would have been a job for me; it seemed like work and pressure that would make you grow old before your time. Good luck to 'em.

After a fine meal I travelled to Bessbrook with the multiple commands for the OC's brief. This was in a CPV; the vehicles everybody knows the troops travel in. It was a screaming red van with a rather obvious skinhead driver.

As we got to the gates of Bessbrook, the OC went out for a run, which was a good start. Around 2000hrs we finally sat down and he began to talk and talk and talk. I had expected to catch the second half of the England game... we finally got out at 0045hrs! I wouldn't have minded, but I only spoke twice!

I stepped inside the NAAFI for a growler and a desk head shouted out, "What are you doing Jim? You should be out on patrol?" I had to count to ten. It was that or kick his head in. Being part of the battalion administration team meant sitting behind a desk, shining a seat with his arse he probably hadn't planned to leave the security base for six months.

Wednesday May 23

My own personal Gazelle helicopter brought me back to R14 this morning. One has to travel in style occasionally!

I had intended to get my head down. As I threw my Improved Northern Ireland Body Armour (INIBA) jacket on to my bed, somebody let out a groan. Guppy, the Light Infantry Commander I was taking over from, was asleep there.

With conditions fairly cramped, I decided not to stay where I wasn't welcome. I took a stroll down the hill and eventually found my way to Phil Phillips' pit. He was a Full Screw like me in Ops (B Company) and we had done Brecon together.

There are a lot of headless chickens in Two Light Infantry at the moment. Two montages (pocket-sized books that contained passport photographs of suspected terrorists) have gone missing, and it's a bad time for this to happen with the Stevens Inquiries taking place. In the 1990s, three official British government inquiries were led by Sir John Stevens concerning collusion in Northern Ireland between loyalist paramilitaries and the state security forces. The Special Investigation Branch has paid several visits to R15, and even the CID popped in today. The rumours are

197

terrible. The lads have been told they may not be able to fly home; even parliament has been mentioned! We are not happy to say the least; in fact this meant there was a major sad on. One lad finally admitted he lost the montages near a bridge in Newry – five weeks after they disappeared. A patrol carried out a search and, surprise, surprise, one has been found. Where's the other one, though?

Clare and Francis are on my mind constantly. If I think about it logically it's a very foolish thing to do. Realising how bad the mistake I'd made by fucking the relationship up and her dropping me like a stone was all very well, but it won't do me any good. I still love them a great deal, that's the problem. I'm finding it so difficult to let it go because one thing's for sure; she isn't having me back. Listening to Janet Jackson's "Come back to me" – some sloppy emotional shit – can't be doing much good. A fool to myself!

Thursday May 24
The ten hours I did on stag today could only be described as the quietest they come. I started at 0400hrs and we had a problem with the comms (we didn't have any), but besides that it was normal.

The intelligence coming from Special Branch is disturbing to say the least. The threat at the moment is very high. At this location a heli shoot is the most likely threat. It's also circulating the grapevine that the enemy intends to take on a multiple (a twelve-man team; a standard unit size on the ground. It either operates as two sixes or as three four-man sub units) on the ground, and that the enemy numbers would be greater. The first thing that springs to mind is a sixteen-man Active Service Unit (ASU), which is extremely frightening at the best of times. The Light Infantry lads are all a bit worried about these reports. If a major incident takes place, their flight could be delayed. Come on, the enemy knows we're coming; four helicopters flew over our location today heading for Forkhill. They know we're not carrying Mars bars!

The police pulled a body out of the canal early this morning, and from here we could see them in large numbers on the edge. No more information has been received about that yet.

The last bit of kit has been handed over. The ammunition in front of me on the table is four hundred rounds (5.56mm) to be loaded straight into my lads' magazines. Oh yes, they arrive at 0400hrs tomorrow morning.

The latest on the missing montage is that, as far as I can see, the incident is closed. The lad who lost them got a £150 fine and twelve days restriction of privileges (ROPs) after leave. The Platoon Commander got £300 and a month's worth of extra duties. The Sergeant will go in tomorrow and Guppy suggested it would be an interview without coffee!

Friday May 25

I went on stag at 0001hrs this morning. It's now almost 2100hrs and I'm going back on. The amount of sleep in-between has been extremely limited. At last the lads got here and the LI blokes could hardly contain their excitement; and quite rightly so. The Wesse came in at 0400hrs and dropped off H, Vic Lloyd, South and Merl. They all seemed a bit shell-shocked, probably because I was talking so quickly. We only had an hour for the changeover. The time passed at double speed and within what seemed like minutes the LI lads were being picked up.

I shook them all by the hand and wished them the best; they had been good to me. This is it now: 1 Cheshire in South Armagh. Straight away the problems began: first with rats in the food and then the water. One of the lads, Murtar, eventually saved the day and the least we could do was cook him lunch. Melling (Six Platoon) went on patrol with Scouse Moran (a legendary

Sergeant within the regiment. He was the scruffiest senior non-commissioned officer in 1 Cheshire with a superb sense of humour) this morning and had no magazine on his weapon for forty-five minutes. Last weekend warmed up considerably for incidents, so let's hope this is a quiet one and we can settle in.

Saturday May 26
Vic and I did our first full stag last night/this morning. We started at 2100hrs and finished at 0100hrs. As expected, things began to warm up as weekend fever set in. A Four Platoon patrol in Corry Square, with Percy as Team Commander, experienced a double-tone 'Antler' attack; somebody was trying to initiate a remote-controlled IED on them. This happened in the Derrybeg area, which is now an out-of-bounds area. The threat of a heli shoot is high at the moment, and because of this all flying has stopped until Monday. Instead, troops will be using the CPVs – dead good!

My first letter arrived today – result! Party invites are to follow!

Wednesday May 30
Nothing much has happened over the last few days, although there have been a number of minor incidents in Newry. Percy's section had another Antler attack from the same operator. He also reported two rounds fired from a low-velocity firearm. Not much luck, hey? Yesterday V20A (the boss) patrolled into Corry Square, Newry. On the way there was a violent joker attack (electronic) in the Derrybeg area.

The days just seem to roll on here. The visibility is zero when the mist comes in on us up in the tower. With this in mind, I decided to place a trip flare on the track and it went off. I'm expecting a fair amount of stick about that, but nothing I haven't heard before. Eventually I got one up; what a nightmare. It wasn't long before it went off again. A sheep, maybe? Who knows... I think I'll shelve that idea.

The Padre visited today bringing writing kit and stamps, good lad. Oh yes, I had a letter from Mark Abbott, which made me laugh. Mark and I had been mates for a few years; mainly through getting pissed in Chester and playing football in the local Saturday and Sunday leagues. He's another good lad.

The Army have at last decided to pay me. A payslip arrived, and that should clear my overdraft. In a few moments I'll begin the one of the worst stags; 2100hrs to 0100hrs. Not quite a Dog Stag but not far behind. Nice, hey?!

Friday June 1
British Summertime is upon us once more, but where is it...?

The sun disappeared about two days ago, and since then it's done nothing but rain. The wind is getting fairly strong as well. It's not too bad when you're on the ground, but it's a different matter when you're a hundred feet up.

This morning I received my invitation to a 'cake and arse party'. The Platoon Sergeant doesn't want to take two lads on the ground, so he has decided to swap them with Vic Lloyd and Suth. There was no notification of this, but hey ho; Woody and Griff, another two likely lads from our platoon made the long trek up the hill with their kit and that's it. The timing isn't too good as the OC is visiting all locations today and will be expecting the troops to know what's what; the arcs, targets and places of interest. It could all be very interesting, Private Ivimey!

The Colour Sergeant from the Royal Irish Rangers (RIR) is also visiting today, so this is a sign that my holiday will shortly come to an end. Ops Company, here we come!

Oh yes, the subject of mail is a touchy one to say the least.

I thought by this stage of the game that writing to everybody in the first few days would pay off. No such luck. I think it's the old story of 'out of sight, out of mind'. I'm sure I've said all this before, was it Belize October '86 to April '87?!

Monday June 4
Well, here we are in this tower again. These ten-hour stags are a slog. I don't really know what we do, but the time seems to pass by. That said, when you're off it seems to go far too quickly and then you're back on!

I've been up here almost three weeks and the handover is in sight, thank goodness! The advance party from the Royal Irish Rangers flies in today. There's no rest for the wicked. Without their feet touching the ground they'll move out to locations this evening. Woody and Griff will move back to Bessbrook as their lads come in, and then it will be left to H and me to show them the ropes. What are we doing up here again?

A major worry seems to be putting on weight, but if you actually sit back and think of the amount of ops B Company will be involved in, there's no problem. This easy living up at R14 will come to an end on June 11. That's the date 2R1R officially take over as Newry Company. We'll then be fucked around in Bessbrook for a while and deployed for our first op on June 14.

I really haven't decided what to do with my Army career yet. I mean, where do we go from here? Senior Brecon (the qualifying course for Rifle Platoon Sergeants) is staring me in the face, but I think I'd like to branch off a bit and do something completely different. The course is run in January, April and August each year and is broken down into two independent phases: tactics and live firing tactical training, but one thing I've always said is, "If you want something enough, just go out and get it". I suppose

202

I'd better do just that.

Out of all these women I wrote to (well, I say 'all these women' – they're just people I know) nobody has replied. I tend to think I've put on the wrong address. Clare is a classic example. Perhaps she and the others don't want to write, I really don't know. Paul has written, as has Mark. It's an old one: you know who your mates are.

Saturday June 9

Well, here I am on stag again. It's now 0530hrs and I'm pushing out until 1100hrs. Since the arrival of the R1R advance party there has been a considerable amount of messing around. The NCOs have changed three times since Monday! They're all good lads, but you just end up spending half the time trying to brief people. It's not only that, either; this week every man and his dog has visited. When the formal brief comes out you know it so well it's like putting a cassette in the back of my head. It's similar to a Small Arms Weapons Instructor on Junior Brecon, it's automatic.

The other day the Engineers did a recce and our battalion's second-in-command decided to come along. He didn't say anything directly to H or me when he was in location, but when he got back to 'slipper city', also known as Bessbrook Barracks (BBK), the buck began to be passed and we were contacted. The word came from the OC asking why we hadn't shaved. It wasn't good, but shaving when you're up a one hundred-foot tower isn't really a priority. I could do without this shit. The faces may change, but the system is still the same; it's bollocks! I really need to move away from this. I've thought about asking the SPSO for an interview because I'd like to know what's out there. We'll see.

The Three Brigadier Commander visited yesterday. As the tower is so small he had to come up alone. This left the CO, OC and the RSM downstairs. The word from the man himself was that mine was "an excellent brief". This cheered me up a bit.

I've seen so many magpies since we've been here, and every time I look at the clock, thirteen is always there. Is someone trying to tell me something? I've thought about writing a letter for Clare and leaving it with H in case anything bad happens. I need time to think.

I've had a letter from Rachel Brown (the only female to have written who is not related to me!), which was nice. She lives around the corner from my mum and we went to the same school. It'll be good if she keeps in touch.

Tuesday June 12

I'm sure it's not really a move for the better, but here I am back at BBK. The main body from the Royal Irish flew in and we were extracted an hour later.

It all began to get tense at R14 yesterday. In Tinnelly's scrapyard (John Tinnelly & Sons), we noticed somebody welding two sets of black tubes onto what looked like a base plate. They were in two sets of five and potentially seemed to be an MK10 mortar. I suppose it's better to be safe than sorry; O was informed and a Gazelle was tasked to have a look within five minutes. It turned out it was all welding equipment, but as I said, it's better safe than sorry. If it had been an MK10 mortar and it had been used, I would have been in the shit.

Anyway, back to BBK. As I walked into Ops Coy lines there was a pile of kit waiting for me to sign my life away again. After two kit inspections and a lot of waffle, I finally got my head down at 0200hrs and as soon as my boots off, we were on ten minutes to move. At least I've got my Military Forces Overseas (MFO) box and now I have sheets and a bed space. Not that I'll see it very much; at 0900hrs today we're on immediate notice to move.

204

Our first op is on Wednesday in Silverbridge. The SAS are here, so something is going down. Let's hope it works.

Chapter 5: Op Harringay

Wednesday June 13 to Friday 15

Our first op was mounted in the Silverbridge area. This is where the last two shootings took place. The Para shot in the leg (covering fire from a GPMG; 84 rounds fired) was one and the other was a Lance Sergeant from the Scots Guard's Close Observation Platoon (COP) (a snipe to the head). The weapon was a Heckler and Koch G3.

We deployed by Wessex and Lynx on the evening of June 13 to cordon positions. Stage one had to be reached by 0330hrs and it was hard going, but we sort of got there. It's not really practical to dig right down; part of the way, yes, and while doing that to build up with sandbags. Anyway, Robbo, a solid and very capable solider was slightly on the edge. There was always the thought that he could flip and kill lots of people – it's always the quiet ones. I also had Steensie. I'm not sure how he made it through basic training; he's not my favourite lad and he knew it. Anyway, we had the Sustained Fire General Purpose Machine Gun (SF GPMG) which was needed in position to cover much of our arcs, so we got ourselves sorted out.

Bear in mind that the Air Reaction Force (ARF) room is now occupied by the SAS. Something is definitely going down in the TAOR. Searsport is where they are watching the main weapons hide, and it's also believed that the SAS are watching two dumper-style trucks that have been armoured (Derryard style). Oh yes, and they've mounted a .50 machine gun in the Lynx. For those who don't know, that is serious shit!

Anyway, on the south of Silverbridge there's an out-of-bounds area. The SAS were in that area for around ten days before we deployed. We had been briefed on cordoning the area for a Searsport op. Read between the lines: there were two shootings in the area and the SAS were based in the south. Do you think the word 'bait' is a little out of place? OK, so we knew; but as all mushrooms do, we are just getting on with it.

Not a great deal happened there, we were 'clicking' (being observed) from various cars, but that's about it. If the SAS found anything they didn't tell us. The information we moved on was a month old, so that could have a lot to do with it.

When darkness finally fell, we got a good tab on into a harbour area. The Lynx came in and lifted the SF GPMG (in tripod) and Browning, but not the Bergans. Saying we just 'tabbed' sounds easy, but it wasn't quite like that. With most people carrying 65Ibs plus, it was hard going and we took around four hours to travel the four kilometres to the new location.

Within minutes of getting there, Robo thought he had lost a round from the belt. After looking around in the heather (akin to finding a needle in a haystack), we found it where he was sitting! Everybody got a few hours' kip and it was certainly needed. At 2300hrs, we (2OP) set off on our intelligence task. That was to check out a possible antenna in a hedge line. It was the first time I had patrolled during daylight hours. To be honest, I felt like I was back in Sennybridge; set off like a bat out of hell! I was all over the place in fact, but I finally got my act together. My call sign overlooked the area while Cheesy (Lieutenant Cheesy Watts) had a look. It was nothing; probably not even an antenna. We patrolled back, and while Crumpy and Woody both fell asleep, Ronnie revealed that he plans to put both of them on a charge. Falling asleep on duty is a big no-no and is classified as gross misconduct. Anyway, we then waited a few hours and the helicopters came in to collect us. On the whole, it wasn't too bad.

When we got back in we staggered up the four flights of stairs for the ritual kit check and de-gunge. We are supposed to be ready to deploy again within two hours and we probably were. There was a lot of mail on my bed, which cheered me up instantly. There was one from Rachel Brown, which was great; we're certainly getting on well with these letters. I only hope it works out as well when we finally meet.

Monday June 18
Today started off as a normal training/patrol pre-day with a weapons training test, terrorist recognition (TR) and first aid – we all put drips in each other! The platoon had intended to play sport in the afternoon, but at around 1350hrs, Ops Company was called out.

Paul Michael Hughes, who is the brother of Sean Gerard Hughes (both IRA players), lives in Forest Park, Drumalee. Acting on the RUC intelligence received, we wanted to search his house straight away. The haste soon went out of the op when we stood in the weaver shed for thirty minutes. The weaver shed is a huge corrugated hut where the covert patrol vans are kept, and where multiples line up and wait before moving down to the helipads for a lift. Eventually we got the Lynx, but not before I had fallen over. I hope it's not on film. Things seemed to go to rat shit straight away. Apparently, Hughes saw the helicopters coming in and went south over the border. As soon as I got on the ground there seemed to be about four call signs too many on the op. We (Y20A) were restricted to about a hundred metres of a small lane.

At this stage, immediately before we got on the helicopters, the sun came out and I took my Gore-Tex jacket and pants off. The thunderclouds came over, the skies opened and it poured down for about thirty minutes! The RUC had to make a forced entry and found nothing. We were eventually extracted at 1645hrs, very wet but in good shape besides that.

This evening we've had orders for our next op, which will

be tomorrow. This is about my third day on the boxing training and things are going well. I'm tired, but it must be doing me some good.

The chapel in BBK is located on the first floor and I found it by mistake. Ops were on the second floor and we trod a familiar path up two sets of stone stairs; either to get to the cookhouse or to deploy. When we had a planned op, for example the phone didn't go and there was no crash out to move at short notice, ARF and then the rest of the company would follow; we would know when we were going out. A set of orders was given the night before, and these were ultimately passed down to team level by me and Ronnie. If we were flying at 0400hrs (it was at usually first light), we would get up at 0230hrs, or 0250hrs in Ronnie's case. We would have breakfast, get our kit and move down to the sheds. When this was the drill, I would pop into the chapel on the way to breakfast. I would sit for a few minutes and I would already be carrying my worry egg (the patrol stone), dog tags and morphine. In my mind this was what I needed... plus a rifle. I would sit for a few minutes on my own going over what I knew: where we were going, who would be there and their capabilities (shooters, bomb makers and so on). I had a think about what I had to do and then I would join the others for breakfast. In six months I never saw another soul in there. I suppose we all had our own ways of preparing to go out.

Each time we flew out my heart would be racing, coming out of my chest. As soon as the 44 call sign had left us and it was quiet I would calm down; I knew what we had to do.

Op Corinto: June 19 to June 24
The whole of this op took place in the 'Jonesborough bowl'. The area is surrounded by high ground, some of which is over the border.

On Tuesday 19, covert ops had to be inserted from our platoon.

Both multiples would be involved. To add to the deception when they were dropped in, we (2OP) also went to the same location but patrolled away from the area to set up a vehicle checkpoint (VCP). Once it was dark we moved back to their location, Slievenaboley, to help construct the op. The weather was terrible and this wasn't a good start, with all the troops and kit getting soaked. Most people got a job and I was positioned on radio stag in the admin area by the Platoon Sergeant. It was a lucky break as I managed to stay reasonably dry.

At 0320hrs, our call sign (Y2OA) was extracted by Wessex back to BBK. This left a multiple in location with people in the area thinking we had all left. It felt great to get back to egg banjos, a shower and a warm bed. What more could a man in South Armagh ask for?! The majority of the day was dedicated to admin and we redeployed to R21 at 2330hrs.

After a quick sort out with kit, we moved out at around 0030hrs to set up a number of VCPs on country lanes. As the sun came up we moved to a harbour area. There should have been a small wood, but where? We just couldn't find it! The countryside is covered by tree lines, but that's about it. Saying that, we did find a nice dry barn to take shelter in.

After a few wonderful hours in the old green maggot (sleeping bag), we moved off to check an antenna. Cheesy did this as the two other teams provided cover. It wasn't on a line, so when they pulled it, it just came out of the ground! Well at least it didn't go off.

The next task (how many!) was a hide check by Ron, which I'm sure was just a grid on the map. This was to check whether this particular location was being used to hide explosives or weapons. Following this, all three teams moved off to recce a possible op position for a close target reconnaissance (CTR) on the bridge. We called it Grant's Bridge for some reason, but it wasn't on any 25k map as that. Anyway, we had several hours to do a job that would take thirty minutes, so everybody had their lunch and a good brew. As it turned out, we did find a good location, but I didn't want to blow it up too much. Guess who would end up missing it?!

We were close to finishing off when the ops room started flapping. A number of men had been spotted laying pipe into the ground down by the Kilnasaggart Bridge. You may say it's just a normal road maintenance job, but this is South Armagh! We got down there as quickly as we could. At one stage my team was picked up by Lynx to set up a VCP right on the border, even though we hadn't asked. We didn't ask to be dropped on it, but we were. If Robbo had moved position to the next bush along he would have been arrested. A Garda patrol sat watching our movements, which I must admit felt quite strange. Anyway, nothing much happened and, after what seemed like a hundred fences, we finally regained the last lie-up position. This was a chance to get our breath back before the tab up to R21.

After a few more glorious hours in our sleeping bags, we moved off in the early hours to place more VCPs. The first of these was in Jonesborough where, on the way, I found an electric fence, which is always interesting when you need to get over it with 65lbs plus on your back.

From there we established another lie-up position, VCPs and a CTR; it's great setting these patterns. It was a long day, but we eventually got back up the hill. This was after Ron stopped Sean Gerard Hughes, who really is the main man in these parts.

A few hours' sleep would have been great before the final phase, but unfortunately it didn't happen. This was all happening at R21. I felt as if I was back in depot, 'get your kit out for a check'. Given the size of an Antler battery, who would want to carry an extra one?! Anyway just as I got back in the sack, the message we had been waiting for finally came: Jimmy Tarbuck from 2OB needs a battery resupply and you're doing it.

What's the point in moaning? We just got on with it. A snap VCP in Jonesborough brought us Sean Murphy, my first player. Result!

All call signs moved through the town down to the country lanes and while we were moving on an independent four-man team, there was a strange incident. A white Hiace-type van began to move towards us with its headlights on full. As soon as it saw troops on the ground, the headlights went out and it reversed away. I think it crossed everybody's minds that we could be taken on and it was a particularly dark lane. Thankfully it came to nothing.

The battery charge was done and a helicopter eventually came to pick us up. The loadmaster had a huge grin on his face on the flight back in. I was listening to the radio as well at the time; Ops Coy were on standby to deploy to Newry.

Two players had been caught setting up a charge on a bridge with all the kit. Four Platoon were deployed because they know the area, so we're still on twenty minutes' notice to deploy.

Sunday June 24

2OB came in during the early hours and I was woken up several times regarding the swapping around of kit. All the rooms need cleaning because the CO is inspecting. What's that about? It's true, we're on an operational tour and we're still getting the accommodation inspected. Everybody got out of bed and the place began to look respectable.

Things seemed to be ticking over nicely with Sergeants' kit inspection at 1400hrs. Then it all kicked off. I'd better explain what's been happening in Newry. Hedgie Hillen and Aidan Mathers (known players) were caught on Friday evening by a bridge. The kit found on their persons and in the area included two boiler suits,

213

two masks, five pounds of Semtex and a battery pack. Yesterday, the Ammunition Technical Officer (ATO) sorted this out and the Scene of Crimes Officer (SOCO) believes there's enough evidence to throw the key away. Today there was a major bomb scare in Newry and the patrol multiple from R15 has moved into the town. Due to this, Scouse has taken his multiple plus a few others to R15 to cover for Op Searsport (an armoured truck threat). Woody's multiple has deployed to Corry Square, Newry, on a crash out with the RUC. As it stands now, I'm attached to Four Platoon waiting for a call out. Anything could happen...

Monday June 25
Today I had to travel to hospital to check out this groin strain of mine. This was an old sports injury which was playing up again – I'm not sure the heavy kit was helping. The move was done in typical 1 Cheshire style; it was slack. I sat in the back of a covert van (a green removal-type van) with no weapon or ammunition. After what happened to those poor signallers, you really would have thought each man would be armed as standard. The truth of the matter is we're not trusted, despite all being trained soldiers. Nothing will be done until somebody else is killed.

Anyway, we got there and I got the all clear. There were a few lads who had to wait until the afternoon to be seen and I didn't fancy hanging around all day in hospital, so I needed some more transport. The Recce Platoon has a few blokes in hospital with bad feet as they had been lying for a number of days with their feet higher than their heads/torsos, which is not good as they are probably looking at deep vein thrombosis, so Mr Waltier, Kev Taylor and Sherry were paying a visit. They asked me if I wanted to cadge a lift with them; great idea.

I'll put the record straight. People take the piss out of the recce, but they do things in style. Mr Waltier had a bag of 'goodies', so we all carried a 9mm plus two magazines and he had a Heckler & Koch (HK) under the front seat. We wouldn't have got to BBK by lunchtime, so we went to Lisburn (NI HQ) instead. It was like being back in England with a huge open camp and women. It didn't feel like NI at all. The strange thing is that the place is full of desk heads and they get the same NI pay as we do; even the same General Service Medal. It made me angry to see a few lard arses playing pool in the NAAFI, one wearing a side arm in a shoulder holster. He wasn't likely to go out on patrol but he looked good. Are there two standards?

Op Relegate (Recce): Tuesday June 26 to Wednesday June 27
The intelligence task was to gather information on six houses in O'Rielly Park (about 2.5kms south of R15). This actually took about half an hour, but Ops Coy spent twenty-seven hours on the ground. This is no joke! What makes it even worse is that it's a recce for an op that will go out on Saturday and we're supposed to avoid setting patterns.

To fill in the remaining twenty-six-and-a-half hours we made up a few of our own tasks: three rummages in woods and several VCPs. The problem was that our movement box was only about 1.5kms square and O'Rielly Park is all of two streets, so we found ourselves meeting the same people several times!

The weather was terrible; it pissed down for hours. This, plus the attraction of England in the World Cup, made R15 the obvious choice. Dream on! The OC didn't buy it and we ended up sleeping at the back of a barn next to a graveyard! What made me feel even sicker was that the pickup point was changed and all call signs had to begin to tab towards R15 once it was light. We were quite lucky that Crab Air decided to fly, as at one stage (0530hrs) the cloud base was so low all flying was stopped.

Everybody is in, showered and has had a kip, so if the OC comes up and asks, "How was it?" they all smile and say, "Great". I've done it myself. As I'm sitting here now, I'm aware that that was one of the biggest wastes of fucking time I've taken part in.

Thursday June 28

A bomb went off on the railway line in Newry during the early hours of this morning. This is the first since Paschal Quigley (another player) began working on the railway. From the off it was believed that it was a device to draw troops (ATO) into the area. There were two positive violent joker (electronic) readings; a secondary device had been left to soak.

Y2OB deployed with ATO last night, just while the tech officer had a look, but they weren't out for long.

For me this is a fairly major incident as the Belfast to Dublin railway is an important link. Despite this, there was nothing on national television. Is it not considered important enough for the British public?

Friday June 29

A patrol in County Down was fired on this morning. It is believed that three gunmen waited in a garden until the four-man team went past and then opened up on their backs. One man was hit in the arms and legs with four rounds. Between fifteen and twenty were fired altogether. The man was rushed to hospital and operated on. He's now past the critical stage, thank goodness.

Op Relegate: Saturday June 30

We got up this morning at 0300hrs (our multiple, 20A) and the first flight out was at 0500hrs. I was lucky as I was on the Lynx; the lads on the Wessex looked pale at the other end. They took off and only five feet off the ground had to go back down again. The loadmaster ordered four people off – including the OC – and the pilot tried again. Apparently, the problem was that it was carrying too much fuel. There's always something.

Anyway, we eventually all got to O'Rielly Park. The whole idea of the op was to support the RUC. They had guaranteed Ian Paisley's safety while he travelled from Newry to border crossing point 5 (BCP5). His eventual destination was somewhere in the south to celebrate the Battle of the Boyne. Great! Well, the op that involved the whole Coy got off to a bad start as it was raining. This continued for some time: Gary Gore-Tex, we love you!

From the drop-off point, my call sign (Y21C) moved at least 75m to the cover of a tree line. From this location our view onto the A1 Dublin Road was good. It was just as well, because that's all we did for the rest of the day. Nine coaches moved south and they all came back again. We drank lots of coffee and talked about all sorts of things. Throughout the day we all managed to sleep a bit as well.

Late in the afternoon the lifts should have begun as, yes, by this stage the sun had come out. The message came over that there were problems with the Lynx and we put the three-hour delay down to Argentina's extra time in the World Cup. Two Wessex eventually picked us up from Forkhill. That was it.

Monday July 2

Most of the platoon (including me) was still lying in bed at 1030hrs. No specific time had been set, so we thought we would just go for it. The Platoon Sergeant said he wanted to talk to the NCOs about this and we prepared our ammunition because we weren't going to fry for this one. As it turned out, he was fairly diplomatic and sparks didn't fly – this time. Oh yes, late last night the message was passed that the commitment for Op Searsport had gone up. There was now a team sitting in a vehicle waiting to go and the rest of us were on so called 'immediate'; we were to get down to the weaver sheds ASAP.

After lunch we were doing a few training periods. Phil and I were doing basic map reading with SF GPMG. We had just done a change with half of the lads when Ops Coy were deployed. A search was going on in the Derrybeg, where a thousand pounds of Semtex was recently found. We had just under an hour to get ourselves sorted and then the first flights went in. It was a massive op. Six search teams, eight RUC teams and the whole of Ops Coy were involved, either in the search itself or the cordon. Two multiples of Royal Irish Rangers (RIR) were there; fuck knows where, though! Our lift was with a Puma, so it was fast onto the ground. Once there, my team was tasked with a satellite on two fields. Tell me about it! I, like most of the lads, was knackered; if I'd had to go much further I would have fallen asleep. As we crossed Fifth Avenue moving towards the railway line, Steensie had an electronic attack for ten seconds. Flap! But it all went quite well. We sent the relevant details on the air and carried on. I swapped and changed the route across the fields, and even doing that we found ourselves in the same places again. Anyway, we eventually got called into the inner cordon. Ten call signs got extracted, so who was left? The housing estate was horrible; it reminded me of Ripe Village (Lydd Training Camp, one of the UK's largest fighting in built-up areas training sites with more than 300 buildings). There were derelicts and murals everywhere. After meeting up with the rest of the multiple we continued to cover the area from a stretch of high ground.

The find was as follows: 1,700 rounds; 7.62 (short barrel); one GPMG; 2.5 kgs of Semtex, one HK G3, three timer and power units (TPUS); one incomplete improvised explosive device (IED);

218

timers; mercury tilt switches; a balaclava; and a set of gloves. Not bad for a Monday evening!

Despite the full moon, we needed night viewing kit and new batteries for the electronic counter measures (ECM). A Lynx flight came in and we got the replenishments. Once that was complete, we moved off to the incident command post (ICP) for food and a brew stop. Wonderful! A quick break, and then fifteen minutes later we moved off to secure the helicopter landing site (HLS). The whole platoon married up there and we finally got in just before 1600hrs. Believe it or not, we were dragged out of bed at 0830hrs! Some things never change.

Op Drumbeat: Wednesday July 4 to Sunday July 8

This whole op revolved around an SP Coy search in the Cullyhanna area. We had intended to deploy at 0500hrs, which would have been an early start, but all flying was put back due to bad visibility. Things finally got going around 1000hrs and we virtually flew on to the position.

For the remainder of the daylight hours, it rained a lot! Basically, we broke down to two six-man teams. With ours we built a beautiful house and put the world to rights eating crackers and cheese.

As darkness came, so did a night move: it was with Y20B to new cordon positions for the new search area the next day. It was all pretty basic except for one incident. We were moving along a country lane when the boss came across a farm complex that was lit up. There was a car in the yard with two passengers, or pax, and no lights. It all looked a bit dodgy, so our team moved around the back to the car. As I approached, the engine started and the vehicle started to move off. It wasn't a case of thinking about it, it just happened. I cocked my rifle and pointed it at the car. The door opened instantly and I told the driver and passenger to get out immediately.

It turned out to be a lad driving his girlfriend home – neither tracked or therefore known to the military – but it's better safe than sorry. Vic had been with me and we were both in the same position with a round in the chamber. We went firm for a few minutes when we took the magazines off, ejected the round, charged the magazine and reloaded. The night move continued and we got into position.

The new location wasn't quite as nice to look at, but we managed to stay fairly dry. During the afternoon the helicopters picked us up.

The remainder of the day and Friday was set aside for admin – as well as plenty of sleep! We redeployed on Saturday morning, first to do a house check/search with the RUC. My team and I were sitting on top of a hill looking at the border. That was 400 metres away and being in the open it was fairly uncomfortable, but we didn't stay long.

After an hour or so the helicopters dropped us at the new cordon position. This was only a few hundred metres from the previous location.

What can I say? I spent most of the time in my sleeping bag. Just call me Z Monster! Ron and I built the 'Corporals' Mess' and we stayed in there. The CO visited and we had a chat, but that was it. We got lifted out on Sunday afternoon in time for the World Cup. It was all very easy. I wonder how many more we'll get like that.

Monday July 9 to Tuesday July 10

Today we (Y20A) took over as the ARF. Easy? Not at all! Things were fairly quiet until the sun went down. A patrol in Crossmaglen (XMG) located what they thought was a pipe bomb hide. That call sign went firm and it was decided that the ARF would fly out with ATO and Weapons Intelligence Section (WIS) to have a look. Is this an ARF task?!

I finally got to sleep just after 0100hrs only to be woken at

0225hrs with a callout. Another task: R21 spotted somebody on 'Snipers Road' signalling with a red torch. We probably could have got out there, but they spent that much time talking about it, it didn't happen. Back to the original task.

We deployed at 0400hrs: ATO, WIS and the Ops Officer in tour. The pipe hide actually turned out to be nothing (surprise, surprise)! There was another task 2.5kms down the road as a possible mortar base plate had been spotted. We had to check it out.

Thankfully the helicopter dropped us on the farm, but the plate was nowhere to be seen. This is the good bit. There was a helicopter inbound in thirty minutes, did we want it? No, apparently not; the ATO wanted to walk. As you can imagine, it wasn't exactly a stroll in the country. It took three hours to get into XMG.

To top it all, the helicopters wouldn't come to pick us up as it's not a flying day. Picture the scene: twelve men trying to sleep in a tiny room, which was the only space we had. Horrible.

We eventually got lifted back to BBK just before 1300hrs. Phew!!

Wednesday July 11 to Thursday July 12

I don't even know the name of this op. We had intended to deploy at 1100hrs to the Newtownhamilton (NTH) area. This is to route check and cover a Protestant march tomorrow. We were all ready with kit and camouflage cream on. Somebody found out that the Ulster Defence Regiment (UDR) had been given the same task. Now the camouflage cream has come off, but we're still on standby to move. I'm sure the OC will get us out there somehow!

This letter I've written for Clare – the one blaming her if anything happened to me – has now been burnt. It's gone now, over, she's not coming back so its time to move on. It's important to write to Rachel and I'm looking forward to seeing her. It'll be good to have something to look forward to.

Now I can continue 'Op Residence', covering the route taken by the Orangemen marching in Newtownhamilton. It wasn't just any march; it was the 300th anniversary of the Battle of the Boyne. Oh yes, and because of the security problem, they haven't marched in the area for twelve years.

The OC couldn't let it lie and we were eventually deployed at 1730hrs to the Security Forces (SF) base. It's a horrible, tiny place right in the middle of town. It's surrounded by streets, and for that reason it gets mortared regularly. I myself wouldn't have minded the crush, but the OC was having none of it and after a brief from OC SP Coy we deployed by foot. Great! Where are we going?!

The tab out was a hard one, but one I'll always remember. A lot of Prods live in the area and we met some kids. They chatted to us, which really made me think that if we can get these people on our side (the young ones) we could be on the right track. None of them seem to have an axe to grind as far as we're concerned. Once on the high ground we met up with Y2OB, who were taking one of our Foxhounds (troops). Steensie had to go.

Our main task during the night was to cover two bridges on the main routes in. After dark we moved in and found this was virtually impossible with only ten men in the multiple. We decided to stay on the high ground and check the bridges once it was light.

We moved position once it was light, but continued to observe the route. The extraction was via Newtownhamilton at 2000hrs.

Saying that, during the afternoon the SAS were inserted due to the movement of a so-called 'armoured truck'. Because of this, nobody was allowed to use the telephone that evening.

222

Friday July 13 to Saturday July 14

At 0800hrs, half of Ops Coy including our call sign (Y20A: our multiple of 12 led by Cheesy) flew to Ballykelly for the range package. It really isn't like Ireland at all, honestly. I could have been at any camp in England, it's so open. There's a swimming pool, a brilliant NAAFI and a football pitch like a bowling green!

The ranges were easy enough for the Annual Personal Weapons Test (APWT) NI, and the great thing is they close down at 1500hrs! Following this was a rather heated game of football. Sergeant Wood and I almost came to blows several times. Anyway, no bones were broken, we shook hands and then we went for a swim. The highlight for me was the session in the NAAFI. What a laugh. Everybody let their hair down. Before I came to Ireland I said I wouldn't drink, but I could never have forgiven myself if I'd let the last night slip by. Lots of beer was downed and there wasn't a hint of trouble, thank goodness.

The following morning was a problem – getting out of bed! In fact, I think I was an hour late. Eventually we got onto the ranges for a bit of a 'cabby': auto fire on the SA80 rifles and SF GPMG (on a tripod). It was all a bit drawn out today, but we still had two hours free in the afternoon. Ronnie, Matty and I went for an adventure on the beach. Well, it was actually a long walk, but the fresh air and open spaces were brilliant.

It was back to the grind this evening. We fly out to NTH in less than two hours for a patrol to cover the extraction of Echo call sign ops. No rest for the wicked!

Monday July 15

We finally deployed just after 0300hrs. Our job was to add to the deception plan. Echo Call Sign ops had been compromised, so they all extracted and we were inserted. Think about it: this isn't a nice

223

area, but our call sign was left on the ground alone and the thirteen of us (we had one signaller) were six kilometres from NTH and seven kilometres from XMG. Lovely!

By the time we got on the ground it was getting light and we needed to find a position quickly on the high ground. Basically, we found a trench-like dip on a hill, and when we were tightly squeezed in we all had cover from fire and view. There were two stagging on positions that we thought would cover the arcs, and with it pissing down we could have sat there quite happily all day before being extracted. At one point we became an easy target as a young lad called Smudge was on stag and I don't know how, but he let a man get right up to the location. The man was that close Smudge could have touched him! If he had had a machine gun that would have been the end of us all, but fortunately he was just mooching around. It was possibly a recce on troops' positions.

Smudge wasn't going to tell anybody! It only came out because another lad got a glimpse of this bloke. With this machine gun team knocking around, everybody's hearts started going. It was time to move. We did our best to stick to the high ground and our skills seemed to improve quickly as we scanned the ridgelines for one! The multiple went firm a few hours later on high ground overlooking St Oliver Plunkett Park. Basically, it's one street in the country plus a church. Around ninety-five percent of the people who live there are tracked, but it was actually one of our tasks to go in. We all had some food and a brew, and then Cheesy and Ronnie's teams moved in. Our job was to cover them as Robbo's firm hands gripped the GPMG.

Things went well. Car details were taken; just photos until one bloke was stopped at our VCP. He must have heard the names of the lads and he came out with: "So you're Woody. You were on stag before. You shouldn't leave things lying around!" He had been up to our original position and picked up the stag list; it had been left under a rock by Smudge. At the time, nobody knew the list had been left, so out of the blue a statement like that made everybody a bit nervous.

The two teams moved back up to us and we went right for the pick-up. We were being 'clicked' (observed) a lot at this stage and none of us fancied staying out. The delay had to come though: first a fault with one of the helicopters, then the weather. At last they came, over an hour late, but at least they came.

Following the loss of this piece of paper, all the umbrellas have now gone up. It really has been a case of passing the buck. Statements have been submitted by Smudge, Ronnie and Cheesy, and it's actually been recorded as the loss of a classified document. The CO wants blood and all three must appear in front of him without coffee!

Monday July 16

Today call sign Y20A took over as the ARF at 0730hrs. Call signs must come on, do their twenty-four hours and then go. Not us. During the evening there was movement from Kevin Tumulty's (player) car around the border. The CO got out of bed and wanted to know why; I can't explain how close we were to being deployed. As we now say, the chip shop tasks always come our way. The line now is, "Do you want salt and vinegar?!"

Oh yes, we found out how much Senior Non-Commissioned Officers (SNCOs) abuse the ARF telephone. Twice I needed to speak to them and twice I had to call the NAAFI and ask to have somebody from Ops Coy on the phone. I could picture people hiding behind NAAFI growlers and cups of tea!

Tuesday July 17

The recce from 42 Commando Royal Marines arrived today. It won't be long now before we head home.

Wednesday July 18 to Friday July 20

The whole area of this op – in fact, that's not the right word, let's just call it a move – was to deploy Ops Coy to various Security Forces bases because the CSE Forces Entertainment show was on at BBK. You see, it wouldn't be right for the 'combat' soldiers to be in camp; only the 'desk heads' can watch shows like that.

Anyway, Y20A deployed to Forkhill. It's the only one we hadn't visited. It's not that bad, in fact it's probably the best of the outstations. It has all the facilities with none of the big arseholes walking around. Wednesday we just mellowed out and got some sun. The idea was to crack all the intelligence tasks in one patrol on Thursday. Cheesy had the idea of covering 18kms with part of the route over Slieve Gullion mountain. No chance! Ronnie and I had to have a chat to put him straight.

The distance was cut by half and we deployed from the base at 0400hrs. Approximately 1km up the road, en route to trivial task number two, we came across a red Ford van sitting on the old Long Road. It was just sitting there with the side door open and the back doors weren't properly closed either. In Chester you wouldn't bat an eyelid, but over here it was dodgy to say the least. All call signs went firm in the baking sun and we sat there for ten hours while checks were made via Belfast, then via London.

It turned out the van is registered to a smackhead in Cambridge. He didn't know quite where he was! Eventually the van was found without number plates and wheels. It was a ringer (stolen), no less!

The RUC deployed from Forkhill with all intentions of solving the mystery, but they wouldn't touch it either. The policy now is

226

that ATO will let vehicles 'soak' for a number of days, and as we didn't fancy sitting out there, it was placed out of bounds. After ten hours in the sun, I still thought we could get a few trivial tasks under our belt. We actually managed one: a rummage of a huge forestry block about the size of 'D' at the Sennybridge training area; it was huge. After a twenty-one hour patrol we got back to the comfort of Forkhill at 0100hrs.

Sleep and admin filled the majority of Friday. Y20A (multiple) was extracted late, as usual, so we headed back to BBK at 2115hrs. Home sweet home.

Chapter 6: Slab's farm

Op Goat: Sunday July 22 to Monday July 23

The background work for this op has been going on for four years. It was mainly information compiled by C13, a surveillance unit within the RUC. They've been watching the area of BCP 28; particularly the yard and complex belonging to Thomas 'Slab' Murphy. Slab is traced and the buildings in the complex are on both sides of the border. C13 have thought for a long time that his smuggling activities are believed to bring in £1 million a year for the Provisional IRA (PIRA). This is thought to take several forms, one of which is the transportation of petrol from the south to the north.

Anyway, they thought the time was right to go in and check this out. The op involved four multiples, plus several of the RUC's mobile support units (MSUs) and C13. Throughout Sunday all call signs were deployed to G20 and G30. Basically, we chilled out and watched videos. We really got underway at 0130hrs when we left the towers.

For the first time during the tour, Ronnie and I didn't have a chip shop task. In fact, it all revolved around us. We had to enter the complex itself with six MSU. There were various fields to cross on the 1.5km route, but we managed it just in time. We had ten minutes on the start line: time enough to switch on the ECM and let the MSU put their elbow and knee pads on. Pads! Then we were off. It was a steady job, but the elephant grass made it hard going. To say I was goosed was an understatement. As we entered the yard it reminded me of The Firm – we were well tooled up. We all had batons and two federal riot guns (FRGs). Ronnie also had chain breakers and I had a 2lb lump hammer and a crowbar. Intelligence had mentioned that there might be up to three dogs or even a night-watchman and we were ready to go.

We charged in expecting a right battle... but there was nothing. There was nothing there, not a soul! You should have seen our faces; even the MSU looked disappointed. Well, that was it. We couldn't exactly go looking for it, the border was only yards away. After a few minutes of looking for trouble, all Army call signs extracted, leaving the police to get on with it. As we took up cordon positions, agencies began to fly in. A digger was even lifted by a Puma.

Slab was sighted in the south, but the Garda weren't really playing ball. Slab is a crafty bastard; he must have known. There wasn't really much there. Yes, there was lots of petrol, but I don't think there was enough to put him away. Evidence was taken, things were dug up and the whole place was videoed. When there was nothing more to do we had to leave.

All call signs were extracted by lunchtime. As we lifted off, Slab and his crew were sighted skulking back to the complex to pick up the pieces. That's it now, we'll have to wait and see what the scientists come up with. Oh yes, the red Ford van in the Forkhill area has now disappeared. Can you believe it?!

Chapter 7: Routine and ops

Tuesday July 24 to Wednesday July 25

During this twenty-hour period our call sign (Y20A) took over as the ARF. What a pain in the arse! When the tour first began, I think we imagined ARF would be lying on our beds waiting for a call out. How wrong can you be?! Really it's a continuation of the chip shop theme. Three men from the 'ten-minute team' had to go down to the battalion ops room and hold the doors open so the shiny arse bastards could get some air. Honestly, it happened. This brought about a premature voluntary release (PVR) from Vic!

Today (Tuesday evening) there was a major incident in Armagh. Four people died, one of them a nun. Another PIRA op backfired, but these people are still dead. I think this has opened our eyes; it's been too quiet here for a long time. Hopefully we'll switch on a bit more now.

Op Mommin: Wednesday July 25 to Thursday July 26

The Gunners (artillery) were flying home and the Royal Tank Regiment (RTR) was taking over. Perhaps it's only the infantry who know the term 'relief in place', so it was left to us to stag on the sangers (static bunker checkpoints) around the perimeter of BBK while they unpacked their kit.

We had a few hours' sleep on Wednesday morning and training tests in the afternoon. The reason for this was simply that they can't fucking leave us alone. Anyway, Y20A – operating as three four-men teams – deployed from BBK on foot to the checkpoints.

It's one of the few times on stag that the NCO gets it pretty tough. There's one man at each end in a sanger and two in the middle, one of whom is the NCO stopping and searching cars. So you don't get to sit down at all. I did the first six hours of the eleven without a break and, while it was quiet, I sat down before I fell! The people are brilliant, however, very friendly. There are a few good-looking women as well, which has brought back thoughts of home!

The hours dragged on, but as it began to get light we all picked up a bit, as you do. A quick handover to the RTR (It was their problem now so, as they say, "Get it down ya neck!"), then patrol back in for us and bed!

Op Gammi: Thursday July 26 to Sunday July 29

For once I can say that we didn't get the chip shop task this time, or did we? We didn't actually deploy on Op Gammi. Our task was to man the ARF with call sign Y30A, under Lieutenant Gilday.

The time passed extremely slowly and we watched a lot of very bad videos. PIRA managed two major incidents within five days; one of which was the shooting of a so-called informant: two rounds to the head, arms tied behind his back. He is said to have been the Ops Officer for Londonderry PIRA with five years' experience. It was mentioned on national news, but I found nothing in the papers. Is the death of a man not considered important enough?

Monday July 30

We dismounted from ARF this morning and were taken over by Y10B. It was back to the grind with the Ops Coy lines full to the brim. This afternoon we had a five-a-side contest. We had a good laugh with no trouble and we managed to reach the semi-finals.

I've been selected by the battalion to travel to 45 Commando RM to appear as a guest speaker as part of their Northern Ireland Training and Advisory Team (NITAT). What good news. NITAT is where you trial before you deploy: real troops as civvies, petrol bombs and live exercises. The NITATs go and speak to a battalion before they deploy and update them on the current situation. This is

232

quite an honour: it's just one Officer and one Corporal (me!).

Op Lid: Tuesday August 31 to Wednesday August 1
This was a planned search of the railway line west of Newry. Two
of our multiples (twenty-four men) would be under the command
of 2RIR. With so much on, everything was thrown together and I
was taking my four-man team to work with Mr Gilday (Y30A). The
team was minus Robbo, who is in the search team, and with Steensie, who is fucking useless!

Orders were at 2000hrs, and with 'reveille' (alarm call) at
0200hrs, I thought it a good idea to get some sleep. Who was I
kidding? The noisiest room in the lines happens to be next to mine.
Lance Corporal Plumb and his team could certainly make some
noise; or perhaps it was me being a little precious about my rest.
I tried desperately to sleep, but it just wasn't happening. With
0200hrs almost upon me, I'd given up, but then Gleavies came in to
tell me the op had been delayed.

Late last night, south of R15 down by BCP 5, a civvie had
reported spotting a dead body by the road. The op was changed
from low to high risk and ATO were called in. This time I managed
to shut my eyes, but 0400hrs came around far too quickly. New
orders were issued after a greasy breakfast and we were put on
hold. A helicopter had to go up to confirm the presence and exact
location of a body.

At 0800hrs, Cheesy came in to say that the whole op had been
binned. The 'dead body' turned out to be a black plastic bag!

Wednesday August 1 (evening) to Friday August 3
During this period, both multiples (Y20A and B) deployed to the
outstations in their entirety. This would enable the other companies
to send men off to the ranges at Ballykinler.

233

Our call sign (Y20A) arrived at Forkhill and we took over on the guards and duties. There are four sangers, three of which are manned. The lads change locations every hour, and considering that it takes fifteen minutes to get round, it doesn't give you much chance to sit down. By 0330hrs I was wasted and Ronnie took over. The transit accommodation at Forkhill is sound; in fact the whole camp is brilliant, so I managed a few good hours' sleep.

During the afternoon I managed a letter to Rachel in the sun, then a good session on the weights. At 1830hrs we moved to Crossmaglen (XMG); chip shop tasks all around. I'll say very little about this, as it'll only annoy me. The camp is wank and so is A Company. We managed to do their fatigues for them, that was all. The less time we spend there the better.

Monday August 6 to Tuesday August 7
All was well during the day. We spent it taking part in a mixture of training and fitness. As the night fell I began to settle down to write a bit more for the 45 Commando presentation.

The next thing I knew is that somebody had mentioned Op Glenanne. It's the first I've heard of it, but apparently it's been an ARF commitment since we got here. It's a good job we didn't get tasked because I knew nothing about it. Anyway, it's a large ammo dump/armoury for South Armagh. The ARF could be on call if it's attacked. That's nice to know after ten weeks!

Basically, because Op Searsport (road blocks for Newry involving the SAS) is effectively over, somebody started thinking, 'What else can they do?' Some knob, I don't know which one, said that the Duty Commander should fly out to recce this armoury at 2150hrs. "But it's dark," came the response. "Never mind, go anyway," we were told.

Nobody was happy, but we got our kit on and made our way

234

to the airhead. On the way, I stopped off in the BM Ops room to tell them we would operate on channel two (I had been appointed Commander). We got the word that it had been called off as we should have left at 2000hrs.

We were being royally fucked around! Anyway, I calmed down and after a sauna was ready to carry on writing. Not a chance. An intelligence message was passed: a mortar attack on either Forkhill or NTH is imminent and this could be followed up by an ASU assault. Flap on! Two multiples were deployed straight away. Our call sign, Y20A, had to be ready to deploy by CPV to any location in the TAOR. No one would believe me, but we ended up doing CPV drills at 0130hrs outside the mill.

Tuesday August 7

We eventually got to sleep, in our combats. The kit had to be collected from the CPVs before deployment to Forkhill the next morning. While unloading our kit, I had a run-in with the RSM about my jungle combats. I took them off and handed them over, and I probably would have got away with it, but then I asked for them back. He went mad! I'm being charged as a result. I wouldn't mind if it was something good, but wearing jungle combats? The upshot is that you're not supposed to wear jungle combats unless you're in a tropical climate, as apparently they don't perform well with flames – i.e. petrol bombs. That said, they dry very quickly, so when you're piss wet through all the time they're pretty useful. Not only that; all the SAS lads wear them, so if they're good enough for the SAS...

I've been talking to people about a possible transfer for a long time, so this was all I needed to spur me on. Later on that morning, I went on Officer Commanding B Company's orders and spoke to a Captain in the Intelligence Corps. The ball is now rolling.

Op Corinto: Tuesday August 7 to Friday August 10

I don't know why we've done two ops under the same name; perhaps nobody could think of a new one. It was more of the same stuff – VCPs – but this time there was more emphasis on search in the Jonesborough/Drumantee area. It was a bit bigger than the last one, involving the Royal Tank Regiment (RTR), Worcestershire and Sherwood Foresters (WSFs), C Coy and Ops Coy. Oh yes, and Close Observation Platoon (COP) and Brigade (BHG) in reserve.

We deployed to Forkhill, but this was only a start point. Y20A tasked out to Drumantee at 0530hrs the following morning. Bear in mind that all other call signs were flown in. We spend the day and most of Thursday around that area. A defensive position was set up on the high ground behind the Three Steps Inn, where Captain Robert Nairac (14 Intelligence) disappeared from in 1977. (They never found his body, and it's believed he was cut up and put into pig food. He was posthumously awarded the George Cross in 1979.) We worked from there, moving out for VCPs on the Newry Road and a number of intelligence tasks. We stopped a few people of interest and they stayed and chatted for a while.

Thursday night was a move up to the one thousand-foot hill on the side of Slieve Gullion. This was done at quite a pace, and everybody was shagged by the time we arrived at around 0200hrs. C Coy, shafting us right up the arse, had all their call signs choppered up and still had the neck to get us up at 0000hrs for the rummages and searches.

Y20A took a WSF search team down, then back up the feature looking for a needle in a haystack. To top it all off, there wasn't a word of thanks from C Coy and they extracted leaving two Ops Coy multiples to go out last. Guess which ones? Y20A and Y30A!

236

Saturday August 11 to Monday August 13

With hardly a chance to catch our breath, the day after getting in from Op Corinto, Ops Coy deployed again; this time to the Silverbridge area. This was the first operation I had missed, but with my R&R approaching, the presentation to 45 Commando had to be completed. So I went over my presentations with Mr Matthews. I'd already written a lot, but we had to link together to ensure it all gelled and that we didn't repeat ourselves. With slides needed to accompany each section, there was quite a lot to do.

We completed a draft copy, which was eventually passed to the CO. He considered a few lines a bit close to the mark and these had to be altered. The regiment had said "write it yourself", but I still felt as if they were trying to hold my hand. We had some fun on the word processor. Some of the spelling was off, but at least we could understand it. The CO saw the finished product with slides and he liked it. For time reasons a few sentences were thinned (we only had forty-five minutes), but it was all right.

Chapter 8: R&R – get the beers in!

Tuesday August 14 to Friday August 24

At last, my R&R. It doesn't matter when you have it, you pro-gramme yourself to last until that date and no longer. By the time Tuesday came around I had had enough and I really needed to get away.

Throughout this time I noticed Hiace vans a great deal, and not only these, but unattended cars. This wasn't because I wanted to be switched on; it had just become the 'norm'. On the Sunday in Claverton's bar, somebody dropped a bottle and I almost hit the roof. Contact, wait out! I was a little bit edgy to say the least.

Anyway, I finally got to meet Rachel. As I thought, she was a very cracking girl. I enjoyed her company and we managed to spend a bit of time together.

Paul's (my best mate from school's) wedding celebrations be-gan on the Wednesday evening: the rehearsal followed by the stag night. I had promised him that I would get back for his wedding and moved heaven and earth to get my leave at this time; i.e. with a different multiple, which is not usually done. We raced back from Birkenhead and didn't begin drinking until almost ten o'clock, but it was still long enough. The Strip-O-Gram in Joe's Wine Bar did us proud; Paul's face was a picture and my only regret was not having a camera. My dad found me on the floor in the kitchen at 0600hrs the following day.

Talking of sleep, I only had more than four hours one of the nights, and that was when I went up to Scotland. I couldn't sleep because I thought I would miss something. I was buzzin'!

Friday was the wedding, and what a brilliant day it was. It's best shown in the photographs. I never realised before how much the best man had to do. I didn't stop until well into the evening, but it was all worth it.

On the stag do itself, I met a young lady with the most beauti-ful eyes I had ever seen. I managed to get in touch with her and on Saturday evening I took her out. It's very difficult not to build things up when it could be nothing at all. She's clever, beautiful and I enjoyed her company, but it could still mean nothing. I saw her again the evening before I flew back. Be steady, Jimmy!

Chapter 9: Girl talk

The girl in question was called Emma. After the customary stripper, we had headed to Blimpers on Station Road in Chester and Emma was there with a group of her mates. She was a trainee orthoptist and was living in nursing accommodation next to the old infirmary, which was near the city walls. We hit it off that night and saw each other again before I went up to join NITAT at 42 Commando in Arbroath. We also met up briefly before I flew back to Ireland. She wrote to me during the second half of the tour and we started seeing each other when I got back to The Dale in Chester.

It was a fiery sort of relationship. She had a temper as bad as mine and was equally jealous, so in that respect we were well matched. That said, it was always going to be our downfall. We were together for about eighteen months, and during that time I was away on exercise in Canada for a month. She seemed less interested when I wasn't there, which is understandable, but it made me worry about what else was potentially going on. We loved and fought each other in equal measure, and when it was really blazing she would slap me. I used to say, "Is that it? Come on, you must have something else there."

On one occasion we went up Snowdon, which was a regular penance for me for drinking too much beer. I really pushed her towards the end, even when she was crying, but she did it – I think to show me she could despite me having a go at her. She came from a farming family in Essex. I liked her family and they were kind to me, often inviting me to stay for weekends. I was never allowed to visit the pub where Emma worked before she started training. Either the locals looked strange or more likely she didn't want to show me off to her old crowd.

Tensions came to a head when she finished her training and moved to Liverpool. This was a new horizon for her, with new objectives. The arguments continued, but now at a distance, and we called it a day. Enough was enough.

The presentation at Arbroath went very well and NITAT were pleased. As they always do, the Royal Marines had this cocksure attitude, but it's not long now and they can see the place for themselves. When I flew back I was on a major downer, but I really didn't have time to think about it.

Chapter 10: Leave's over, crack on

Op Restraint III: Saturday August 25

Within a few hours of getting back I was preparing my kit for the latest op. Call signs had originally intended to insert at 0600hrs, but the weather was so bad we went back to sleep for a few more hours.

We finally got going just after 1000hrs. The whole platoon was working together for a change: us plus Y20B. We flew up to the north of Slieve Gullion and set up a harbour position on the high ground. To be honest, it was quiet, despite being a Pro-PIRA area. There wasn't much happening in the VCPs and there was no obvious clicking. We were extracted at 1750hrs from the high ground.

Monday August 27

Today I finally got my act together regarding this transfer. I found out for myself that everything that has been said about the Army building you up to knock you down is true. After so much talk of Sandhurst and a commission, the command structure is now telling me I need O-level maths. Bollocks. I only need that because it suits them. Despite this, I still said I wanted to go to the Intelligence Corps. Now I'm just waiting for the CO interview.

Oh yes, the incident with the jungle combats finally came to a head. I was charged £10 via the OC by the RSM. Arse!

Op Melston: Tuesday August 28 to Wednesday August 29

This was a search op in the Crossmaglen area. Y20A flew to an area four hundred metres from the border near the Concession Road. It all felt a bit dodgy, but we took up a defensive position on the highest ground possible. This was only three hundred feet up and it was overlooked by a higher feature to the south, but we had no choice.

243

About an hour after taking up the position, one low velocity round was fired at us. No position was located and it didn't hit anybody, so we carried on digging.

Four of us went out during the afternoon for a VCP and encountered some heavy clicking. At one stage, eight people were observing the call sign from the border. It was far better to keep the cars on the road, thereby reducing the chance of a contact. We didn't hang about too long. We closed down fairly quickly and moved back up to the defensive position.

That night I took out a four-man team to put a lurk in (gain effective visibility) on the Drumboy Road/Concession Road junction. It was Vic, Matty, Jonno and me. All our hearts were going a bit, but the lads' personal skills were excellent. The junction was approximately 400 metres from our position and it took more than three hours to get down into the lurk. The whole idea was to be able to react to the road in case of a rat trap. Nothing happened, and just after 0200hrs we moved onto Concession Road to set up a VCP. One of the cars almost knocked me down and Victor ended up cocking his rifle. Besides that it was all fairly quiet. We moved back to the high ground at 0330hrs.

Everybody had worked hard and I was pleased with how things went. We got some well-earned sleep and then, later that morning, the same four plus a cameraman went out for more VCPs. Even though it was a dodgy area, I think we all enjoyed it. As soon as we got in, Cheesy went out for some house checks on the border. On the way back in he discovered a stash of fertiliser bags. In Northern Ireland, it's illegal to import and/or take possession of fertilisers that contain more than seventy-nine percent ammonium nitrate unless licensed by the Northern Ireland Office. He also found burnt clothing and blank ammunition.

After a good op with some excellent intelligence, we were the last call sign to extract from the cordon position at 1950hrs.

Op Lechdale: Friday August 31 to Monday September 3
This was a planned, four-day search in the Silverbridge/
Crossmaglen areas. We deployed on Friday morning to an area
north-east of Silverbridge. Working in conjunction with Y30B,
our call sign would set up an op for the first two days while they
patrolled, then we would swap. The first position was facing out
towards the locks along Newry Canal. The SF GPMG (capable
of firing 1,800 metres) was up on the high ground with the rest
at the rear in dead ground. I must be honest, throughout this op –
including this phase – I did get a lot of sleep. I think I was in my
bag before the GPMG was dug in!

We should have moved a few hundred metres forward at 2200hrs
and set up a covert op, but it wasn't possible. There was a feeling
that troops had been seen in the area so we dug in a sustained fire
position on the high ground for the GPMG. I must admit, the
position was quite good for us. We had a pit on the low ground and
I dug and dug with Mat until it was finished and the kit was in.
We got back into a routine involving plenty of sleep. The weather
was good to us and the moon was a wonderful sight; like a
glowing beacon.

The hours passed by with food and lots of brews. We had a
small radio, but it was a shame that all we could pick up was Terry
Wogan! The football scores came in and Scouse Moran was most
interested! Anyway, that night both call signs got together and at
2200hrs we moved out to a new area just south-east of the Newry
Road/New Road junction.

Troops haven't really gone into Silverbridge since the 'Planes,
Trains and Automobiles' incident. (This was when an IRA gun team
was chased by an Army helicopter and started throwing their kit

out of a moving vehicle. When the RUC joined in they turned up at these players' houses and they were all in the shower with their kit in the wash to get rid of any gunshot residue). As we always said, we know who they are; it's catching the fuckers in the act!

That night we changed all of that. Going across country would have taken all night, so instead both call signs tabbed down the Newry Road and straight through Silverbridge. What a picture the locals' faces were. They were gobsmacked! They saw twenty-four troops with full kit on tabbing down the road without a word. Brilliant! As this happened, the clicking picked up fivefold, traffic on the road increased, and at one stage we cut off just to see what the reaction would be. Eventually we got to the op position for Y30B. There was a quick swap of viewing kit for ECM and then we were off. We didn't really go very far, just to the high ground on the other side of the road. The position was probably the best we'll ever come across in South Armagh: a beautiful line of trees in a square covered in baby elephant grass and not a mine (cow shit) in sight. Bashers up! (This was when we put up a poncho to sleep under.) Then we got back into a routine.

I didn't do a stag that night, although I had intended to. As we all know, Ronnie is difficult to get up, to say the least. But Steve, the Royal Military Police (RMP) cameraman, didn't have any knowledge of this. Steve thought he had succeeded in getting him up, and they actually had a conversation in which Ronnie convinced him he was awake! Bollocks! I woke up at 0650hrs quite confused and embarrassed, not really knowing what had happened. Vic looked at me from his basher but didn't really speak. In the end we found out what had happened and carried on as normal.

We had to keep hold of this position at all costs, so on each patrol a four-man team stayed in location and eight went out for the tasks. Ronnie and I did one each. It's just not a nice place; the people aren't nice and it doesn't feel right at all. The time I went out we had a number of VCPs to do and I felt much better being back on the high ground inside the trees. Oh yes, on the Newry Road/New Road junction there's a memorial to PIRA members who have been killed in action, plus a big sign saying: "You're entering a war zone". The next time we visit we've promised to take some paint!

That evening the call sign moved over the Newry Road up onto the S62 feature (a large hill). This had been the ICP area and we extracted that night by Lynx to the base of the G40 observation tower.

Once on the ground we tabbed across the Cully Water and up to the high ground to set up a patrol harbour. It wasn't a bad area, but the OC wasn't happy and we had to move locations the following morning. The reason for this was that we had been fucking around with the kit on the ground; some of which we had swapped with Y30B. We all had one eye on the weather, so anything we didn't need was shipped off and sent back to BBK. Anyway, he wasn't happy, and in the end it did rain that night. Bloody typical.

We only did one patrol that day and we had an RUC man attached. Paddy and Ronnie and his team did it and I listened to the radio. There was another move that afternoon over the Cully Water and up to the ICP area on extraction from the base of G40. It was a relief to get back in and when we got on the Wessex everybody was buzzing!

That evening we had a few beers, but only a few. Cheesy had been promoted to Lieutenant a year early. We had to celebrate, so there were beers and lots of good stories. This wasn't how Ronnie and I had set our stall out for the lads at the start of the tour, but this was a real reason to celebrate.

Chapter 11: Gathering intelligence

Op Cheese: Thursday September 6 to Friday September 7

This op came entirely out of the blue. On Wednesday afternoon
(I think I'd been training in the morning), a phone call came up to
Ops Coy lines: "Tell Corporal Ivimey to get down to the Battalion
Ops room in civvies." Initially, all I was told was that I would take
out a four-man team to observe a specific target in Camlough.
I immediately thought: 'Isn't this an OCP task?!' Not that they're
any better, but they always go on about this type of work. Anyway,
I was doing it and I had to decide who I would take. Mat was
in, but a lot of the Coy had deployed, either to Forkhill or on a
search in Newry. That's where Robbo was. I wanted to make some
changes for this one, so Hendo came in. That gave me Vic, Mat
and Hendo – all good blokes.

The op involved lots of people: us four, an Ops Coy multiple,
multiples for A Coy, R11, R12, R13, G30, the RUC, C13 and the
Garda. But what was it about? Well, it was about our old friend
Slab Murphy, who had been buying petrol in the north and selling
it in the south, making a £1 million profit every year. Fuel was
being supplied to Murphy by all the major manufacturers until the
government put an exclusion area on his farm complex, right on the
border. When they wouldn't supply him, the sly bastard bought his
own tankers and decided to collect his own fuel. The idea was that
my team would go in an op near the fuel depot in Camlough armed
with various viewing equipment and a list of 'Slab tankers'. Percy's
multiple would take us in and have a movement box to work in
close by, just in case we needed help quickly. We would report this
movement, the R towers would pick it up and track it, and A Coy
would ambush it inside the exclusion area.

Anyway, that was the idea. We all got up at 0400hrs on Thursday and intended to deploy by 0515hrs. I had comms problems with my radio and we didn't actually start tabbing until almost 0600hrs. Camlough is only about 2kms away and it was still dark, but the moon was bright and we got into position just before 0700hrs.

Lack of time the day before had prevented me from doing a drive past, but the OC did one and I had seen all the photos of the area.

Our position was 690 metres from the target area on a fairly steep hill looking down into Camlough First we tried sitting against a wall with camouflaged net over our heads; it wasn't very comfortable. Mat saw a good position and we eventually moved a few yards back so we could lie down behind a small wall. It gave a little cover from view and fire. Despite this, we all agreed it was the coldest we'd ever been in Ireland. It was freezing! Everything was on, Gore-Tex as well, and I was still gibbering. The first day the rain and wind was terrible, and with no chance of putting up a poncho we had to just lie in it.

We lay there all day until after 1700hrs when the place shut. We drank coffee from flasks, ate lots of sweets and laughed about silly things. We had lots of tankers coming in and out, and after a few Mat got to grips with the swift scope. Our reporting, including views, was good. We didn't see a Slab tanker come through and I asked to extract just after 1700hrs. Talking about inserting and extracting, it wasn't done exactly how I wanted it to be, but I'm sure it could have been worse. Percy had commanded a patrol to take us into the op position. They were supposed to tab past our location and my team would just go firm and stay put as they carried on. On the first drop, Percy (Corporal Potter) got about 50 metres past our location and the whole patrol stopped to take five. We had a word about this later. As I say, it's not ideal, but it could have been worse.

Anyway, we got back to BBK for a bit of rest and were up again at 0400hrs. This time there were no comms problems and we were

away by 0515hrs. I had put forward a proposal to the Intelligence
Officer (IO)and OC that we move forward to one hundred and fifty
metres in front of the target area; exciting stuff. But if compromised
in that position, we would have problems getting out. They both
backed me, but the CO turned it down. It wasn't as if Slab would
go away and it wasn't worth risking a team. Right answer!

Despite this, the OC asked me to recce positions closer in case it
runs again. For this reason the patrol Y10A with us went right into
Camlough up to the target area, then tabbed up to the high ground.
I did notice one position about one hundred and twenty metres
from the target area, but it was right next to a house. If the situation
ever came up we could get in there. Besides that, not much else
was right. There were good hedge lines, yes, but with high trees
in front of the complex the job would be impossible. So it was
back to the same field. The call sign patrolled up and past, then
out across the back of the field. As I said, Percy didn't get it
quite right, but we finally made it.

Again we saw plenty of tankers and reported back to Call Sign
O (control).

The weather was far kinder to us. The wind was still very sharp
and this meant that all the kit went on, but it didn't rain too heavily.
During the afternoon I was looking up towards R13 when I noticed
an old bloke walking about fifty metres from the op position. We
all stayed low and hoped he hadn't seen us, but he obviously had.
About ten minutes later he was within five metres of us. We had
covered all the viewing equipment and just sat tight. He must have
been thinking, 'Why is a four-man team looking at Camlough?' or
'Is this the SAS?!' Old as he was, he could have been working for
anybody. He had a good look at the front of the position and seemed
to be looking for other troops in front of us before walking into
Camlough. All of this was reported to O and the decision was left

with me as to whether we should pull out. I thought we might as well see the job through and it turned out to be a good call.

A few hours later we sighted a white rigid Ford BP tanker moving into the complex; one of Slabs'. Call Sign O asked me on several occasions to confirm the vehicle registration number (VRN) and it was definitely one of his. We all got fairly excited and it seemed the plan had all come together.

It moved off west on the Newry Road, where the R towers picked it up and tracked it moving towards the exclusion area to Larkins Road. A Coy call signs were in a lie-up six hundred metres from the road. The idea was for them to stay covert and move into ambush positions. Nobody really knows what happened, whether it was the call signs moving or the helicopter overhead, but four hundred metres short of the area the truck just stopped dead in the road. As before, Slab seemed to be one step ahead. There were two reported Citizens' Band (CB) radio break-ins. The tanker had a CB and that was it; it wasn't going any further south.

What followed can only be described as 'Planes, Trains and Automobiles part three'. The call signs lost sight of the truck. They picked one up again, but it was the wrong one. Chasing it from this point didn't really make any difference. It was just a lorry and nothing illegal had happened yet.

In my opinion, A Coy fucked it up, but in time it'll all come out.

My call sign got a well done from OA (the OC Ops Company; the boss) himself: on the air as well as in person. We were extracted by Y10F back to BBK.

The op could well run again in a week or so, and hopefully we'll get involved.

On Friday September 7 the General Office Commanding (GOC) visited South Armagh. He had jungle combats on.

Chapter 12: The pressure's on

Saturday September 8
Today we had the Ops Coy photo taken. There's still a long way
to go, but this is a sure sign that home is around the corner. Everybody is smiling and all the talk is of home.

Op Ewhurst: Monday September 10 to Friday September 14
This is an op I didn't really want to do. With my blokes away, it
meant working with another multiple. Everybody has their own
way of doing things and I didn't intend to change now. Anyway,
I had to go and that was it. I was attached to Mr Askew (Four
Platoon) from Y10A, my old platoon before I left the regiment.
It wasn't so bad after all.

The task for the whole company was to set up a number of covert
op locations and watch selected targets. We were all spread out
around the Crossmaglen/Silverbridge areas. Our target was Vincent
McLoughlin, a known member of PIRA, who uses a big telescope
to watch troops.

We flew into a lie-up just north of a .749 feature, the top of which
would be our position. The tab up was a brisk one, led by Macca,
and on top it was kit off and the ground was prepared. The ground
was perfect: it was a hollowed area surrounded by bracken. We dug
down so that eventually the admin/sleeping area was below ground
level. As well as this we had a rear stag position that looked down
into Mullaghbawn and the main op position.

McLoughlin's house must have been a good thousand metres away,
so we had brought in 20/120 Nikon binos and a thermal imagery (TI)
kit. We spent the next four days crawling around on the floor.

It began to get very cold; a sign that the winter will be a hard one
and that more warm kit is needed. I began to read a book, which is

quite rare. Macca, Foxi (Lance Jack in B Company – a good lad) and I set up the screws' Mess and we ate and drank as much as we could. Oh yes, we had a mini TV, what a laugh. Trying to get a picture was a nightmare. The main objective was to get a clear picture for Home and Away!

Mr Askew had to be lifted out on Thursday evening as he was playing hockey for the infantry on the mainland. This left me in charge. Nothing altered besides the stags and we just carried on. The OC's four-man team visited that night as well. Our position was just big enough for us and we advised them to sleep in the bracken. Macca had been for a crap while it was dark and the OC woke up next to a 'covert op!'

Before I finish, we had been set a number of intelligence tasks during our time in the op. How can you stay covert but patrol from a position?! You can't, so the patrols were done from inside the boss' bivi bag (sleeping bag cover) and in his head!

The position remained covert until it was crashed early on Friday. Vincent McLoughlin then took a great interest. 'How long have they been here?' he must have wondered. Our call sign, along with the OC's group, flew from the top of the feature at 1240hrs on the Friday.

Op Inch Pin: Saturday September 12
Saturday was a pretty mellow day involving fitness and some TV. I even managed a chat with the OC regarding a transfer to the Intelligence Corps.

I was settling down for a night in front of the TV to watch a Bond film, write a letter then catch the world title fight. Crash out! The whole company had to move just before 2000hrs. The initial report was of a contact shooting near BCP 5 (Dublin Road beyond R14/15). There was a fair bit of flapping, with lots of people running around. This time I was attached to Scouse (Y30B).

As soon as I found out about deployment, it was a quick trip up to the NAAFI. "Give me lots of chocolate!" I entreated.

Call signs flew in; every man and his dog moved to an HLS about five hundred metres north of BCP 5. The story gradually began to come together. PIRA had set up an illegal VCP near a garage about two hundred metres from the border. Their intelligence was brilliant; they knew exactly what vehicle they wanted. It contained RUC officers and prison officers returning from a fishing trip.

The recce was excellent. The garage roof was in direct line of sight and they knew this when the IRA did their recce and appreciation of the ground; therefore, the incident that took place at that exact location on the road was dead ground from R21 and it couldn't be seen from the tower. It was also out of sight of R14, some 4kms up the Dublin Road. The driver had been left, while two officers had run and eventually got a lift to R15. It's believed there were twelve gunmen in combat jackets with AR15s and they abducted three people: two prison wardens and one RUC officer. They asked for the RUC man by name. It's believed he shot a player three years ago and had been on sick leave ever since. Later that night the two prison wardens were dropped in a village, apparently well beaten. There was no sign of the RUC bloke.

We took up a position just south of the garage on the road forming the inner cordon. To begin with all vehicles were turned away, but this was overruled from a higher formation. The prison warden's white van, still in the middle of the road, was cordoned off, but traffic was allowed to pass by. On hearing this we got into a field and got some sleep! I don't know whose bright idea it was, because during the night three people were caught looting and somehow an ITV film crew got right up to the vehicle. Anyway, at 0700hrs, ATO's kit began to fly in: the remote-controlled wheelbarrow, etc. We already knew there was nothing there, but we went by the book anyway. It took all day! We all thought we would be out by 1200hrs. No chance! Royal Engineer Search Advisors (RESA), Royal Engineer Search Teams (REST) and ATO played around all day and we got photographed a lot. I appeared on TV and in the *Daily Mirror* looking wet and fairly cold. Once the vehicles were clear (one belonged to the looters), call signs began to extract. A Puma came in to lift ATO's kit off the road and troops flew in via Lynx and Wessex.

In my mind, the RUC bloke was probably over the border by the time we extracted, and he was probably dead as well. I wouldn't wish that on anybody, but these were evil men. I only hope they didn't torture him.

Back in warning order (which meant we were warned there would be a deployment, but not before a specific time), there was no move before 0600hrs. A possible body had already been located near Belleek, but it had to be left to soak. If it did turn out to be a body, the person was already dead, so there was nothing immediate we could do. It could have been booby-trapped, so this cautious approach was taken to minimise the risk. It was possible that a device could have been made with ammonium nitrate fuel oil (AMFO) and left there.

Call signs were deployed along the border to different locations on house checks with the RUC. Whoever lived at our particular house must have heard the helicopters and skipped over the border; all we found was about five hundred empty barrels, but of course knew about Slabs' petrol smuggling activity. All of a sudden there seemed to be a rush to extract all call signs. Something was on the cards. It was decided that we would go in and clear the body in Belleek. The op would involve the whole of Ops Coy as well as a number of other call signs and support troops. The fly out would start at 1600hrs. We got our kit on and it was down to the helipad. We were all primed to go when we heard it had been called off.

It's now believed that the find in Belleek is a possible booby trap. It probably isn't a body; it's likely just to be a dummy. As well as that, A Coy is cordoning an unconfirmed body in the Concession Road in XMG.

Everybody is back in the lines, cleaned up but waiting to deploy. Watch this space...

Just to change the subject, I've had a number of really nice calls from Emma as well as a number of letters. I'm looking forward to seeing her and those beautiful eyes!

Tuesday September 18

This incident is still ongoing and W Call Signs are blocking the road around the suspect object in Belleek. I think they were getting a bit worried about being out on the ground. Come on, they had been there for thirty-six hours. So it was Ops Coy to the rescue. Three multiples (I was attached to Y30B) deployed to satellite around them. It was only for a few hours in the afternoon, but it was still more deployment for blokes who had been working on and off for a few days. Belleek was said to be a staunch Catholic area and it probably is, but the odd person gave us a little wave. Anybody who hasn't been out here wouldn't think it was much, but it does make a difference. Overall, the area was very quiet. The people knew why we were there and obviously stayed out of sight.

A bloke stopped by Gleavies in a VCP said we should take care in these country lanes and asked us what we were doing on the road!

The loadmaster was probably the best we've had as he really knew his job. He was about fifty, but he did the business. He often smiled, which is important, and he kept the door open and observed the arcs. If we're doing our job, so can the rest. Y30B extracted

257

from Belleek at 1940hrs. The poor RUC sod was eventually executed; he had been tortured and shot in the head.

Wednesday September 19

It was probably just before midnight that we took over as the ARF. I say we, because I was back with my lads in Y20A. They were all feeling fresh after their R&R and were ready to push through to the end of the tour.

Anyway, ARF was much the same as before. I wonder how many more of these we'll get.

Op Crab: Thursday September 20

This operation was coordinated by A Coy. It got off to a bad start with them saying they had nothing to do with it. In all honesty, I don't consider them to be as good as us in B Coy.

Anyway, it was a planned search of specific houses and the surrounding area in connection with the kidnapping of the RUC Officer, Robinson.

B Coy had three multiples on the ground: Y10A, Y20B and us. Y20A were to satellite and act as the outer cordon. This was the first time back on the ground for my blokes and Cheesy set off at a fair lick. Ronnie and I calmed him down with a brew and things seemed very much as they were before.

As all three teams were crossing the Newbold, Vic saw Gabriel Grant heading north in a white Hiace van. Some time later, that vehicle was located on the New Road/Newry Road intersection, but nothing came of it.

During the morning an Ammunition Technical Officer (ATO) flew in, followed by WIS and SOCO. One of the search teams had located what they thought was an off-route mine. It couldn't have been much because WIS only spent ten minutes at the scene.

258

ATO was messing around so much, which meant that timings for extraction were put on and off like a light switch. ATO flew out along with Y10A and when we were the furthest call sign from XMG (at a VCP in Silverbridge), it was decided that the weather was too bad and we had to tab in. Bastards! We had been used to cover their extraction, that's all.

The tab in was a hard one; about 8kms in the pouring rain, never mind the wind. It was difficult not to drop your head and to just put one foot in front of the other.

As we (Y21C) had just crossed the Cregganduff Road in Cully-hanna, Newry, a red Mitsubishi Saloon carrying one male pax came to a screaming halt. He quickly put it into reverse and at the second attempt turned around and drove off. If only we had been on the road we would have had him. The driving was like something you might see in a stunt film; I wonder what he was carrying. The Intelligence Officer was informed, but he didn't seem very interested.

Eventually we got back to the XMG. We thought they would give us the washing up to do, but even they couldn't do that twice. There was a quick intelligence debrief before extraction, or so we thought. The Wessex came in pissing fuel and had to shut down on the pad.

We thought we would be staying, but somebody got their act together and decided to bring a Lynx onto the football pitch behind the Security Forces base. Last out, I took the nine of us onto the pitch. The ARF were supposed to secure the area, but they were nowhere in sight. At least we got back.

Op Fastball: Friday September 21
This was a C Coy op in the Jonesborough bowl. Search teams, along with the Divisional Mobile Support Units (DMSO), were clearing the route taken by the ATO last Saturday.

Three Ops Coy multiples were used: two as satellites and Jimmy Tarbuck's (the Sergeant's) multiple going back up to Slievenaboley to op the ground. It's an area we know quite well after Op Corinto and the ground was familiar. We had one RUC attached and that helped with a number of house checks. Well, he knocked on the door instead of us.

With so many troops on the ground the area was very quiet. By luck, Y21C stopped Damian Finnigan, another player, in a VCP. He stopped to talk to us for about half an hour and call signs extracted at 1400hrs.

Saturday September 22

Ops Coy had a series of lectures planned for today. They were being given by the multiple commanders and we all sat quietly and listened. It was nothing we didn't know; in fact, they covered what we had been doing for the past four months. There was no way of getting out of it, so we just got on with it.

Just as we were coming to the end, with the company's second-in-command still due to talk, we got crashed out. Thank goodness we missed his lecture! The initial report came back as 'contact' with a Security Forces casualty. The ARF deployed immediately to the contact area and a further four multiples deployed to the surrounding areas. There were far too many troops on the ground the week before and we (Y20A) took over on the ARF.

More details came through on the contact. It actually turned out to be an SP Coy patrol just north of Crossmaglen, which was a fair way from home. As the call sign moved to set up a VCP, they were opened up on by two automatic weapons: A GPMG as cover and an AK47. They fired specifically at the gunner, 'Murph', who was ex-B Coy. He was hit by one round in his side, but thankfully the bullet had already hit a fence and had slowed down considerably before ploughing into his webbing.

The GPMG apparently fired more than seventy rounds and the AK around sixteen. The call sign returned fire. Surprisingly, a bloke from the Mess moved out of cover and returned fire with the other gun. It was this fire that made the gunmen withdraw.

When Murph was flown in he was conscious and talking. They operated that night and he'll be alright. He was very lucky.

As darkness fell, the firing point was located by Y20B (Jimmy T). Originally, because of the high surrounding ground, the REST and RESA wouldn't go in without a 'suit', but Jimmy T managed to hang out of the barn and get some empty cases from the firing position.

I was in the ops room at the time and the CO wasn't happy about troops being on the ground. He extracted all call signs at 2200hrs, under darkness.

While this was all going on, R21C located what they thought was an illegal VCP on Edenappa Road just south of Jonesborough. We were there on Friday. Ronnie, who was on the 'immediate' (stand by to move) took off, but the pilot wouldn't land without an HLS recced. While in the area, R21C located two blokes moving east from the road to the border. The lads were made ready in the helicopter; weapons were cocked. This put a round in the breach; safety catches on; weapons are ready to fire. It was very frustrating.

Sunday September 23

The call signs involved yesterday flew into the area of the shooting for a 'high-risk' clearance at first light. They extracted at around lunchtime.

Mat was on stag at around 2000hrs down at the ARF hut when he heard what he thought was high-velocity fire from the housing estate. This was confirmed by the new guard room, so W Call Signs and the ARF deployed. We tabbed around Bessbrook and set up a VCP, but that was all. The kids in the area were interested, but there were no gunmen. With sound travelling much more at night it could well have been a test fire.

I'm not happy working in the same platoon as Jimmy Tarbuck. We had history as he thought he could talk to me like a CROW when I rejoined the regiment. Ronnie has moved to Four Platoon and I'm sorry to see him go. What'll happen to the 'Screws' Mess'?!

Op Longus: Tuesday September 25 to Wednesday 26
This op was a two-day planned search of the lakes area. SP Coy was running the show with Y Call Signs setting up ops and satellite patrols. Our Y20A patrol area was about 2.5kms southwest of Cullyhanna. It was fairly shitty ground.

There was a heavy fog on Tuesday morning and flying was delayed. We finally got going at around 0800hrs. Looking out over the search area there were still blankets of fog on the ground. People in the surrounding houses could hear the helicopters, but they couldn't see us.

I think everybody was still very much on edge after the shooting last weekend. Skills were sharp and people seemed switched on, which was good to see. I located two beer kegs as we moved towards the high ground, but they turned out to be nothing more than containers for cow feed.

I've never seen such obvious clicking. Throughout our time on the ground, people came as close as possible to our positions. Were they all looking for the same calf (that old line about losing a cow)? PJ Carrigan Jnr and Peter McShane, more players, visited. We set up a harbour area on the high ground and sent out two VCPs from there. It wasn't a great position as there was cow shit everywhere. With our warped sense of humour we always referred to this as the ground being 'mined'. In this case it was a heavily mined field: anti-personnel (AP) plus MK7s – the big buggers!

Our VCP went out during the early evening. I wouldn't say it was quiet, but we had to stop a woman on foot to get a Charlie 1 (personnel check)! It was another 'Planes, Trains and Automobiles' incident. The boss located a car and one male pax moving to a wooded area. With overhead protection (OHP) it was ideal for a hide area. We tabbed down and stopped a bloke with a shotgun on the way. He had no licence: Charlie 1! Finally, we found this bloke who had such a bad stutter he could hardly speak. A full Charlie 1 and body search followed.

As this was happening, I found a Perspex pipe with wooden ends; ideal for a transit hide for weapons or explosives. I tried to pass this information on over the air, but the interference was terrible. The OC got upset and that was the last thing I said on the radio.

As darkness fell we moved towards Kiltybane Road. Two VCPs went out between 2200hrs and 0100hrs, but between them only one car was stopped. Stag on. On Wednesday we had food, laughs and plenty of brews, then extracted at 1830hrs from the high ground.

At 2215hrs I was just about clean when the word came. There was contact on the helipad at NTH: there were two single shots with a burst of automatic. Apparently, a Foxhound has been hit in the backside. Everybody is sick of this; we're all getting pretty tired now.

This shoot came as a Lynx was landing at NTH and the landing site is just outside the Security Forces base. As it was dark, the GPMG wasn't manned by the air gunner. As the troops debussed they opened up from a four by four van on the high ground with a green Russian tracer. It looked as if they were going for the Lynx, so the chopper did one sharpish. As the troops moved for cover, one of them was hit in the arse.

Thursday September 27

At 2030hrs, all call signs were ready to deploy on Op Restraint II. Contact! The G20 tower had been shot at from across the border with two or three automatic bursts. The number of rounds returned was between two and three hundred! Ops Coy crashed out and were lifted out onto the ground, but it eventually calmed down.

'Light Scales' i.e. belt order (rifles and webbing) have been re-packed in Bergans and Op Restraint will still go ahead.

Op Restraint II: Thursday Sept 27 to Saturday Sept 29

We finally got out as the time approached midnight. The op was a VCP/intelligence-gathering period in the Camlough and Newry areas. We were deployed to an area approximately 2kms northwest of R14/15, along with Y20B. As Jimmy T was away, Phil was left in control of that call sign. We both dropped on the same grid and set up a patrol harbour together. Everything was mellow.

We moved off to the high ground and towards a huge forestry block, where memories of Brecon came flooding back! It was fairly tight and very dark, so to get some depth we held onto each other's Bergans as we moved. When we got about fifty metres in we set up a harbour. Everybody just got tight and got in their bags. Stag on!

At 0630hrs our call sign had to move off. We climbed the one thousand-foot feature to a small wooded copse and set up our own harbour area. It wasn't that we didn't want to stay, but all call signs had specific roads to VCP. In order to react, we had to get a little closer to our target area. The wood was perfect, and the 'Screws' Mess' was quickly set up. As usual, Vic was voted in.

Once we had set up – the stag positions were sorted and the guns were made ready – a mellow time was had by all. The road we had been targeted to VCP was dead; it was unbelievably quiet. For the remainder of Friday and Saturday we couldn't have stopped more than ten vehicles. Good work by intelligence!

The op had been set to run until Sunday evening and we should have moved via R15 on Saturday night, then down to the fathom line for more VCPs on Sunday. The information came over the net that a huge out-of-bounds (OOB) area had been set up. It ran south from R15 to more than 6kms over the border. What a shame he had to knock it on the head. With three illegal VCPs in less than a week, the Tactical Command Group (TCG) had sent in the SAS, supported by COP teams, to set up an ambush. Well, that's what we all assumed as the SAS have been seen again in the area. Go on lads!

The weather was closing in, but we all remained hopeful and moved to the pickup point (PUP). It just wasn't happening. From there we were tasked to R15 to just head down and go for it. We burned along the road. At last the PUP was in sight as we moved north down the Forkhill Road. This was a place I had watched for four weeks from R14, and it felt quite strange to be on the road looking up.

Inside R15 we met up with some of the COP. It was strange to see them in uniform! Then it was brews all round, as well as egg banjos. Extraction was by CPV during the early hours.

Sunday September 30

At 1000hrs this morning we took over as the ARF. What a day to take over the ARF hut! Buzzard – the flying HQ block in Bessbrook – was being knocked down and then rebuilt; a job that would take ten months or so. The day we took over was the very day the kit had to be moved. We didn't have to move far, just to a Portakabin on the other side of the road. Actually, it's not too bad. It's a bit bigger and has carpeted floors.

The battalion has decided to make a video about the tour. Of course they needed a bit on the ARF, so I'm in. Action!

Monday October 1

Phew! October at last, so it's not long now – touch wood!

We dismounted from the ARF between 0830hrs and 1530hrs. This was a chance to get a shower and sort ourselves out. Everybody already knew we would be pushing it out until Friday.

During my time off I thought I had better get a good training session in: weights and some good work on the bag. By the time it got round to 1530hrs I was ready to get my head down. Then crash out! Bloody hell, not again! Are you sure? This was at 1700hrs.

Via intelligence, we heard that it took the Garda twenty-four hours to work this one out, but the previous evening Brian Tumilty had moved south over the border and up the Fathom Line in Newry. There was also one other pax. He was only over the border for about two minutes, so obviously he didn't go far. On the way back the Garda decided to stop him. Well, he had a big smile on his face and two boiler suits in the back of his car. As I said, it wasn't until twenty-four hours later that it was decided he might have put something in a transit hide.

Hey Y20A, does anybody want salt 'n' vinegar?! (It was another chip shop task!)

Chapter 13: What makes squaddies laugh?

At this point I think military humour is worth flagging, because it's strange and warped and there is a close bond between service personnel. That said, if you make it known that you have a weakness – your hair, your big nose, your skin colour, etc – this will be exploited to the nth degree. Despite the fact that the people around you are more than happy to dismantle you piece by piece, if you're out and it's coming on top or if someone is in trouble, you all stand together and never leave anyone behind.

There was a continual feeling that we were being royally fucked around. Shit always runs downhill from the top. Everyone has something to say to the person below them in what is one of the most autocratic structures in society. By the time it reaches the pond life (us), no one has a clue what's going on. Over the years there have been a series of phrases that have been put into the mix to describe the futility of some of the things we have been asked to do:

Hurry up and wait

You're in your own time now

Get on the bus, get off the bus

You've been invited to the cake and arse party

Mushroom club: kept in the dark and fed on shit.

I remember when the Lockerbie disaster happened. The Cheshire Regiment was based in Chester in the Dale Barracks. We were shortlisted to go and pick up the wreckage despite being about five hundred miles away – go figure. The general rule is that much of the work we do is shit, painstaking and boring, but if you don't laugh you end up crying.

The frustration felt was best summed up through various sets of bluff orders, sketches and 'improvements' to maps carried out by my old mate Ronnie Wilding during this tour. I've included a few, which still bring tears to my eyes today.

Chapter 14: The final push

Anyway, back to the op in hand. We flew out on some hot intelligence with two dogs to sweep the area. We covered 2kms north of the border and, yes, you've guessed it, we found nothing. When it was time to leave, there wasn't a helicopter in sight. I put a lot of this bad treatment down to the Ops Officer having a 'sad on' with my boss.

Oh yes, before we left the Fathom Line, Mat took a car apart. Have you ever seen a car in bits on a road? I must point out that neither team had comms. When checking IDs we all had a chat about who we thought it was. We decided one bloke was tracked and he got the good news!

Anyway, we tabbed on our way to the aptly named Windy Road, encountering the sort of hill you never want to see again. Steep doesn't come into it! We finally got to the PUP and on came the CPVs. It's not really very covert and usually consists of a white van with chocolate or crisp boxes in the back windows. It was very dodgy. I didn't like sitting in the road with the boss covering me at all; my only other weapon was a red filter torch in my hand! We had no choice, and we got extracted at 2200hrs. I had to sit on the road because that's the deal. If the weather is shit and they can't or won't fly it's our only chance to get in. They send a squaddie in civvies to be at a PUP at a given time. We need to patrol to that location (usually somewhere quiet) and ensure he sees us. This usually means either me or Ronnie on the road with the rest of the patrol hidden in the bushes.

Thursday October 4
It was another day on ARF; our fifth on the trot. Cheesy was away on a tactical exercise without weapons (TEWT) and the multiple

commando for the day was the RSM. I didn't really know what to expect with him, so I just thought of the worst possible scenarios and made sure everything was squared away. As it turned out, he was really mellow. In fact, when I was taking over for lunch he said I could read his bird-watching book!

In the afternoon we went on Eagle VCPs , something I hadn't done before. We get a Lynx to zip around the countryside, and if we spot something we don't like or want to take a look at we ask for a quick put down and that's what they do; usually onto a piece of land the size of a fifty pence piece! The pilot will either wait, or if it takes more than a few minutes he'll take off and come back when we're ready; then we'll go somewhere else. We flew into the Camlough area with the RSM's team on over-watch in the Lynx while we dropped in on two roads with the Wessex. It was brilliant. The pilot was excellent, he was throwing it around. After we had left a few surprised faces on the roads, we bugged out quickly and flew on to Silverbridge to drop off a GPMG with Y30B. On the way back I think the combat flying had told on Steensie. His lid came off and he looked pale; he was almost sick!

Op Carrive Grove: Sunday October 7 to Monday October 8
This was a search op set up by A Coy. However, the area being searched meant it was far easier to deploy from Forkhill, so we flew there on Sunday afternoon. For the remainder of the day we chilled out with MTV and plenty of sleep. In the evening there was even the chance to watch a classic film: Raging Bull.

Ops Coy call signs were us (Y20A) in a static position with Y20B satelliting. At the same time, Y30A/B were involved in a C Coy mini op to the east of the Security Forces base. Anyway, we deployed at 0500hrs and moved west for about one thousand five hundred metres. That took us through the bog, which I found! Then we moved onto the side of Croslieve to a 1017 feature with G40 on top. Despite the tower, we had good arcs with better observation from east through south to west. The sustained fire GPMG was dug, Junch (a CROW) made a brew and we stagged on. I had the last radio watch, which meant four hours' straight sleep to begin with. Smudge got me up at 1200hrs and I was still trying to get my head together when I heard on the net that call signs were beginning to extract.

A Coy had finished early, and made a poor attempt to make out that they have worked hard for the whole tour.

On the route back in I was determined to avoid the bog. I moved south aiming for the Fairview estate. En route we hit a small stream. I saw a bridge but decided to stay professional and cross at a shallow point. Being about five feet wide I had to go for a rock to make it across. Big mistake! One foot on and that was it, I slipped and was straight in with all my kit. Vic couldn't help himself. He dropped down and roared with laughter.

After taking a few minutes to sort myself out we set off again. What happened next did piss me off. We went firm and let the boss catch up, but he went through us and moved straight on to Gate Five. I had already told him they couldn't open two gates at once and we found ourselves sitting tight in Fairview estate – lovely! When we finally got going we doubled into Gate Three and it wasn't open! It could have been nasty, but we all got in eventually. Then there was more MTV and sleep, and I had a chance to dry off. At 2100hrs we extracted back to clean sheets at BBK.

Chapter 15: The beginning of the end

Wednesday October 10

The first part of the advance party from the Royal Marines arrived today. Our blokes (ARF) deployed to the back field for the Chinook to come in. As they got off, nobody ran – and where were their helmets? Is this the shape of things to come? To be honest, they're welcome to it. Next week it'll all be theirs. Some of our blokes got away and inside myself I wished I could have been one of them, but at least it's a start. I can't remember if I've used this expression before, but it's the beginning of the end.

Friday October 12 to Sunday October 14

Everybody was taking it fairly easy and we were all getting used to staying in camp. No deployment was expected until Tuesday, so I had been weight training and played a bit of football as well. I had my heart set on a shower, then a good sleep, in the afternoon. As I stood in the shower, the message I got simply said: "NTH at 1300". That was it, we were off.

The multiple got all the kit together and we flew out just after 1300hrs. There had been an illegal VCP north of NTH on Thursday evening. This was just inside 2UDR's area and they immediately placed it out of bounds. Nobody had decided whether it was PIRA or the Ulster Volunteer Force (UVF), so we were tasked into the area. It's a shit task, I know. That's why we got it!

We tabbed out at 2000hrs and were given a number of VCPs to set up throughout the night until 0700hrs. The weather was terrible and after the first set it all went out the window. It wasn't raining, it was just very foggy. There was nothing on the roads, or if there was we couldn't see anything. At least with visibility like that nobody could see us either!

We moved into a forestry block and got our heads down. The only problem was that with light scales there wasn't a sleeping bag in sight. We all gibbered a lot!

Cheesy and I lied like cheap NAAFI watches on the radio, reporting that VCP2 was in position!

We had a stroll on Saturday morning and got a few looks as we passed the market area and had a hard target (run) in. We washed our faces and then got plenty of sleep.

That night we deployed again at 2000hrs, this time to the south of NTH. It was a similar task to the one on Friday: a series of VCPs, originally on crossroads. Whose idea was that!? Anyway, we set off and the roads were far busier, so this made the time go much quicker. We took it in turns for the VCPs and we were on the Dundalk Road at around 0230hrs. Despite the time, there were a few cars, one of which belonged to a Peter Murphy. He stayed to chat for a while because we made him! The British Army can hold an individual in location for up to two hours if needs be. He had been travelling south and there were about three cars waiting to go through in that direction. Then a vehicle came up, dropped down to third gear and screamed through the VCP at about seventy mph. I called Robbo, who was a little way up the road in cover on a cut-off position onto the road, but there wouldn't have been much left of him if he had got in the way.

We got the vehicle registration and it came back as a Metro from Belfast, but the car that ran through our location was a Peugeot. Time flies when you're having fun: we spent more than an hour on the road. We tabbed north towards NTH, through the Protestant housing estate and back to base, where we went straight to bed.

The Coy 2i/c had put the bid in for our flight back. We didn't expect anything and didn't get it either. We flew back to BBK at 1800hrs.

Chapter 16: Last op – Selfless

Tuesday October 16 to Thursday 18

This was our last op. The multiple was originally placed on Brigade Reserve, but we had yet another massive kick in the bollocks and ended up going out. Y20A deployed with Y20B to set up a platoon-sized harbour in the locks area. There were another two multiples doing exactly the same to our south. Oh yes, and there was also the OC and his four-man Sabre team.

We got to the DUP at around 2030hrs, with two Royal Marines, our Officer and Corporal Jones (Jonah) in tow. The drills we carried out were exactly the same as all the times before; we knew what we were doing. In the meantime, the Royal Marines really kicked the arse out of it with plenty of really slick drills. All the blokes were looking on, me included, but we knew it wouldn't last. It was time to chill out, kick back and be mellow! To tell the truth, I had had enough. I was too young to die and I just wanted to come home.

Anyway, like so many times before, the recce was map-based. Once Jimmy T arrived, our first task was to carry out a VCP on the high road to our west (Aughanduff Road). The ground was terrible and, crossing the three rivers as we did, I probably got wetter than I had done during the rest of the tour. We actually got to within yards of the road, but because of the bad ground and the timing, the boss decided to bin it. Moving up to the platoon harbour wasn't easy either; it was like climbing the Matterhorn! We came close to binning it and leaving it until the morning when Jimmy T found a track and we were up.

For the first time since we had been on the ground my boots came off. We were all soaking, so we got into our dry socks and into the maggot. I had a good sleep.

We (Y20A) were patrolling on the first day and set off at 0700hrs, moving south through the valley. As I've said, I didn't really want to be there and didn't make any particular effort. I just got on with it and we had quite a mellow time. The boss did a VCP and I carried out a number of house checks. I had expected people to spit in my face, but they were all very nice. I wonder, did they know we were going home? It was a beautiful sight seeing the helicopters flying over: Pumas, Wessex and Lynx. Funnily enough, A Coy had been extracted. Who says they can't fly in bad weather?!

As far as I was concerned, 1600hrs couldn't have come around quickly enough. We moved up to the harbour, but to all intents and purposes the op was over. We all had a really good kip, but I couldn't eat because I was too excited.

On Thursday morning we got the message to say extraction had been delayed and the depression set in. Then I can only assume that a lot of wheeling and dealing went on. It was decided that extraction from NTH would take place under darkness. Why didn't they think of that before? Brigade Reserve were still down on the border, so Ops Coy were being lifted.

"The 44 Call Sign will be at your location in five," we were told by Call Sign 0. Panic! At this point Vic, who had been bitten by some insects, asked me if I had something for the irritation. I gave him two Piriton tablets (the wrong dose) by accident and he could hardly keep his eyes open. He needed a bit of a shake to get his head together.

The HLS was secured and seeing the helicopter come in was wonderful. The loadmaster seemed to panic himself about the amount of kit we had, but once it was on and we'd lifted he looked over and asked if I was all right. It was as though a huge weight had been lifted off my chest. I had a bit of a lump in my throat.

I'd never seen anything like it before; there were looks of relief all round and the attic room was filled with smiles. Ammo and kit

(Left to right): Me, Bomber, Robbo and Bratch on Ripe Village NI training

Y2OA (multiple) – Ripe Village NI training

THIS COPY IS FOR CHESHIRE NCO TAKING OVER

ISSUE & RECEIPT VOUCHER
Army Form G 1033 (Small-in Pads of 100)
Voucher must accompany stores if practicable

ISSUE Voucher No. & Date	RECEIPT Voucher No. & Date
Account OP AMMO	Account NEWRY COY

UIN STAMP (See footnote)

Issued BY
CPL ROSS
A COY
2 LI

Issued TO
CPL IVIMEY
NCO i/c R14

Authority for issue QM 2LI

Date & Mode of Conveyance 17 0590

Signature (See footnote)

Sheet No. 1

No. of Sheets 1

Carriers/Convoy Note No. & Date

Ledger Folio (1)	Catalogue or Part No. (2)	Section or Sub-Section / DESIGNATION (3)	Qty. (4)	Description and Marks on Packages (5)	S. (6)	R. (7)	D. (8)	U. (9)	Rate (10)	Value £ (11)
P14	ADAC 12701	ROCKET 15 ILLUM	8	PW2/86	4	9	4			
P26	ADAC 54041	PAD AND JACK ASSY	8							
P18	ADAC 13201	FLARE TRIPWIRE	13							
		RD 7 62mm 4 BIT	400	RG85						
		RD 5 56mm 4 BIT	500	RG88 OR RG RG 88						
		— LAST ITEM —								

NOTE—On original and triplicate forms, the stamp and signature will be those of the consignor; on duplicate forms, those of the consignee.

My receipt for ammunition at R14

Ronnie documents the Slab Murphy tanker debacle in his own inimitable way

DAILY Mirror

Tuesday, September 18, 1990 **COLOUR NEWSPAPER OF THE YEAR** *(INCORPORATING THE DAILY RECORD)* Sale w/e September 1: 3,944,265 22p

COLIN WALLACE — THE KINCORA SCANDAL

HIS OWN AMAZING STORY
● Centre Pages

WIN 100 TICKETS TO SEE TINA TURNER – Page 22

Jailed Irish to face trial in Iraq

THREE Irishmen are to stand trial for trying to flee from Iraq without exit visas.

They were detained two weeks ago and kept in a hotel, the Foreign Affairs Department in Dublin revealed yesterday. Now they are in jail.

The three, who have not been named, are thought to be the first westerners to face trial for trying to escape from Iraq.

Two were arrested near the town of Mosul in northern Iraq when soldiers found they didn't have the visas.

They were working as electricians at a petro-chemical plant 130 miles from Baghdad.

One is married and the other a bachelor. Their employers are Kent Construction, of Clonmel, Co Tipperary.

Visited

No details were available last night about the third man.

A spokesman for the firm said last night: "We have been in touch with the men's families.

"We have a manager out there who is in regular contact with us."

The three have been visited by officials from the Irish Embassy in Baghdad and lawyers have been appointed to defend them.

A Foreign Affairs Department spokesman said it was expected that their case would come before the courts in the next few weeks.

● The Irish ambassador in Iraq is to protest about the detention of diplomat Dr Niall Holohan in Kuwait.

He was held for three hours by troops who raided the Canadian ambassador's residence.

BLUNDER!

THE WATCHTOWER ON BOMB ALLEY: MP Ian Paisley claims it was unmanned – but the Army deny this

Were watch towers empty when IRA snatched cop?

By JOHN HICKS

A MASSIVE security blunder was blamed yesterday for the callous IRA murder of off-duty RUC constable Louis Robinson.

The unarmed officer was shot after being kidnapped from a van travelling along the most heavily-guarded road in Ireland.

Top politicians condemned the Army for allowing ten armed Provos to set up a fake road block close to two giant Army watch-

VICTIM: Louis Robinson

towers on the main Dublin to Belfast border crossing.

MP Ian Paisley claimed last night the watchtowers were unmanned.

He said men who had been with the murdered officer ran to them for help, but there was no one there.

But the Army said his claims were nonsense. "These observation points are fully-manned 24 hours a day," an officer said.

Local MP Seamus Mallon, deputy leader of SDLP, said: "These lookout posts are cosmetic. They just there to be seen – rather than to be seen from."

The three-mile "no-man's land" stretch of road – known as " bomb alley' - has claimed 11 lives in three years.

And on Saturday the IRA once again showed they could operate under

● Turn to Page 2

A report on the abduction and murder of RUC officer Louis Robinson, who was snatched by the IRA on the Newry Road. They stopped him at an illegal vehicle checkpoint after finding a section of the road that was in a blind spot from Army observation towers

Newspaper reports on RUC Louis Robinson's abduction – one shows me with an RUC officer on the cordon when we found his body

SOBBING WIFE BEGS IRA GANG TO FREE SICK COP

Security slammed

By FRANK CURRAN

THE WIFE of kidnapped cop Louis Robinson last night pleaded with the IRA to spare her sick husband's life and release him.

Distraught Anne Robinson, 39, choked back tears as she begged: "He is a human being. He has not been well. Please, please let him come home."

Police and churchmen backed her call for the release of the 42-year-old RUC officer, who was snatched by a dozen gunmen on the main Belfast-Dublin road as he returned from a fishing trip with five prison officer pals.

Mr Robinson has been on sick leave for three years suffering from depression, high blood pressure and rheumatism.

Struck

As fears grew for his safety, Newry and Armagh MP Seamus Mallon said:

"The whole community is appalled and demand he be released immediately."

And he slammed the lack of security which allowed the cop to be snatched a stone's throw from a police station and two army look-out posts.

The gunmen, who struck in the border bandit country of South Armagh, are believed to have been trailing Mr Robinson.

Three of the prison officers fled when their van was stopped but Constable Robinson, of Newry, and the two others were bundled died into the boots of waiting cars.

The two warders were badly beaten before being dumped seven miles away.

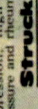
VICTIM: Louis Robinson

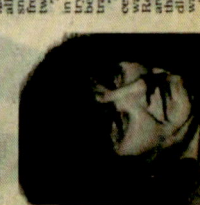
DISTRAUGHT: Wife Anne

observation posts on the hill-

Victims of the A1: a family of three were killed in this explosion in 1988 (left), and the van in which Louis Robinson was travelling

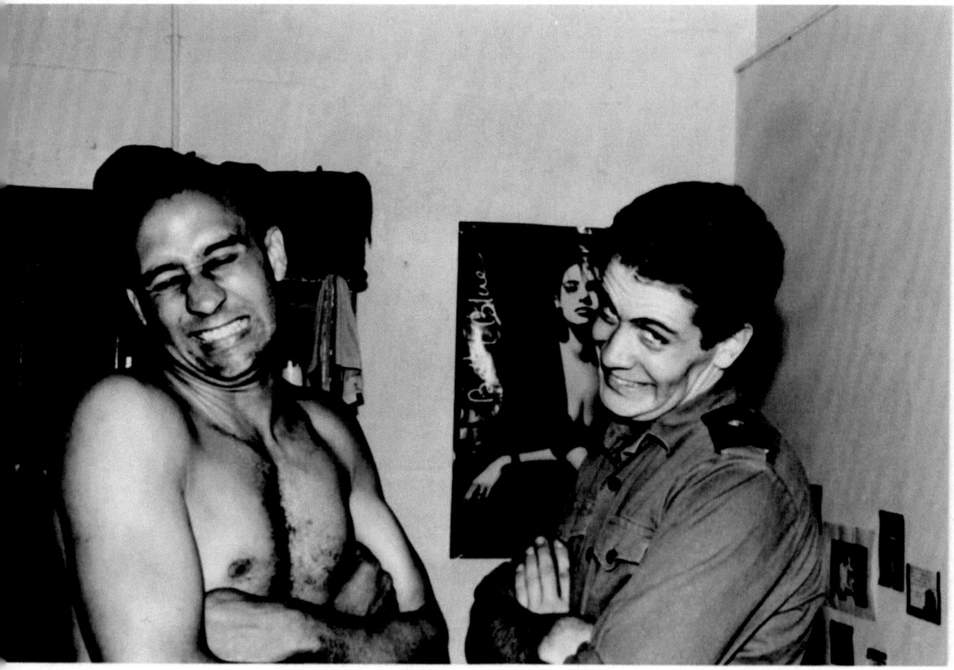

Me and Cheesy in Ops Coy lines, Bessbrook Mill

Setting a trip flare at the base of R14 tower, 5km outside of Newry

Me with Tony Harris
at the base of the 100ft
R14

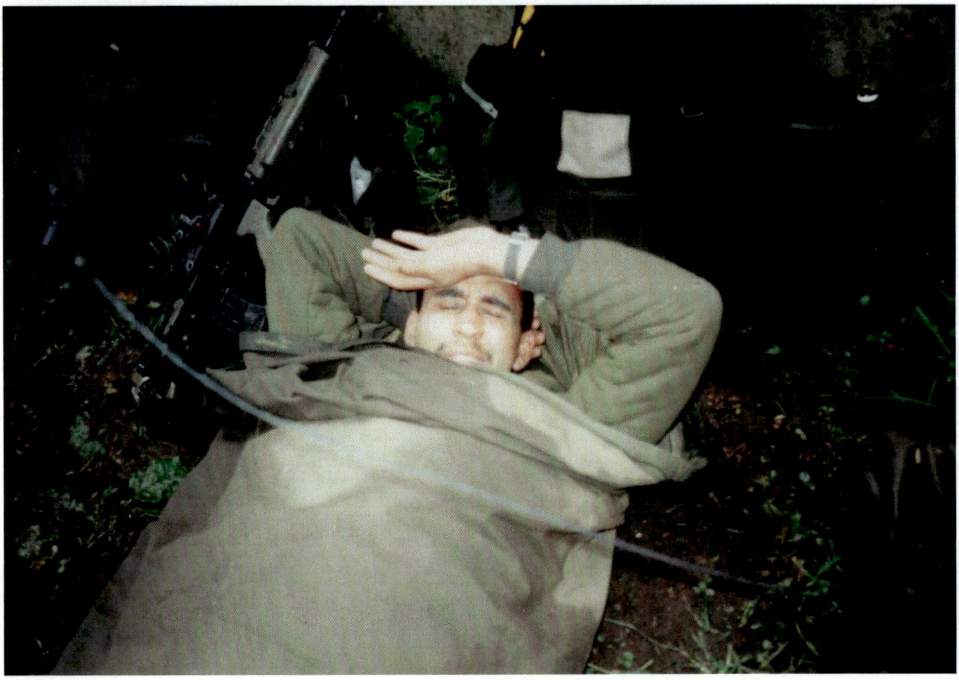

Waking up from a kip in my bivvi bag, on patrol in South Armagh

On my pit in Ops Coy Lines, Bessbrook Mill

Having a kip in the ARF Commander's Chair – Operations Room Bessbrook Mill

CPL (Vince)

School of Infantry
NORTHERN IRELAND TRAINING ADVISORY TEAM (UKLF)
Lydd Camp, Lydd, Romney Marsh, Kent. TN29 9JD

Telephone Army Network Shorncliffe Military } ext 8545
GPO Folkestone 49541

Fax Machine   ext 8549

See Distribution	Your reference
	Our reference UF/3/1
	Date 16 Jul 90

NITAT (UKLF) PRESENTATION TO 45 CDO RM
20/21 AUG 90

1.   Introduction. The NITAT (UKLF) Presentation Team will visit 45 Cdo RM in Arbroath on 20 - 21 Aug 90 to give the Main Presentation for the Commando's forthcoming tour. The presentation is designed to give junior ranks a flavour for operating within Northern Ireland. This letter outlines the administrative requirements for the presentation. The programme is at Annex A.

2.   Preparation. The area for the presentation should be fully blacked out prior to NITAT's arrival. A space of at least 6m should be left clear at the front of the auditorium for the erection of video eqpt, and staging provided for the mounting of two lecterns on either side of the screen. In addition 45 Cdo RM are requested to provide the following:

    a.   5 x 6' Tables GS.

    b.   1 x Roll of black tape (4").

    c.   1 x LSW c/w BFA and 20 x 5.56mm (blank).

    d.   1 x 9mm Pistol c/w magazine.

    e.   6 x Blankets.

3.   Composition. The NITAT (UKLF) Presentation Team will consist of the following:

    a.   Maj D V Walsh (David), KINGS - OC NITAT (UKLF).

    b.   Capt D L Strawbridge (David), RE.

    c.   Capt T Butterworth (Terry), DWR.

    d.   Insp Turbitt (Irwin), RUC - RUC Officer NITAT (UKLF).

    e.   WO2 (QMSI) M D Grant, SASC.

    d.   Cpl Govans, RE.

    e.   2 x RCT Dvr to be nominated.

    f.   There will also be guest speakers from 1 CHESHIRE and 2 UDR who will liaise direct with the Battalion.

1

Docs relating to the Northern Ireland Training and Advisory presentation to 45 Commando, Arbroath

ony Harris and me on operation to cover the 300th anniversary of the Battle of the Boyne

Left to right): Ronnie Wilding, Vic Lloyd and me waiting for a fast lift on the helipad, Bessbrook
Mill

TURN ARMY LOOSE ON IRA KILLERS

Take out the chiefs

By MICHAEL YARDLEY,
a former Army officer now a psychologist and author specialising in terrorism

FOR more than 20 years the Provisional IRA has been getting away with murder.

Parts of Northern Ireland have become a battle zone and the quality of life in Britain has been damaged.

We've tried to contain the IRA with improved security. It hasn't worked.

It's time for a new approach, one which recognises the need for some prudent security, but which also sees that the only way to control the IRA is to persuade its leadership that terrorism is not in their interests.

It's also time to realise that politics will not provide answers at present.

Ultimately, the godfathers of terror need to know they put their own lives at risk when they sponsor terrorism.

Fanatics

They have declared a shoot-to-kill policy on us. They should expect nothing less in return.

The people that count in the IRA know they're secure from justice. It will be the young fanatics they dispatch to murder and maim who will take the fall.

The Army has never had the opportunity to fight the war that it is uniquely capable of winning. Every soldier who served in Northern Ireland will tell you that almost all active members of the Provisional IRA are well known to the Army.

Many of the terrorists are kept under round-the-clock surveillance by men from specialist units such as 14 Int (Intelligence) Company.

If the Army and our intelligence services were allowed to **ACT** on the information the Provisional IRA would probably suffer casualties in the region of 70 to 80 per cent of personnel.

Britain should make a secret declaration to the IRA Godfathers that from now on, for every murder they commit, one of their own will lose their life.

And to sow seeds of fear, we should warn them that if they commit an atrocity in say, Belfast, then our reprisal could come among the IRA barons in "bandit country" of Armagh.

As Al Capone was finally brought to book for tax offences, Britain should use every device available to make ever, moment of these men's lives a nightmare.

We will investigate how they pay their bills. And if there is no legal explanation for their financial affairs—few work but all seem to live comfortably—then they must face repercussions.

Abandon

I am not suggesting the suspension of democracy, because that is an IRA aim.

What is suggested is a measured response made in the gravest extreme to a problem which will not respond to other actions. It amounts to the declaration of a limited war in peace.

Many politicians have said that there cannot be a military solution to the Ulster problem.

But many policemen and soldiers believe that without a military victory there can be no political solution.

Westminster needs to recognise the problem for what it is—a **WAR**—and to abandon the policy of fighting with civilian means.

There's a need to create new Army units, drawing together small teams of counter terrorist specialists. There's also a need to close the IRA's major source of funds—its criminal activities.

But we also need to recognise that many people in Northern Ireland do have a hard time and are entitled to a better standard of living than they enjoy.

We should offer massive financial investment conditional upon peace being established.

Every day that a policy of mere containment is pursued, the IRA become more deeply embedded in the local community.

TARGET . . . time to turn tables on the killers

WEDNESDAY OCTOBER 3 1990 • WEATHER: UNSETTLED

INSIDE TODAY

BILL WYMAN

STONE ALONE
Bill Wyman's own story

Danger man on run after Stonehenge ambush

IRA CELL TRAPPED BY POLICE

By ALUN REES

FOUR people from a suspected IRA murder squad were ambushed by armed police last night in the shadow of Stonehenge.

At least one more man is on the run on Salisbury Plain. Police say he is "armed and extremely dangerous" and have sealed off dozens of square miles around Salisbury.

Forensic scientists are examining two cars after the dramatic arrests in the car park next to Britain's most famous ancient monument.

And the latest intelligence files on Britain's most wanted man, notorious expert Patrick Sheehy, were being studied after it was realised one of the gang had escaped.

Murderous

One of the arrested four tried to escape by driving off at high speed in a grey van, but CID men closed fast and blocked his way.

The three men and one woman are held at a secret location being questioned about attacks including the bomb murder of Eastbourne MP Ian Gow.

The arrests came a week before the Tory party conference opens 70 miles away at Bournemouth.

They are the culmination of a months-long manhunt that took police yesterday to the heart of Britain's big-gun military base, Bulford Camp near Amesbury, Wilts.

MURDERED: Gow   WANTED: Sheehy

Called Operation Trojan, it led to all our days being cancelled for a week in the Wiltshire, Hampshire and Dorset police forces.

But the suspects had been trailed for weeks on end, sources said.

A CID man revealed: "We lost them, but we knew what car we were looking for — a blue Ford Sierra with a distinctive number plate we know to be false.

"Over the weekend there was a huge sweep of streets and lanes to find the target.

"Then today at about 3pm it was spotted in the Bulford area.

"The two persons in the Sierra were seen meeting with the occupants of another car and armed detectives moved in to make the arrests.

"That was the most delicate moment. I can tell you that a lot of people are breathing more easily."

The suspects were trailed to Stonehenge from the heavily fortified Bulford camp five days after a specialist undercover team spotted them near the home of an unnamed VIP on the Wiltshire-Hampshire border.

A source said: "They were observed through night sights and filmed on infra-red cameras.

"Something at the house spooked them — it may have been a car and a blue Sierra was seen driving away to their vehicle and left the scene."

"It was a blue Sierra with the registration A962 RNU. Later on the same car was observed near the home of a retired general who had served in Ulster and now lives on the edge of Salisbury Plain.

A detective team member cracked out the story: "When they departed from Hampshire we thought we had lost them.

"But one of our units a couple of miles away saw them drive past and clocked the number."

Peppered

"We remarked that as it was a false plate the late three letters — RNU — might have been somebody's idea of a pun on the Defence Secretary Tom King's name as they stood for a huge target."

Wiltshire is peppered with possible targets for the IRA. Northern Ireland Secretary Peter Brooke lives only eight miles from Stonehenge in the village of West Lavington, and at least five retired Northern Ireland army commanders are in the area.

This evening's operation was centred on the little Salisbury Plain village of Amesbury.

Villagers there said there had been rumours of IRA activity in the area for **Page 2 Column 1**

Danger man alert sparks new appeal

By MICHAEL ATCHINSON

POLICE have issued a photograph of a man they want to question over the bungled IRA attempt to bomb a top anti-terrorism conference.

Scotland Yard issued the picture and description of James McGarrigle, in a desperate bid to trace him. They are convinced he is still in London.

McGarrigle, 21, from Belfast, disappeared from his job as a kitchen porter at London's Royal Overseas League Club soon after the device was detected.

Attacks

The police appeal is the latest move in the hunt for the IRA terrorists responsible for 24 attacks in the country in the past two years.

McGarrigle is pictured wearing round, gold-rimmed glasses and a white, open-neck top. He has thick, dark-brown eyebrows, thick, short hair and dark stubble on his chin.

Club official Robert Newell refused to reveal how McGarrigle had been employed but he said he was vetted.

Staff said the mystery

WANTED: McGarrigle

Irishman had been well-liked, friendly and approachable.

One added: "He never once mentioned Ireland. the IRA or any dislike of the Government."

The Provos later claimed the 2lb of plastic explosive, packed into a lunchbox and hidden in the speaker's lectern was aimed at Foreign Office Minister William Walde-grave, who was due to speak at the conference.

Softly-spoken McGarrigle, is described as 5ft 6in tall, slim with brown hair, blue eyes and wears glasses. He had been employed at the club for a year.

But he vanished after the bomb was discovered and defused in the conference 200 yards from the Carlton Club, the Tory stronghold blasted earlier by the same terror gang.

The bomb was found an hour before the conference was due to start by a technician checking the microphone on the lectern, prompting a row over security.

It was planted after the police carried out an initial security sweep but before private security firm Group 4 began checking admissions.

The Scotland Yard hotline is Freephone 0800 789321.

Dawn arms raid

SECURITY forces on both sides of the border launched a massive search for an arsenal of IRA arms and explosives yesterday.

Operations were concentrated on a farm straddling the border in South Armagh "bandit country" near Crossmaglen. After months of undercover surveillance, police and troops landed by helicopter before dawn.

One man was held for questioning.

Newspaper clipping - IRA activity during the tour

Ronnie and me outside the ARF Hut- helipad Bessbrook Mill

Ops Coy home – Bessbrook Mill

From: Major D V Walsh KINGS

Cpl I

School of Infantry
Northern Ireland Training Advisory Team (UKLF)
Lydd Camp
Lydd
Romney Marsh
Kent TN29 9JD

Folkestone (0303) 49541 Ext 8530

DO/DVW

Good work.
OC B *18/9*
OC C *:/,*
/12/9.

Lieutenant Colonel K Skempton
Commanding Officer
1st Battalion The Cheshire Regiment
British Forces Post Office 811

5 September 1990

Dear Colonel Keith

Thank you for making Paul Mathews and Cpl Ivimey available for the 45 Cdo RM presentation. They were quite excellent, pitched their talk at exactly the right level and maintained the Battalions reputation for high grade briefings established by Nick Chapman at the Commanders' Cadre in July.

I had a long talk with Paul and sense a slight frustration that the tour has not been more eventful. Whilst apparent inactivity may be due to a number of reasons, in my opinion, it is usually due, to some extent at least, to sound tactics acting as a deterrent. Whatever the reason, long may it last.

Thank you again for sending two high grade commanders. They made a significant contribution to the Royal Marines introducion to the training.

Yours aye

David.

Cpl Jones
Photo copy for Cpl Ivimey, then send the copy to C Coy.

Docs relating to the Northern Ireland Training and Advisory presentation to 45 Commando, Arbroath

Arms cache drivers jailed

TWO men arrested as they drove a van containing a one-ton cache of IRA arms and explosives were given long prison sentences by a Dublin court yesterday.

The haul included seven assault rifles, 10lb of Semtex explosive and more than 32,000 rounds of ammunition, most of it for use in a heavy machine-gun.

Ciaran O'Dwyer, 35, was jailed for 12 years and John Carmody, 25, was given a ten-year sentence by the anti-terrorist Special Criminal Court. Both men are from Limerick.

They were convicted of having the assault rifles, ammunition and explosives on May 25 this year.

Special Branch detectives, acting on a tip-off, stopped the men on a Limerick housing estate, the court heard.

A loaded Kalashnikov rifle and revolver were in the front of the van and the other arms were in boxes in the back.

Troops fall foul of border error

Eleven British soldiers were dropped from helicopters on the wrong side of the Northern Ireland border yesterday after a map-reading error.

Irish police said officers went to the scene, a field near Castleblaney, Co Monaghan. The names and units of the 11 soldiers were noted and they were then allowed to walk back into South Armagh.

Newspaper clippings of IRA activity during our tour, including the second Cheshire to be shot at Newton Hamilton SF base

Soldier survives IRA gun ambush

A SECOND Cheshire Regiment soldier is recovering in hospital after being shot in a terrorist ambush in Northern Ireland.

Corporal Darren Jones is in the same hospital as Private Mark Moorfield, who was shot at the weekend.

Meanwhile, a third soldier, Trevor Bell, 26, has returned to his Hawarden home with a fractured collarbone after rioters set upon him on Sunday.

The latest victim, Corporal Jones, was shot on Wednesday night whilst on guard duty in the Newton Hamilton area of South Armagh.

by JAMES JACKSON

"Corporal Jones came under terrorist gun fire and sustained a bullet wound in his buttocks," an Army spokesman said.

Corporal Jones, from the Liverpool area, was rushed to hospital for surgery and is believed to be in a stable condition.

His wife Jenny was expected to be by his bedside today.

Private Moorfield, 25, from Birmingham, was making good progress today, doctors said.

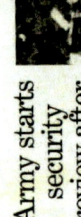

THE INDEPENDENT

*** Published in London   35p

THURSDAY 25 OCTOBER 1990

No.1,259

IRA uses human bombs

Army starts security review after attacks kill six soldiers and civilian

By David McKittrick
Ireland Correspondent

A MAJOR REVIEW of security procedures is expected to take place in Northern Ireland in the wake of the emergence of a new IRA "human bomb" tactic which yesterday led to the deaths of six soldiers and a civilian.

In a significant escalation of its terrorist campaign the IRA forced three Catholic civilians, whom it called "collaborators" with the security forces, to drive large bombs to military installations while their families were held hostage.

Five soldiers and a civilian died when a huge bomb went off at a border vehicle checkpoint near Londonderry, just after dawn, partly demolishing the installation. Almost simultaneously another soldier was killed in a similar incident at a checkpoint near Newry, Co Down.

In a third attack, several hours later, the IRA strapped a man into the driving seat of a carvanette containing bombs and ordered him to drive into an army camp in Omagh, Co Tyrone, following him in their own vehicle. At the base the man wriggled free: later the bomb's detonator went off but failed to set off the device.

The tactic clearly poses a grave new danger to the security of military and RUC bases and checkpoints, raising the possibility that civilians acting under duress may deliver large bombs which explode without warning.

The use of "human bombs" shocked MPs, who heard the Secretary of State for Northern Ireland, Peter Brooke, tell the Commons that the tactic "marked new

The checkpoint near Londonderry. The main road runs lower left to upper right. The triangular checkpoint enclosure behind it has an accommodation block in the middle and two "sangars" — fortified

SUMMARY

Polly Peck to ask for administrator

Directors of Polly Peck International, the troubled electronics and food group run by Asil Nadir, will today ask the High Court to appoint an administrator.   Page 28

Rover pay offer

The Government suffered a blow to its anti-inflationary policy when Rover car workers were recommended a basic 11 per cent rise.   Page 2

Pollution bulletins

Air quality reports are to be included routinely in Met Office weather bulletins..... Page 3

440 children die

Road safety has worsened with injuries to children up 3,000 to about 48,000 a year. Of those, 440 were killed.   Page 3

Benefit pledge

Child benefit "is and will remain" a strong element in government support of the family, the Social Security Secretary said, announcing an increase for the oldest child.   Page 6

Problem drinkers

Young professional women are seeking treatment for drink problems.   Page 8
Leading article, page 26

Summit 'silence'

Jacques Delors, European Commission President, urged that disputes over economic and monetary union should not be allowed to spill over at this weekend's EC summit to avoid a clash with Margaret Thatcher.

Hot air bubble, page 27

Dolphins dying

A virus related to that which wiped out 18,000 seals in the

Newspaper clipping about IRA human bombs striking at two locations, including vehicle check point R15 just outside Newry.

Ronnie and me getting some sleep during operations, Y20A Screws' Mess, South Armagh

Vic Lloyd holding court, Screws' Mess, South Armagh

Newspaper report of 1 Cheshire's deployment to Fermanagh and County Tyrone at very short notice in 1991.

DAILY TELEGRAPH - 20-March 91

More troops for Ulster as checkpoints close

By Chris Ryder, Irish Correspondent

FIVE HUNDRED soldiers from the 1st Battalion, the Cheshire Regiment, have been deployed for an indefinite tour of duty in Co Fermanagh after a decision by Mr Brooke, Northern Ireland Secretary, to close two of the 18 permanent vehicle checkpoints along the border.

The extra soldiers will initially be used to provide cover for the teams of Royal Engineers and helicopter crews who will dismantle the two heavily fortified posts at Boa Island and Derryard.

Security sources said the future of the other 16 checkpoints was also under review and there could be more closures.

Senior security commanders are deeply committed to the policy that, whatever the consequences, the lives of their men on the ground will not be risked unnecessarily.

In the light of the IRA's new "human bomb" tactic of holding a family hostage, then forcing one member to drive a vehicle with a bomb on board to a checkpoint, the commanders have decided the risk to the soldiers manning the posts and the helicopter crews servicing them is now significantly outweighed by the intelligence benefit from maintaining them.

A number of other roads crossing the border will also be closed with barriers, to prevent terrorists using them to mount attacks or smuggle arms and explosives into Ulster from the Irish Republic.

Mr Brooke: denies he is giving in to the IRA

After the Boa Island and Derryard posts are dismantled, the Cheshires will participate in a more intensive programme of mobile patrols in the sparsely populated countryside, designed to reassure the local community about their security and safety and to deter further IRA activity.

Mr Brooke said: "I took the decision to remove these checkpoints after the most careful consultation with the Chief Constable and the General Officer Commanding on how to make the most effective use of resources to counter terrorist activity in the area.

"I also took fully into account views expressed to me by elected representatives and other members of the Fermanagh community who were able to offer me first hand local views about the value of the permanent vehicle check-points in Fermanagh." Last December, Mr Brooke ordered the indefinite night-time closure of four border checkpoints, at Boa Island, Derryard, Clonalty Bridge and Killyvilly, to save lives.

Mr Brooke denied that the Government was giving in to the IRA. He said that his decision was a response to the "bestiality" of the IRA human bomb attacks at several checkpoints a month earlier.

Recognising that the closure would cause inconvenience and hardship to those living in the immediate border areas, Mr Brooke said that advance notice of the decision could not be given because it would have alerted the terrorists.

"There are eight to 12 soldiers in each of the permanent vehicle checkpoints," he said. "If a dozen people had been killed in the course of the night I would have lived with those dozen lives on my conscience for the rest of my life."

Since the first human bomb attacks during November, in which seven people died, including six soldiers, a major rethink of security at the highly vulnerable posts has been taking place.

An intercom system was installed for emergency traffic at night. Travellers had to communicate with the guard force at the posts, who had full discretion whether or not to let them through.

Gates and traffic lights were installed to control access by vehicles and reduce the risk of human bomb attacks.

My £10 charge for wearing jungle combats, as reimagined by Ronnie Wilding were handed over. I left my kit on the floor and was still dirty, but I phoned Mum and Emma to let them know I was in off the ground.

Chapter 17: Girl trouble

Throughout this book I've mentioned my relationship with numerous women. This is a difficult one for me, because in my experience every relationship I had during my time in the military turned out to be disaster. The only ones who really got it were my mum, bless her, and Jen – my wife and partner of more than twenty years. More about Jen later, but when I met her I knew she was too clever to be dragged around the world with me and my priorities changed. It suddenly became less important to me and was no longer all-encompassing, so I left.

My mother had experienced all of this first-hand, way before I arrived. She was married to Dave, a Royal Marine who served on HMS King George V and was in the Pacific for the best part of three years during the war. I know she knew what the military meant to him and the sacrifices service personnel make for their countries. So when I was calling her on a monitored telephone landline from South Armagh, for example, we both knew I couldn't talk about the ops, but she let me have a rant for a few minutes about how it was going pear-shaped and that some people weren't performing. After I'd got it off my chest she asked if I felt better and then told me to keep my head down and get on with it. I put her though the mill and I think she aged, as she had to accept the fact that I was doing what I had to and that she wasn't in a position to protect me any more.

Despite the lack of understanding of my Forces vocation from the women I met, it didn't stop me trying! That said, I told it straight. I refused to pretend to be a tree surgeon or a plumber when I was out on the piss with the boys. That was the sort of line I often heard when lads I worked with went out on the pull. Mine was a 'take it or leave it' attitude. I was shy anyway, so I balked at any attention, but if what I said didn't fit with what they wanted, that was fine.

That evening we all had a few beers; some a few more than others! All of those things the LI had said were true: it does go very quickly, but so much had happened.

Chapter 18: Last one on the Herc lift the ramp!

Friday October 19

We didn't really get off to a good start as the Chinook broke down! Pumas and Wessex were called in and we got lifted by our normal form of transport to Aldergrove. As we got off it was exactly as it had been when we arrived: a stick of Royal Marines waiting to get on. They all looked at us fairly hard, but that wasn't going to win the war. For the record, there is generally animosity between any and all units from all three branches of the armed forces. I was badged a Cheshire and would die one. Any of their lads would say the same.

The Hercules was packed with troops and kit, and nobody minded the noise. Ops Company along with the CO were the last Cheshires out of South Armagh on the tour. The Herc flew us to Speke Airport in Liverpool, where the coaches came onto the runway. We got straight off the plane and onto the coaches and they drove us to the Dale in Chester. We were home!

It has been said for the past twenty years, and I'm sure it will be said again, but the solution to the situation in Northern Ireland will never be us walking around with heavy kit waiting for something to happen. We've done our bit now. We all went and all came back, so that's something to be proud of. But how many more lives must be lost before it ends?

To illustrate how serious the threat in South Armagh and else-where across the province was, ten days after we got home there were two simultaneous attacks: one in Londonderry, the other at R15, the permanent vehicle checkpoint on the Dublin Road just outside Newry. Families were taken hostage and two men were told to drive 'human bombs' – cars filled with explosives – to these two separate locations. Five soldiers were killed in Londonderry and five were seriously injured. At R15 (the place I had walked to down the hill from the tower to get a shower during the first month of my tour), a 65-year-old man drove his van containing a bomb to the checkpoint but managed to leap out and shout a warning just before the bomb went off. The checkpoint was blown to pieces and Royal Irish Ranger Cyril John Smith, aged twenty-one, was killed. Eight others – seven soldiers and a policeman – were injured. Bastards.

Chapter 19: Politics and music in 1990

January 13: Some fifty thousand people demonstrate on the streets of London to support Britain's ambulance workers as the ongoing ambulance crew strike continues four months after it began.

January 18: The first MORI poll of the decade shows that Labour have a twelve-point lead over the Conservatives, with forty-eight percent of the vote. Liberal support is at its lowest level for more than a decade, with just five percent of the vote.

January 29: Lord Justice Peter Taylor publishes his report on the Hillsborough disaster, which claimed the lives of 96 Liverpool FC supporters on April 15, 1989. He recommends that all top division stadiums are fully seated by 1994 and that the rest of the Football League follows suit by 1999. He rules out the government's proposed ID card scheme to combat football hooliganism, claiming it is "unworkable".

February 20: Three people are injured by a bomb explosion in Leicester city centre.

February 26: Fourteen people are killed as storms hit Britain.

March 31: Two hundred thousand protesters take part in London's Poll Tax Riots in the week preceding the official introduction of the Community Charge.

June 1: An army recruit is shot dead and two others are wounded by two suspected IRA gunmen in Lichfield, Staffordshire.

July 20: An IRA bomb explodes at Stock Exchange Tower, the base of the London Stock Exchange.

July 24: A Roman Catholic nun and three police officers are killed by an IRA landmine in County Armagh.

July 30: An IRA car bomb kills British MP Ian Gow, a staunch unionist, after he assured the IRA that the British government would never surrender to them.

September 18: Air Chief Marshal Sir Peter Terry survives a murder attempt by IRA terrorists at his home near Stafford.

December 13: Russell Bishop is sentenced to life imprisonment (with a recommended minimum of 15 years) for the abduction, indecent assault and attempted murder of a seven-year-old girl in Brighton earlier this year. Aged twenty-four, Bishop was cleared of murdering two other girls in 1987.

December 25: Storms on Christmas Day leave more than a hundred thousand British homes without power.

December 26: The fatwa (order to kill) against *The Satanic Verses* author Salman Rushdie is upheld by Ayatollah Ali Khamenei more than a year after it was first issued. Rushdie is in hiding.

What I was listening to in South Armagh:

Desire by Talk Talk (as we left the room before we went out on a planned op)

Heaven or Las Vegas (album) by The Cocteau Twins (I had a feeling this is what angels would sound like if it all went wrong)

Chapter 20: Other deployments and vetting problems

Later, during the posting to Chester, we were deployed again; this time to Fermanagh and County Tyrone. The regiment was shooting at Altcar Rifle Range near Liverpool at the time. The next moment the word came around like wildfire: clear your weapons, get on the coaches and get back to camp. We did this as quickly as we could and were told to go to the gym. Once the whole regiment was assembled, CO Bob Stewart came in, I remember it well. He said: "I can't tell you where you're going or what you're doing, but you now have forty-eight hours to prepare your kit and be ready to move." Then he walked out. The excitement was tremendous walking back to B Coy lines.

We flew to Aldergrove airfield in Ireland on Saturday night/ Sunday morning via Hercules from Stafford. There is no shutdown facility there for Hercs, so when they dropped the gate there was a Lynx up as top cover as we ran off.

This was a politically sensitive job. We were there to support the Engineers as they destroyed a number of checkpoints on the border. On December 13, 1989, the IRA had attacked the Derryard check-point manned by the King's Own Scottish Borderers (KOSB). During this attack, two soldiers were killed and two were left injured.

Part of this deployment was patrolling out of Carrickmore Police Station, which usually contained a handful of coppers who were barricaded inside. This is the location where, on November 12, 1983, one police officer was killed and several injured during a mortar attack. We were around and about for three weeks or so before they flew us home. This wasn't until after an incident on the border when A Coy were attacked and returned fire with several hundred GPMG rounds. Good effort.

Of course, during the tour of South Armagh I'd already taken advice from SAS-trained Para Major Rusby, who was OC Ops Company. He had said it was the right time for me to either go to Hereford to join the SAS or perhaps try the Intelligence Corps. For me it was a fairly easy decision. I didn't think that the physical fitness required for SAS selection would be a problem, but the mental ability to cope with that kind of work was. I had already been knocked back for a commission by the CO in South Armagh, so when I got back to Chester I put in my paperwork for the Intelligence.

I travelled to the Intelligence and Security unit in Salisbury and they accepted me. One problem was the positive vetting (top secret), or PVTS, which is a detailed look at the individual, their background and their family. As I had been adopted at birth, I asked my birth mum for details of my real father, but these weren't forthcoming. There was a fucking shit storm and that was the end of that. I had put my heart and soul into the Cheshire Regiment, but it hadn't always gone to plan and I had decided I needed to do something else. Perhaps in hindsight I should have gone to Hereford and tried my luck with the SAS, and this is a decision I have played over in my mind several hundred times. Despite not being as mentally tough as I needed to be from a pure soldiering point of view, it'll be something I will think about – with all the ifs and the buts – until I leave this place. Anyway, at the time I had convinced myself Intelligence was the place to go; it was, after all, the place where the intelligence was gathered (14 Intelligence) for the major Special Forces ops. But due to not knowing the details about my dad (I still don't know who or what he is to this day), I wasn't able to go. This was a huge kick in the bollocks.

Chapter 21: Partner in crime

I knew it was a game-changer when I met Jen in Chester. She was and still is the love of my life, my number one, my partner in crime. We met at a school reunion in 1992. We had known of each other as I was in the same school year as her sister, Sarah. However, I'd only known her to pat her on the head and say hello to as she's a few years younger than me.

It was fate the way we got together. I was still serving in the Army and only heard about the event as my sister, also called Sarah, had heard about it. She was pregnant with her son George but was planning to come up from Devon for the bash.

It was pretty exciting until the actual day, when the prospect of losing a night out with the lads dawned on me. Mum said I had to go because Sarah had gone to so much trouble, and that was that.

Around teatime I drove into town in my 1972 red Beetle and parked it by Chester Cathedral to get some cash out of the bank. As I ran up the road, a bloke shouted: "You'll get a ticket parking there." I, in turn, was just about to tell him to "f off" when I saw it was Ken Croall, Sarah and Jen's dad. We knew each other of old as he was a lecturer at the local college and was involved with the school. He knew I was a bit of a lad and he also knew I'd been in a bit of trouble. I asked if Sarah was going to the bash at the school and he said that she wasn't, but Jen was. I kept this in mind.

Jen had just got back from a month of InterRailing that day and, though she'd originally planned to go, she was tired and was going to skip it. She told her dad so and he said that she had to go because he had told people that she would be there. So that was that!

At the school, it was polite conversation and a few ales. Of course, there is always the odd person who kicks the arse out of it: Nobby was that man. He was battered and was barracking the

new Deputy Head. You know the sort of thing: "Oi, fish face!"
Unfortunately for Jen, she was standing right next to him and the
assumption was made that they were together. I knew Nobby of
old, and when Jen was looking round for someone to help she
caught my eye. That was it; it was love at first sight. I quietened
Nobby down and then Jen and I spent most of the night talking.
That was September 19, 1992 and we've been together ever since.
We were married in 2000.

Anyway, back to that first meeting. Jen had said that I should
call her as she was at a loose end having finished university and
didn't yet have a job sorted. I left not long after as I didn't want to
get bladdered and thought that if I made a quick exit I could still
get into town to find the boys. The next morning I got the phone
book out, found Jen's number and then had a re-think. As I said,
Ken knew I'd been in prison. My conclusions were that he thought
I was an OK sort of bloke, but not a good enough one to take his
daughter out. I didn't make the call.

A few weeks later, I was out on the town, suited and booted on
a Friday night, and we headed in to Scruples near the cathedral. I
was just going to get a round in and the next thing I knew, Jen was
in front of me, collecting glasses. I was in grovelling, apologetic
mode for most of the night; so much so that I stayed sober and
went back to see her after the bar shut. Jen eventually agreed that I
could take her out and we went to Alexander's Jazz Theatre bar for
a few drinks one evening. I was training, so when I arrived I asked
for a glass of wine, which I could sip slowly because I didn't want
to kick the arse out of it and get too pissed. When Jen got there I
asked her what she wanted to drink and she said a pint of lager!
Five pints later I walked her down to get a taxi, and as hers arrived
she asked me if she was going to get a snog! Our first proper date
was to see Liverpool play Spartak Moscow in the European Cup

Winners' Cup. We got beaten two nil and Mike Marsh got sent off in the eighty-seventh minute. What a romantic I am!

Jen is a woman for all seasons. She put up with a lot, especially in the early years as I was still very much in military mode and my temper could kick in at the drop of a hat. She always supported me in whatever I wanted to do, even when I wrote to Bob Stewart to ask if I could rejoin the regiment to go to Bosnia. Despite all of this, I knew in my heart of hearts that my Army career was over when I met her and I couldn't have both lives. I opted for Jen and I know I made the right decision. For me it's a young man's game; I joined young and gave it my all. Enough was enough and I wanted to be with her, not the regiment. Good choice.

Jenny Ivimey is a sexy and very clever lady. She was when I met her and has grown more beautiful with time. She is now the mother of my two children and has, if anything, become more gorgeous as the years have gone by. She's one in a million.

Chapter 22: Life away from the regiment

By this stage the regiment knew I wanted out and offered me the carrot of a promotion to Sergeant at twenty-four (the youngest in the regiment at the time) to try to dissuade me from leaving the regiment. I was also offered a posting to Crewe as a Recruiting Sergeant. The thinking from the Army was that young men and women wanted to speak to young people, and the new policy was that recruiters should be under thirty years of age. I took it, but it was the final nail in the coffin for me and my regimental life. I lived a cushy life of home cooking, with minimal training and lots of food and drink. It wasn't very conducive to a combat lifestyle. That said, it was a good life. I fell in love with Jen and have never looked back from that.

In good faith, I tried to get back into it on more than one occasion, but it didn't happen. The Cheshires were in Fallingbostel in Germany as a mechanised infantry battalion. To avoid amalgamation with another regiment (which happened in the end), Bob Stewart took a fast ball to be the first regiment into Bosnia, and six weeks later they were there. I was gutted that I had missed this one and as mentioned I wrote to him personally to ask if I could come back in any capacity to rejoin them on tour. He very kindly wrote back (handwritten and included in this book for reference), but as expected he said no; I had a job and was expected to get on with it.

I did eventually get shipped back to the regiment, but missing out on Bosnia obviously gave some people a preconceived idea about me before I got off the plane. This was in December 1993 and it was a bloody disaster. I had no car and knew no one in the Mess. I played rugby against the officers (and scored) and I got to serve Christmas dinner to the lads in the cookhouse, which was my highlight. As I had not completed Senior Brecon I was marched in to the RSM and told that as they were going back to the UK (Oakington Barracks in Cambridgeshire), the regiment would reduce in size. As I was only an Acting Sergeant I would be reverted back to Full Screw – fucking cheers.

I took a shit-stick job to escort the Mess silverware back to the UK in an artic truck container. The weather was so bad on the crossing we nearly had to turn back.

I trooped it and fucked off to join the Territorial Army as a regular instructor back in Chester. It was a very sad end to my time with the regiment and I finally realised that whatever I did out on ops or on the sports field, I was just a number. The regiment didn't give a shit about me and that goes for every poor sod who came before me and the thousands who will come later, long after I'm gone. It's about your mates, the lads; how you do your job in their eyes and how you're remembered... hopefully fondly.

When the war in Afghanistan started in August 1990 I went to the careers office in Blackheath, Lewisham, and went back on the reserve. I was feeling noticeably old as most of the kids in the shop were young enough to have been my own! It was put to me that I could sign up for a six-month tour, which would have been great if I didn't have a wife and young baby on the way.

A report on the news said that three out of ten reservists weren't prepared to deploy, which for me is shit; if you take the shilling, that's it. I wasn't going to volunteer, but if they wanted me I was back in the mix. I knew pretty well that there were plenty of young lads who were likely to be in the frame to be killed before me. This is a harsh reality, but if the Army had called and wanted me to do a job, I would have done it.

Since leaving, I went to the Regimental Tent at Chester Racecourse in May every year expect one because it had been raining for a week and would have been like a swimming pool. Anyway, this was the only real contact I had with the lads I served with and, to be fair, in most cases we had little in common by this point anyway. That said, we lived in such close conditions we had the memories of the days gone by. Jacko and his brother Bob, Steve Baldwin, Kev Taylor, Carl Fin, Jamo and I sank a few ales at the races and were able to reminisce about what we did.

Each year I made no promises, but I gave them all a hug (probably a bit too much), wished them well and prayed they would be there next year. If you looked around the tent you could see groups of men, wives and girlfriends. The guys had Cheshire regimental or County ties on and most of these groups were in their twenties and thirties. In some cases they're in their sixties or seventies, but in their minds – just for a few hours – they were twenty-one again.

I get slapped on the back of the head a lot and called all sorts of names, but this was the nature of the day. One year someone came up to me and asked me if I remembered when we broke into the cookhouse (we were starving, so we walked up the storm drain and got in the back). I thought about this for a minute and realised this took place in Hong Kong twenty-five years earlier! Happy days.

There was one lad, Jonah, who served as a Private when I was a Full Screw with Four Platoon. I didn't really rate him at the time as he was always looking for an angle. Anyway, I saw him years later in the Regimental Tent and he had made it to Lance Jack in the Recce. Anyway, I asked him how it was going and he said it was fine, but that occasionally the lads would moan about him giving them a hard time. His response was: "If you think you're getting a hard time now, you should have tried working for Jimmy I." That was lovely for me to hear. I was a little choked about it, because it was lovely to be remembered at all, never mind fondly.

On September 1, 2007, the Cheshire Regiment merged with the Staffordshire, Worcestershire and Sherwood Foresters Regiment to become the Mercian Regiment; the Cheshires being the 1st Battalion. I've missed the fun at Chester Racecourse (Roodee) in Chester, but to my mind, if you're badged a Cheshire, you'll always be a Cheshire. I have yet to find camaraderie and bonds like the ones that are forged in the Army; I've stopped looking now. It was a chance in a lifetime and I took it. I played the game, got stuck in and loved it. Of course, it's not always like that. As the years go by you seem to gloss over the fear, hunger and pain you went through – that every infantry solider goes through – but this was a journey that was not to be missed.

Chapter 23: Cheshire Regiment luminaries

Bob Stewart was the best Commanding Officer I served under during my military career. He assumed the role as the figurehead for the regiment, but he also fearlessly defended the Cheshires; so much so that he took a posting to become the first British battalion in Bosnia at unfeasibly short notice, just to avoid amalgamation. Given the autocratic nature of the military and its rank structure, we never walked up and spoke to him directly, that just wasn't done. But he was unusually approachable and made himself available to the troops. He took great pride in commanding the regiment and it showed; the lads had the utmost respect for him. He was a one-off.

David Colebourn was the first Company Commander I worked under when I arrived at the battalion in Hong Kong in February 1985. The B Coy commander was a larger-than-life character who seemed pretty cool to a young eighteen-year-old CROW. He spoke like a gentleman and had the accompanying box of tricks, including a motorbike. He came along the border on it to see me at a tower to ask if, at eighteen, I would do the NCO's cadre (the Non-Commissioned Officer's promotion course) and I said no. He also played regimental rugby – you get the idea. He was a big bloke who used the now-famous (in my mind) line: "Close in B Company, I don't want to shout." There were others: "It really grips my shit." Oh yes, and: "If any of you fuckers want a go, I'll take you around the back, and if I can't do it I'll get Fox to sort you out" (Mickey Fox was the battalion's heavyweight boxer).

On one occasion we were on exercise in Fiji and his mother had come (don't ask!). Anyway, as we debussed, she called out to him in a thick Scouse accent – brilliant! Later during that time in the field he went off horse riding in the bush with an AR15 ArmaLite rifle on his back! He was James Bond in waiting, a cracking bloke! He came to see me before I boxed in the finals in Hong Kong. I was in the changing rooms shitting myself and he stuck his head around the door in his Mess kit and had a word about what I needed to do; not for B Company, but for myself.

Bede Etherington was a first-class platoon commander. He and I got on exceptionally well; I was more than happy to work for him. Equally, we could go on the piss and sink a few beers, no problem. He identified straight away that I was a stroppy bugger and made allowances for my moody outbursts. That aside, he knew his stuff and commanded Five Platoon well. He led from the front and made the platoon the desired location for any poor buggers who were sent to B Coy when they arrived at the battalion. We had some great tours: Belize (the kangaroo court) on patrol will not be forgotten by Corporal Broomhall (Prof). He oversaw adventure training when we did no sport, drank rum (sometimes with a parrot!) and learnt the local bupsie dance. We also managed a trip to a Mayan pyramid, and Bede broke a bit off – I have a photo!

We toured Cyprus, where we worked and played hard. This was in 1987, when eight hundred people had died in Greece during the summer because it was so hot. It was mad dogs and Englishmen on exercise. On the live-firing platoon attack he managed not to shoot me despite me running across his arc of fire. Cheers Bede.

Alex 'Cheesy' Watts was my Multiple Commander (Y20A) when we were in South Armagh. He gets a mention because anyone who

296

can put up with and get the best out of me and Ronnie Wilding at the same time deserves one. Neither of us was shy about coming forward or speaking our minds about what we were being asked to do (from a tactical perspective); particularly Ronnie. Yet Alex did a good job. He always took on board what we were saying and at times adjusted tack to implement our ideas; he showed solid leadership. That said, when we were operating as a twelve-man team (multiple) it was his call and, if it went tits up, the buck would stop with him.

I remember fondly when we got back from South Armagh and we were all at home on leave in Chester, so I called him to see if he was coming out for a beer. His mum picked up the phone and asked who it was, and I confirmed that it was Corporal Ivimey. She said she wanted to thank me for looking after her son. It wasn't strictly true, but these were very kind works that I never forgot.

Ronnie Wilding was my mucker in South Armagh. He operated as I did; as a team (four-man, or occasionally, six-man leader) in Y20. He was a brilliant soldier with a temper that would give my own a good run for its money! He was the grumpiest man in the world first thing in the morning, and when we had a planned op and lift (say 0400hrs), we would be up at 0300hrs to get our kit sorted, eat breakfast and then go. Nobody, including me, wanted to go near him at that time in the morning, and we would draw straws to decide who would get him up. But he had the best sense of humour I have seen in a solider.

On one op in Ireland we hit the road under darkness (it was never done in the day) and tabbed hard. On reaching our location we would set up the bashers to get some kip. Vic and I had a hot chocolate on the go and Ronnie, being the perfectionist, had made

297

the perfect basher. Unfortunately, just as Ronnie finished, Matty tripped over one of the bungees and collapsed it. Ronnie knocked the shit out of him in front of me and Vic. Neither of us said a word; we just carried on hugging our drink.

Jason 'Vic' Lloyd was one of the best soldiers I worked with. He was a great bloke, a good squaddie and a drinking pal of old. When I was a team leader, Vic was one of the senior toms (lads). If you needed something doing and you asked him, it got done. More than capable of looking after himself, Vic boxed for me in Chester when I ran the B Coy team at the Dale.

In Ireland, on the few occasions I could choose my own team, his name was always the first, like the time I took him on a lurk at the crossroads in Crossmaglen. He was brave – after one night tab along a country road we saw a suspicious car parked up, so we dropped our bergans and he followed me around a farm building to take a look. He was with me all of the way and reacted just as I wanted him to as we both cocked our weapons and got into the alert to prevented the car from leaving the location. On another occasion I asked him to stop vehicles on a dark road one night and he stopped an eighteen-wheel truck by flagging it down with a red torch. It braked late and stopped just inches away from him. He didn't move.

We had a brilliant laugh, and when we went firm (stopped moving on the ground and held a position) in South Armagh and managed to get some rest it was mainly Cheesy, Ronnie, Vic and me under a basher in the hastily constructed Screws' Mess. On the last sighting of Vic, he was working as a contractor in Iraq. Take care, mate.

Simon 'Jacko' Jackson. This one goes without saying. We were out one night in Hong Kong having a few beers, doing what lads do, and the next we were in a world of shit. We stuck together because we had to and we came out the other end. I have seen him many times since in the Regimental Tent and there is only one event we never speak about. We both know what happened and that's enough.

James Marc Ivimey
Enlisted: December 19, 1983
Discharged: September 21, 1994

Chapter 24: Glossary

44 Call Sign – Helicopter lift

A 1017 feature with G40 on top – A big hill with a military tower on top

Alcalde – Magistrate/village top man

Antler/violent joker – Electronic counter measures equipment

APC – Airport Camp

APWT – Annual Personal Weapons Test

ARF – Air Reaction Force

ASU – Active Service Unit

Attap – A traditional house found in Brunei, Indonesia, Malaysia, Singapore and Belize

ATO – Ammunition Technical Officer

BBK – Bessbrook Barracks

BFT – Basic Fitness Test

Bondhook – Rifle

Buckshe – Spare

Bupsie – Local Belizean dance

Buzzard – Flying HQ block (Bessbrook)

Call Sign 0 – HQ Command

Cas evaced – Casualty evacuation

CBF – Commander of the British Forces

Charlie 1 – Personnel check

Chip shop tasks – Shit, dead-end jobs

Choggies – Shop/café

Clicked – Being observed/monitored

CO – Commanding Officer

Colour Bloke – Colour Sergeant

Connor – Food

CPV – Covert Patrol Van

Crab Airways – The RAF

CROW – Combat Recruit of War

CSM – Company Sergeant Major

CTR – Close target reconnaissance

Dog Lydon (Sergeant Major, B Coy) – So named because he once allegedly ate a whole hay box of range stew

Dog Stag – Guard shift between 0200hrs and 0400hrs

DSO – Distinguished Service Order

ECM – Electronic counter measures

Foxhound – Troop

FRG – Federal riot gun (with plastic bullets)

Full Screw – Corporal

G20, G30 and G40 – Golf and Romeo watchtowers

Garda – Irish Police Force

Gary Gore-Tex – Waterproof overclothing

Glasshouse – Prison

GOC – General Office Commanding

Gonk bag – Sleeping bag

Gook – Illegal immigrant (Chinese national) trying to cross the border (on the 1985 tour of Man Kam To, Five Platoon wore 'Gook Buster' T-shirts)

Gook stick – Baton/pole

Green eggs – Carlsberg

Green maggot – Sleeping bag

Growler – Meat pie

Gweilo – Non-Chinese person

Hiace van – Used to mount a heavy machine gun or mortar

HK – Heckler & Koch

HKMS – Hong Kong Military Service

HKVF – Hong Kong Volunteer Force
HLS – Helicopter landing site
ICFT – Infantry Combat Fitness Test
ICP – Incident command post
INIBA – Improved Northern Ireland Body Armour
IO – Intelligence Officer
Lance Jack – Lance Corporal
Lines – Accommodation
Lurk – To lie or wait in concealment
Mine (in the context of NI 1990) – A cow shit
Moonies – New Belize-based troops
MSU – RUC's Mobile Support Unit
Multiple – Twelve-man team operating on the ground; either as three fours or two sixes
NAAFI – Navy Army Air Force Institute
NBC – Nuclear, biological and chemical
NCO – Non-Commissioned Officer
NIG/Niggi – New (in Germany)
NITAT – Northern Ireland Training and Advisory Team
NTH – Newtownhamilton
OC – Officer Commanding
OHP – Overhead protection
Op – Job/task
OP – Observation Post
Op Searsport – Armoured truck threat
Pads – Married soldiers/married soldiers' accommodation
Pax – Passenger
PG – Punta Gorda
Prof – Corporal Broomhall
PTI – Physical Training Instructors

PUP – Pick-up point

PV – Personal vibes (personal stereo)

PVCP – Permanent vehicle checkpoint

PVR – Premature voluntary release

R&R – Rest and recuperation

RE – Royal Engineers

RESA – Royal Engineer Search Advisor

REST – Royal Engineer Search Team

RHA – Royal Horse Artillery

RIR – Royal Irish Rangers

RMP – Royal Military Police

ROP – Restriction of privileges

RPL – Ramped powered lighter (landing craft)

RSM – Regimental Sergeant Major

RTU – Returned to unit

RTR – Royal Tank Regiment

RUC – Royal Ulster Constabulary

Sabre team – Major Rusby's four-man team on the ground

SEZ – Special Economic Zone

Shau Kei Wan Flyer – Bus

Shark eye – Powerful torch

SF – Sustained fire

SF – Security Forces

SLR – Self-loading rifle

Snap – Food

SNCO – Senior Non-Commissioned Officer

SOCO – Scene of Crimes Officer

SOP – Standard Operational Procedure

SPSO – Special Personnel Selection Officer

Stimms shop – NAAFI shop (stimms = pop)

Tab/bash – To march

TACBE – Sends an electronic distress signal of a constant danger message to Airborne Warning and Control System planes, however, it can also be used as a short range communications device with local aircraft.

TCG – Tactical Command Group

TI – Thermal imagery

TR – Terrorist recognition

TWET – Tactical Exercise without Troops

UDR – Ulster Defence Regiment

UVF – Ulster Volunteer Force

VCP – Vehicle checkpoint

Vengeful – A system used by the British Army to identify vehicles of interest; linked with the Driver and Vehicle Licensing Agency in Northern Ireland

Vis – Visibility

VOA /OA – OC Ops Company

VRN – Vehicle registration number

WOCS – War Office Controlled Stores

WRVS – Women's Royal Voluntary Service

XMG – Crossmaglen

About the author

James Ivimey is married with two children and lives in South London. Before joining the Army at 16 he attended Queen's Park High School in Chester. He now works in the real world.

This is his first (and probably last) book, which he has written as a piece of social history. Many people, his father included, served and did what was asked of them for their country. They weren't heroes, but all were prepared to risk their lives to do what needed to be done. This book is testament to those soldiers and their unsung exploits; unless these stories are recorded, when these people die, so will their stories.